Programming Web Services
with XML-RPC

Programming Web Services with XML-RPC

Simon St.Laurent, Joe Johnston,
and Edd Dumbill

O'REILLY®

Beijing · Cambridge · Farnham · Köln · Paris · Sebastopol · Taipei · Tokyo

Programming Web Services with XML-RPC
by Simon St.Laurent, Joe Johnston, and Edd Dumbill

Published by O'Reilly & Associates, Inc., 101 Morris Street, Sebastopol, CA 95472.

Editor: Valerie Quercia

Production Editor: Ann Schirmer

Cover Designer: Ellie Volckhausen

Printing History:

June 2001: First Edition.

ISBN: 0-596-00119-3

[M]

Table of Contents

Foreword

My name is Dave Winer. I wear a lot of hats. I'm the CEO of a company, a programmer, a columnist, a weblogger, and a developer of things that turn into standards. The last role was the biggest surprise. I've been developing software since the late 1970s, and all the time I wanted most to create a standard—to develop something that's so compelling and simple that its goodness propels it to success. I'd say now, with XML-RPC becoming such a widely adopted protocol, that it's happened. It's a strange feeling, for sure. Now, three years after the publication of the initial spec, it's an interesting time to pause and reflect how we got here, and then I'd like to offer some ideas for where we're going.

In 1998, my company, UserLand Software, had just finished porting Frontier from Macintosh to Windows. Our software made extensive use of networking, so we had a problem—with two versions of the software, how would they communicate? We could no longer use the networking software of one platform: Apple Events on the Mac or DCOM on Windows. So we decided to use two standards of the Internet, XML and HTTP, to form the communication protocol for our software. By February 1998, we had a deployed protocol for Frontier-to-Frontier communication simply called RPC, and it worked pretty well.

As I often do, I wrote a public essay about this and offered to work with others. Usually, I make those offers and no one responds. This time, I got a call from Bob Atkinson, who I knew from work we did with Microsoft on COM in the early 1990s, and he asked if we would like work with them on XML-over-HTTP. I remembered that it had been a lot of fun working with Bob in the past, so without hesitation, I said yes.

I flew up to Redmond, met with Bob, and met Mohsen Al-Ghosein (of Microsoft) and Don Box (of Developmentor) for the first time. We sat in a conference room. I had a projected laptop. I opened Notepad with an example call from our earlier protocol. As people expressed their ideas, I changed the example. It was one of the most productive brainstorming sessions of my career.

When I got back to California, we set up a web site and a private mail list and got busy writing clients and servers. That's when *betty.userland.com* came into existence (it's mentioned in the chapters of this book). Mohsen wrote JavaScript code to call my server. We talked about it on the mail list. One day Mohsen called and described a much more powerful serialization format. Until then, we had only been passing scalars, but with Mohsen's idea, we could move much more complicated structures. We upgraded our implementations, and a few hours later we were talking structs and arrays.

A few weeks into the process, I wanted to release the software to our users. It was already much more powerful than what we were shipping. Wire protocols are a delicate area, and serious breakage would surely happen if we waited much longer. So we forked a release, called it XML-RPC, and continued working with Microsoft on what would become SOAP 1.1. But that's another story and another O'Reilly book. ;->

As the book at hand, *Programming Web Services with XML-RPC,* explains so well, XML-RPC is XML over HTTP, and a great way to develop Web Services. But there's actually more going on here—there's a philosophy to XML-RPC that's different from other software projects. The philosophy is choice, and from choice comes power, and, interestingly, a disclaimer of power.

In the past, your choice of development environment limited your power as a developer. If you chose to do Java development, that meant, for the most part, that your code could only communicate with other Java programs. The same was true of Microsoft and, in practical terms, many open source scripting environments.

However, when you build applications with XML-RPC as the connecting glue, all of a sudden you're not locked in. If you want to switch from Java to Python, for example, you can do it gradually, one component at a time. This kind of fluidity allows developers more choices and relieves platform developers of the responsibility of being all things to all people. By supporting XML-RPC, the platform is offering you a way out if you don't like the way they're going. Choice here is power for developers.

We've learned the lessons from lock-in; XML-RPC takes it the next step—where it's supported, you are guaranteed choice.

Having XML-RPC in place also means that new environments can come along, and even if they don't wipe out all previous environments (they never do, of course), they can still find a user base that appreciates their qualities, and their work can interoperate with the larger environment.

Viewed another way, XML-RPC turns the Internet itself into a scripting environment, much as Visual Basic turned Windows into a scripting environment and AppleScript turned the Macintosh OS into one. It makes our worlds come together—makes the bigger world smaller and more approachable. And it's inclusive; no one need be left out of the XML-RPC revolution.

And you can pick it up by a different thread, and it's one of the most ambitious and successful open source projects in history. Most of the XML-RPC implementations are open source. Leaders of the open source world, from Eric S. Raymond to Tim O'Reilly, are big fans of XML-RPC. The Slashdot guys love it. Why? Because it's simple, low tech, and it gives developers freedom to choose their development environment.

The joy of XML-RPC for the programmer and designer is that we can learn how other people do what we do. I know almost nothing about the non-UserLand implementations, yet my software is part of the network defined by all the languages that support XML-RPC. It's like visiting a foreign country where they don't speak your language. They still eat and sleep and do all the other things we all do, but they do it differently. It's a passport that takes you anywhere you want to go.

So in my humble opinion, XML-RPC the ultimate leveler. It teaches us about each other. It's what we have in common. Perl, Python, Tcl, C++, Java, Microsoft, Sun, O'Reilly, sole proprietors, LittleCo's and BigCo's, open source teams, consultants and contractors—everyone can be on the bus; everyone can contribute to the environment and benefit from it. Sure, it's also XML-over-HTTP, but it's also a ticket to freedom and power for all developers.

Looking toward the future, here's a list of issues that are on my mind (re: XML-RPC in April 2001):

Applications

As we continue to work on interop, we're also creating public services in XML-RPC. For example, our Manila content management system has a full XML-RPC interface, as does xmlStorageSystem and mailToTheFuture. This means that every Manila site is a server that you can run XML-RPC scripts against. There are so many cool things we can do here. The apps are linked into the Services section of the XML-RPC directory. The list is relatively short now—one of our goals is to make the list really big.

Tools

One of the most exciting possibilities of XML-RPC is that writing and illustration tools can seamlessly connect to servers, turning the Web into a fantastic, easy, creative environment, open to all.

Deployment

> I'd like to see scripting environments bake XML-RPC into their releases. Net-working is an important function for all developers. UserLand has included full XML-RPC support in all of our products and encourage others to do so, too.

Community

> Please join the XML-RPC community. We have an active mail list and web site—all the resources are pointed to from *http://www.xmlrpc.com/*.

XML-RPC is the work of many people. There were four designers working on the initial April 1998 specification: Bob Atkinson and Mohsen Al-Ghosein of Microsoft, Don Box of Developmentor, and myself. After that came implementors: people like Ken MacLeod, Fredrik Lundh, Hannes Wallnöfer, Edd Dumbill, Eric Kidd, and many others. Thanks to these people, as well as those who have followed them: application developers and people who have built networks and companies on XML-RPC.

Finally, thanks to O'Reilly for supporting the XML-RPC community with such an excellent book. And thanks to Simon St.Laurent, Joe Johnston, and Edd Dumbill, for studying, understanding, and documenting XML-RPC in the depth they have. Such commitment and talent is rare. We're really lucky to have them working to make XML-RPC more broadly accessible to Internet developers.

Now I turn you over to their capable hands. I hope you enjoy XML-RPC and join the community, and let's use XML-RPC to create a fantastic new Internet scripting environment.

—Dave Winer
UserLand Software
April 2001

Preface

XML-RPC takes web technology in a new direction, giving you a new way to create simple, but powerful, connections between different kinds of programs. After wasting more hours than I care to admit developing and documenting network formats used to exchange relatively simple kinds of information between programs, I was very happy to discover XML-RPC. It would have made all that work much easier.

Whether you integrate systems within a single network or provide services and information to the public as a whole, XML-RPC provides critical layers of abstraction that make it simple to connect different kinds of computing systems without needing to create new standards for every application. Because XML-RPC is built on commonly available HTTP and XML technologies, the costs of implementing it are low. Because XML-RPC focuses sharply on solving a particular kind of problem—making procedure calls across a network—it is very easy to learn and implement across a wide variety of systems.

Audience

Any developer who needs to share information between programs running on different computers will find this book useful, but two classes of developers will find it especially worthwhile:

Integrators
> Developers focused on making distributed, and often dissimilar, systems communicate with one another may find that XML-RPC solves some of their thorniest problems in an easier way.

Web developers

> Developers wanting to make the information they provide on human-readable sites more widely available will find XML-RPC a useful tool for sharing information that can be processed by task-specific programs, not just browsers.

XML-RPC provides an enormous amount of flexibility for both groups because it allows them to build services without having to know in advance what kind of client or server is on the other end of the connection.

This book assumes that you have programming skills in the language(s) you plan to use (we cover Java, Perl, Python, PHP, and ASP) and that you have general experience with web technologies. You should know what web servers and firewalls do, for instance, and have at least a user's grasp of TCP/IP networking.

This book includes appendices that explain the amount of XML and HTTP needed for XML-RPC, so you don't need to understand XML or HTTP to get started with XML-RPC. To use XML-RPC, you don't need to know an enormous amount of the detail underlying the specification, but it can help in many situations.

Organization

The first two chapters of this book orient you with XML-RPC concepts. The subsequent five chapters discuss implementing XML-RPC clients and servers using various popular programming/scripting languages. The final chapter gives a broader view of the XML-RPC landscape. The two appendices provide useful reference material for some associated technologies. Here's the chapter breakdown:

Chapter 1, *Introduction*, gives an overview of what XML-RPC does, its origins, and what it's good at.

Chapter 2, *The XML-RPC Protocol*, describes the sequence and structure of requests and responses required to invoke computations on a remote machine using XML. The chapter also covers the various XML-RPC data types.

Chapter 3, *Client-Server Communication: XML-RPC in Java*, demonstrates how to build XML-RPC clients, servers, and handlers using the Java programming language.

Chapter 4, *XML-RPC and Perl*, walks you through the development of XML-RPC clients and servers using the Perl scripting language and shows you how to embed an XML-RPC server in a web server.

Chapter 5, *Integrating Web Applications: XML-RPC in PHP*, covers XML-RPC clients and servers created using the PHP scripting language. The chapter also demonstrates the integration of two web applications into a single web service, connecting O'Reilly & Associates' Meerkat technology database and a custom XML-RPC discussion server.

Chapter 6, *XML-RPC and Python*, explains how to make XML-RPC calls using the Python scripting language. It also describes how to set up a standalone XML-RPC server.

Chapter 7, *Bridging XML-RPC and COM: XML-RPC in ASP*, demonstrates how to build XML-RPC listeners and clients using the ASP library written in VBScript.

Chapter 8, *XML-RPC and the Web Services Landscape*, puts XML-RPC in a bigger context.

Appendix A, *The XML You Need for XML-RPC*, and Appendix B, *The HTTP You Need for XML-RPC*, provide a reference to these supporting technologies.

Conventions Used in This Book

The following font conventions are used in this book:

Italic is used for:

- Pathnames, filenames, and program names
- Internet addresses, such as domain names and URLs
- New terms where they are defined

`Constant Width` is used for:

- Command lines and options that should be typed verbatim
- Names and keywords in programs, including method names, variable names, and class names
- XML element tags

`Constant-Width Bold` is used for emphasis in program code lines.

`Constant-Width Italic` is used for replaceable arguments within program code.

How to Contact Us

We have tested and verified the information in this book to the best of our ability, but you may find that features have changed (or even that we have made mistakes!). Please let us know about any errors you find, as well as your suggestions for future editions, by writing to:

> O'Reilly & Associates, Inc.
> 101 Morris Street
> Sebastopol, CA 95472
> 1-800-998-9938 (in the U.S. or Canada)
> 1-707-829-0515 (international/local)
> 1-707-829-0104 (fax)

You can also send us messages electronically. To be put on the mailing list or request a catalog, send email to:

> *info@oreilly.com*

To ask technical questions or comment on the book, send email to:

> *bookquestions@oreilly.com*

We have a web site for the book, where we'll list examples, errata, and any plans for future editions. You can access this page at:

> *http://www.oreilly.com/catalog/progxmlrpc/*

For more information about this book and others, see the O'Reilly web site:

> *http://www.oreilly.com*

Acknowledgments

All of the authors would like to thank Dave Winer for nurturing XML-RPC and believing in its capabilities. We'd also like to thank John Posner for his contributions to this book and the entire O'Reilly tools and production crew for helping to get this book out so quickly.

Simon St.Laurent's Acknowledgements

I would like to thank John Osborn for believing in this project at the outset and for finding us the support we needed. Val Quercia and Paula Ferguson have improved the project substantially with their comments. Edd Dumbill helped get this project rolling, and his experience as an implementor of the specification was invaluable. Joe Johnston and John Posner helped us through the jungle of diverse implementations, and Joe's assistance with many of the chapters has strengthened them. I'd like to thank the XMLhack editors for their continuing support and the xml-dev mailing list for continuing to explore new and exciting applications for markup. Most of all, I'd like to thank my wife Tracey for keeping me going.

Joe Johnston's Acknowledgments

Deceivingly, only three names are listed on the cover, but this book is the result of many people working together to make it a reality. O'Reilly editor John Osborn is directly responsible for bringing me into this project. Although John left the project early on, he shouldn't be allowed to escape the culpability of his actions without a proper reckoning. The inheritor of this project, Valerie Quercia, maintained her grace and sense of humor despite being brought in on short notice to tame the wild manuscripts of physically (and mentally) remote authors. Another eleventh-hour hero is veteran O'Reilly editor Paula Ferguson, who deftly separated the content wheat from the fatuous chaff. It has been my privilege to work with Simon St. Laurent, whose quiet but firm leadership navigated this project through its often wild and turbulent course. Thanks are also due to Edd Dumbill and John Posner for bringing their technical expertise to this effort. Greg Wilson's comments on the Python chapter were both insightful and instructive.

I would not be a technical writer today without the encouragement, support, and friendship of O'Reilly's Jon Orwant. For many hours of proofreading and syntactic bravado, Caroline Senay has my gratitude. If anyone deserves to see some payoff from my writing, it's my family, who have tolerated me beyond any reasonable person's expectation. To the regulars of the IRC channel #perl, this kick's for you. Thank you all.

Edd Dumbill's Acknowledgments

I would like to thank the contributors to XMLhack, who constantly provide encouragement and a new perspective on the XML world; Ken MacLeod and Bijan Parsia for their criticism and debate; the members of the PHP XML-RPC mailing list; and my wife Rachael, whose support, as usual, makes my work possible.

1

Introduction

Have you ever wanted to publish information on the Web so programs beyond browsers could work with it? Have you ever needed to make two or more computers running different operating systems and programs written in different languages share processing? Have you ever wanted to build distributed applications using tools that let you watch the information moving between computers rather than relying on "package and pray?"

Web services are a set of tools that let you build distributed applications on top of existing web infrastructures. These applications use the Web as a kind of "transport layer" but don't offer a direct human interface via the browser. Reusing web infrastructures can drastically lower the cost of setting up these applications and allows you to reuse all kinds of tools originally built for the Web.

XML-RPC is among the simplest (and most foolproof) web service approaches, and makes it easy for computers to call procedures on other computers. XML-RPC reuses infrastructure that was originally created for communications between humans to support communications between programs on computers. Extensible Markup Language (XML) provides a vocabulary for describing Remote Procedure Calls (RPC), which are then transmitted between computers using the HyperText Transfer Protocol (HTTP).

XML-RPC can simplify development tremendously and make it far easier for different types of computers to communicate. By focusing on computer-to-computer communications, XML-RPC lets you use web technologies without getting trapped in the focus on human-readable content that has characterized most previous web development. Most of the XML-RPC framework will be familiar to web developers, but as a web developer, you will probably use off-the-shelf packages to connect your programs.

The rest of this book explores this simple, but powerful, approach more thoroughly using various development techniques. Chapters 3 through 7 explore the XML-RPC libraries available for Java, Perl, PHP, Python, and Active Server Pages, and Chapter 8 takes a look at XML-RPC's future. But before we can dive into the details of the XML-RPC protocol in Chapter 2, we need to lay some basic groundwork. The rest of this chapter covers what XML-RPC does, where it excels, and when you may not want to use it.

What XML-RPC Does

At the most basic level, XML-RPC lets you make function calls across networks. XML-RPC isn't doing anything especially new, and that largely explains why XML-RPC is useful. By combining an RPC architecture with XML and HTTP technology, XML-RPC makes it easy to for computers to share resources over a network. This means that you can give users direct access to the information they need to process, not just read and reuse systems you've already built in new contexts, or mix and match programs so that each can focus on what it does best.

Remote Procedure Calls (RPC)

Remote Procedure Calls (RPC) are a much older technology than the Web. Although the concept of computers calling functions on other systems across a network has been around as long as networks have existed, Sun Microsystems is usually given credit for creating a generic formal mechanism used to call procedures and return results over a network. RPC fit very well with the procedural approach that dominated programming until the 1990s.

Say you have a procedure that calculates momentum. This function knows the speed and name of the object, but it needs to know the object's mass to calculate the momentum. It needs to call a procedure that returns the mass for a given object. For a local procedure call, this is fairly straightforward. Programming languages let you divide your programs into procedures (or functions or methods) that call one another. The syntax is different, but generally, you can pass parameters and get a result:

```
mass=getMass(objectID)
```

Now imagine that **getMass()** is implemented on a remote system. In this case, calling the procedure requires your program to know a lot more about a more complex process. Your program needs to know which remote system to contact, how to package and send the parameters, how to receive an answer, and how to unpackage and present that answer to the routine that called it originally.

Although the RPC approach involves considerable extra overhead, with libraries on both sides of the connection creating and processing messages, as well as the possibility of delays in crossing the network, the approach does permit distributed processing and sharing of information.

The RPC approach makes life easy for you as a programmer because it spares you the trouble of having to learn about underlying protocols, networking, and various implementation details. RPC libraries are generally designed to be relatively transparent and are often operated with a single function call rather than a complex API. The abstraction required to implement RPC has another advantage for developers; because there has to be a defined protocol operating underneath the RPC system, it's possible to create alternate implementations of that protocol that support different environments. Programs written on mainframes, minicomputers, workstations, and personal computers, even from different vendors, could communicate if they had a network in common.

Effectively, RPC gives developers a mechanism for defining interfaces that can be called over a network. These interfaces can be as simple as a single function call or as complex as a large API. RPC is an enabling mechanism, and as a developer you can take as much advantage of it as you like, limited only by network overhead costs and architectural concerns.

Letting Computers Talk: XML and the Web

Although half of XML-RPC's heritage comes from RPC, the other half comes from the World Wide Web. The Web's growth over the last decade has been explosive, moving rapidly from techie curiosity to ubiquitous consumer tool. The Web provides an interface that is easy for developers to build but still simple enough for ordinary humans to negotiate. Although the Web was initially a tool for human-to-human communications, it has evolved into a sophisticated interface for human-to-computer interaction, and is also moving into increasingly complex computer-to-computer communications.

As fantastically successful as HTML was, it was only really useful for transactions presenting information to people. As HTML's limitations became clearer, the World Wide Web Consortium (W3C), keeper of the HTML specification, hosted the development of Extensible Markup Language (XML), a markup language that fits into the same environment as HTML but provides far more flexibility for communications between programs. XML allows developers to create documents whose contents are described far more precisely than is possible in HTML. XML makes it possible to create messages intended for computer interpretation, not just presentation to readers. XML lets you create a set of tags for your data, such as <title> and <author> for book catalog information. XML-RPC uses its own set of tags to mark up procedure calls. Because XML was built to fit into the same framework that carries HTML, it has created new possibilities for the Web, including XML-RPC.

Reusing Web Protocols and Infrastructure

XML-RPC reuses another key component of the Web, its transport protocol. The HTTP protocol was built into an enormous number of development environments, from web servers proper to micro-servers intended for use directly inside of programs. Developers are used to the process of assembling documents for transport over HTTP, and network administrators have supported web servers and web-friendly firewalls for years.

In many ways, HTTP is an RPC-based protocol, opening with an identifier for the method being called and then providing parameters that determine what that method should return. HTTP's relatively open approach, based on the MIME (Multipurpose Internet Mail Extensions) set of standards for identifying and encoding different kinds of content, has given it enough flexibility to carry the many kinds of content needed for web sites. That flexibility provides it with enough strength to carry the kinds of payloads an RPC protocol demands.

Building a Different Kind of Web

XML-RPC allows you to implement the RPC approach described previously while taking advantage of existing HTTP tools and infrastructures. Because HTTP is available on all kinds of programming environments and operating systems, and because XML parsers are similar commodity parts, it's relatively easy to assemble an XML-RPC toolkit for any given environment.

Most web applications are designed to present information to people. With XML-RPC and web services, however, the Web becomes a collection of procedural connections where computers exchange information along tightly bound paths. Instead of having humans surf through hypertext links, computers follow previously arranged rules for exchanging information. This exchange doesn't have to follow the client-server model established by the Web. XML-RPC supports peer-to-peer communications as well as client-server approaches, taking advantage of HTTP's facilities for sending information from the browser to the server more often than most web browsers do.

XML-RPC clients make procedure requests of XML-RPC servers, which return results to the XML-RPC clients. XML-RPC clients use the same HTTP facilities as web browser clients, and XML-RPC servers use the same HTTP facilities as web servers. Those roles aren't nearly as fixed as they are in the regular web world, however. It's common for the same program to include both XML-RPC client and server code and to use both when appropriate.

Although you can build XML-RPC handlers using traditional web techniques, there is little need to drill that deep. As a developer, you may never even need to see XML-RPC's internals or know that the RPC system you use is running over the Web. Most XML-RPC implementations hide the details of XML-RPC from those using it, requesting only a port number to communicate over. You may need a web site administrator to set up the initial system, or you may need to integrate your XML-RPC servers with web server features like secure transactions, but once that initial setup is complete, XML-RPC is much like any other RPC system.

Where XML-RPC Excels

XML-RPC is an excellent tool for establishing a wide variety of connections between computers. If you need to integrate multiple computing environments, but don't need to share complex data structures directly, you will find that XML-RPC lets you establish communications quickly and easily. Even if you work within a single environment, you may find that the RPC approach makes it easy to connect programs that have different data models or processing expectations and that it can provide easy access to reusable logic.

XML-RPC's most obvious field of application is connecting different kinds of environments, allowing Java to talk with Perl to talk with Python to talk with ASP, and so on. Systems integrators often build custom connections between different systems, creating their own formats and protocols to make communications possible, but they often end up with a large number of poorly documented single-use protocols. Each piece might work very well at its appointed task, but developers have to constantly create new protocols for new tasks, and reusing previous protocols can be very difficult.

XML-RPC offers integrators an opportunity to use a standard vocabulary and approach for exchanging information. This means that developers can create open programming interfaces. Sometimes a project has clearly defined needs for connecting two or more specific environments together, and a small set of XML-RPC packages can help create a complete solution. In other cases, developers want to publish a service but don't necessarily know what kinds of clients they have to support.

XML-RPC makes it possible for services like Meerkat (*http://meerkat.oreillynet.com*) to provide an interface that can be accessed from several different environments. Meerkat, which aggregates news and announcement information from hundreds of sites, can be searched through a traditional web interface or through an XML-RPC interface (documented at *http://www.oreillynet.com/pub/a/rss/2000/11/14/meerkat_ xmlrpc.html*). Developers who want to use Meerkat information in their own applications can call functions on the Meerkat server, and Meerkat's maintainers don't need to know anything about the details.

Because XML-RPC is layered on top of HTTP, it inherits the inefficiencies of HTTP. This does place some limitations on its use in large-scale, high-speed applications, but inefficiency isn't important in many places. Although there are definitely high-profile projects for which systems must scale to millions of transactions at a time, keeping response time to a minimum, there are also many projects to which systems need to send information or request processing far less often—from once a second to once a week—and for which response time isn't absolutely critical. For these cases, XML-RPC can simplify developers' lives tremendously.

A Quick Tour of the Minefields

Before moving into the details of XML-RPC and exploring its capabilities in depth, it's worth pausing for a moment to examine some possible areas where using XML-RPC may not be appropriate. Although RPC and tunneling over HTTP are both useful technologies, both techniques can get you into trouble if you use them inappropriately. Neither technique is exactly the height of computing elegance, and there are substantial scalability and security issues that you should address at the beginning of your projects rather than at the end.

RPC Issues

RPC architectures have some natural limitations. There are plenty of cases when RPC is still appropriate, including some when combining logic with data in objects is either risky or excessively complex, and messaging might require additional unnecessary overhead. On the other hand, RPC lacks the flexibility made possible by the other approaches because of the relative simplicity of its architecture. The level of abstraction in RPC is relatively low, leading to potential complexity as the number of different requests increases.

Although the descriptions in the previous section might suggest that RPC is just a message-passing mechanism, the messages can't be arbitrary. Remote Procedure Calls, like procedure calls in programs, take a procedure name and a set of typed parameters and return a result. Although developers can build some flexibility into the parameters and the result, the nature of procedure calls brings some significant limitations for development, flexibility, and maintenance.

Development methodologies have spent the last 50 years moving toward looser and looser connections between computing components—on both the hardware and software sides. Looser connections mean more flexibility for consumers of computing products and their developers. XML-RPC provides some flexibility, abstracting away differences between computing environments, but the procedures to which it is applied supply only limited flexibility. Careful API design can help developers create maintainable systems, but changing APIs is often more difficult than adding additional information to a message. If different systems need to see their information in different forms, API complexity can grow rapidly.

Protocol Reuse Issues

Although XML-RPC reaps enormous benefits by using HTTP as its foundation, many developers see such reuse as misguided, wrong, or even dangerous. In some sense XML-RPC's genius lies in its perversity, its creative reuse of a standard that was designed for relatively simple document transfers. Although XML-RPC's reuse of the software infrastructure makes sense, there are definitely those who feel that XML-RPC conflicts with the infrastructure that supports the protocol.

Although reuse issues come up on a regular basis on nearly every mailing list that touches on XML-RPC or SOAP, the most detailed discussion of reuse issues is Keith Moore's Internet-Draft titled "On the use of HTTP as a Substrate for Other Protocols" (*http://www.ietf.org/internet-drafts/draft-moore-using-http-01.txt*).

HTTP isn't very efficient

HTTP has some limitations for building distributed computing environments. It was originally created to ship HTML from servers to browsers, although later versions added support for a wide variety of file formats and for limited communications (through forms from the web browser to the web server). HTTP grew in fits and starts from a very small base, and some approaches it uses reflect compatibility needs rather than best practices. Although HTTP is easy to use, it's not really designed for performance.

XML-RPC isn't your average web page

An XML-RPC processor will probably be referenced using a URL such as *http://www.example.com/RPC/*. That URL looks awfully familiar—it might, in fact describe an HTML page that just happens to be retrievable from *http://www.example.com/RPC/*, rather than an XML-RPC processor. There might even be a form processor lurking there, waiting for POST requests. There is no way to tell from the bare URL that it references something outside the realm of ordinary web browsing behavior.

HTTP already supports significant diversity for URL behavior by allowing the GET, POST, and other methods, each of which may return different information. XML-RPC takes this diversity to a new level, however, by moving outside of the normal format in which POSTed information is sent and by creating a new set of structures for defining behavior. The same URL might have hundreds, or even thousands, of different methods available to service XML-RPC requests; a big change from the "one form, one program" common to most POST processing, and potentially larger in scale than even the most ambitious generic form processors.

XML-RPC also provides no default behavior for users hitting an XML-RPC processor with a GET request. Sending an HTTP error message is one possibility, breaking the connection is another, and sending a polite web page explaining that this URL is for XML-RPC use only is another. Developers might even choose to hide an XML-RPC processor underneath a regular HTTP URL, responding to GET requests with web pages and to XML-RPC requests with XML-RPC responses. (Don't consider this security, however!)

Breaking through firewalls by reusing HTTP

Part of XML-RPC's promise is its subversion of network security rules (making it possible for developers to bypass firewalls), but that is also a critical part of XML-RPC's danger and raises vehement opposition. Although there have been plenty of security warnings about web browsers over the years, the need for people on various private networks to read the Web has given HTTP and port 80 a greater degree of freedom than most other protocols. Network administrators rely on filters, proxies, or a simple pass-through to avoid the raft of user complaints that emerge when web access is denied.

XML-RPC takes advantage of this common practice—and states that it does so, right in the specification—to let it establish tight bonds between systems that are on supposedly separate networks. XML-RPC already provides very little security for its transactions, and its firewall-breaching capabilities raise serious new security threats for network administrators who thought they had plugged all the holes. Adding an XML-RPC interface to the computer that holds a company's financial information may not be so smart if that computer can be reached from outside networks. Because HTTP is effectively privileged, the odds of that computer's XML-RPC interface being exposed are much higher than the odds of an interface built on a protocol where security is traditionally of greater concern.

To some extent, these issues aren't too hard for network administrators to address. Many firewall and NAT setups already block incoming requests, only permitting responses to requests that originated on the internal network. Although this block would allow outgoing information flows, it would prevent the outside world from making requests of the systems on the private network. In other cases, typically those in which port 80 is considered an "open" port, network administrators may have a lot of additional work to do in figuring out how best (and if) to allow XML-RPC transactions and how to block them, if desired.

Because of these "wolf in sheep's clothing" issues, some developers prefer to see XML-RPC and similar protocols take a different approach. Some developers find HTTP to be too insecure, too inefficient, and generally too inappropriate as a base for these application protocols, but few call for an outright ban.

Keith Moore's "On the use of HTTP as a Substrate for Other Protocols" (*http:// www.ietf.org/internet-drafts/draft-moore-using-http-01.txt*) outlines a list of practices he considers appropriate to proper use of HTTP, nearly all of which XML-RPC violates. XML-RPC provides no explicit security model, "masquerades" as existing HTTP traffic, uses the "http" URL scheme and port 80, doesn't define explicitly how the client and server interact with proxies, and allows the use of HTTP errors for certain situations. As we'll see in the next chapter, XML-RPC also provides its own mechanism for reporting procedure call faults.

We'll consider these issues again in Chapter 8, after we've explored XML-RPC more deeply. That chapter also covers some alternatives to XML-RPC that have emerged, such as the Simple Object Access Protocol (SOAP); Universal Description, Discovery, and Integration (UDDI); and Web Services Description Language (WSDL). For now, these warnings are worth keeping in mind, especially if you have to explain how and why you're using XML-RPC to an unsympathetic network administrator. In simple situations, especially when you control both the network and all systems on it, these issues probably won't cause you any harm.

2

The XML-RPC Protocol

This chapter describes the XML-RPC protocol—that is, the sequence and structure of requests and responses required to invoke computations on a remote machine using XML and HTTP. It also covers XML-RPC's data types, a subset of those commonly found in programming languages. If you plan to use an available XML-RPC library to create XML-RPC clients and servers, you don't need to understand all the details of the XML-RPC protocol. However, when you need to debug your service, you'll find it quite helpful to know about the protocol details. This chapter also provides the information you need to implement your own XML-RPC library, should there not be a library for your particular environment.

This chapter, and the rest of the book for that matter, assume that you have a basic understanding of both XML and HTTP. This knowledge is critical to your ability to understand XML-RPC. If you don't know much about XML or HTTP, or if you just want to refresh your memory about the basics, you should check out Appendix A and Appendix B.

The current chapter explains the XML-RPC specification (found online at *http:// www.xmlrpc.com/spec*), which is the first point of reference for the technology. In addition, the chapter draws upon current practice to recommend guidelines for implementation and use, and to highlight areas for future specialization or extension of the technology.

Choreography

An XML-RPC call is conducted between two parties: the *client* (the calling process) and the *server* (the called process). A server is made available at a particular URL (for example, *http://example.org:8080/rpcserv/*).* To use the procedures available on that server, the following steps are necessary:

1. The client program makes a procedure call using the XML-RPC client, specifying a method name, parameters, and a target server.

2. The XML-RPC client takes the method name and parameters and then packages them as XML. Then the client issues an HTTP POST request containing the request information to the target server.

3. An HTTP server on the target server receives the POST request and passes the XML content to an XML-RPC listener.

4. The XML-RPC listener parses the XML to get the method name and parameters and then calls the appropriate method, passing it the parameters.

5. The method returns a response to the XML-RPC process and the XML-RPC process packages the response as XML.

6. The web server returns that XML as the response to the HTTP POST request.

7. The XML-RPC client parses the XML to extract the return value and then passes the return value back to the client program.

8. The client program continues processing with the return value.

There is nothing to stop a process from being both a server and a client, making and receiving XML-RPC requests. It is important, however, to recognize that in any single XML-RPC request, there are always the two roles of client and server.

The use of HTTP means that XML-RPC requests must be both synchronous and stateless.

Synchronous

An XML-RPC request is always followed by exactly one XML-RPC response; the response is synchronous with the request. This happens because the response must occur on the same HTTP connection as the request.

Furthermore, the client process blocks (waits) until it receives a response from the server. This step has consequences for program design: your code should be written in such a way that the potential blocking of a response for some time will not affect its operation, or else your program should restrict itself to calling remote methods that execute in "reasonable" time. "Reasonable" may vary, according to the needs of your program. Methods that are called frequently in time-sensitive environments may be unreasonable if they take more than a fraction of a second; methods that are called occasionally to return large volumes of information may be perfectly reasonable even if they take a few minutes to return the full collection of information requested.

---

* That is, an HTTP server responding on port 8080, on the machine whose name is *example.org*.

It is possible to implement an *asynchronous* system, where the response to a request is delivered at some point subsequent to the time of request. However, this implementation would require both processes to be XML-RPC client and server enabled and to contain a significant amount of code for handling such asynchronous responses. Systems that require asynchronous responses can build such systems on the synchronous foundation of XML-RPC using multiple request-response cycles. One simple way forward would be to have the server process return a unique identifier and the calling process implement a special XML-RPC method that allows the transmission of results corresponding with the request. If the transactions are conducted over the Internet, this also means that both processes must be accessible through any firewall that might be in place.

In general, synchronous requests are capable of fulfilling many processes' requirements, and the overhead of creating an asynchronous system is probably prohibitive in most cases.

Stateless

HTTP is an inherently *stateless* technology. This means that no context is preserved from one request to the next. XML-RPC inherits this feature. So, if your client program invokes one method on the server and invokes it again, XML-RPC itself has no way to treat them as anything other than two isolated, unconnected incidents. This avoids the sometimes massive overhead involved in maintaining state across multiple systems.

But there are good reasons why you might want to preserve state. For instance, one request might create a certain object inside the server, and subsequent requests modify that object. Users of HTTP have gotten around its statelessness by storing state server-side and using identifiers held in cookies, or in the URL of the page itself, to indicate to the server a continuation of a session of requests. Although this is often necessary for projects like web-based shopping carts, the program-to-program communication of XML-RPC doesn't need this infrastructure for the simple processes it supports.

Although XML-RPC itself provides no support for preservation of state, you can implement a stateful system on top of XML-RPC. For instance, you could make the first argument of all your procedure calls be a session identifier. The procedures would need to have some kind of state management system, perhaps a database, in the background. They could then keep track of which calls came from where and perhaps use the history of previous calls to determine responses to current calls.

Data Types

XML-RPC calls closely model function calls in programming languages. An invocation of a remote method is accompanied by data in the form of *parameters*, and the response to that method contains data as a return value. Although a request may contain multiple parameters, the response must contain exactly one return value.

To represent these values, XML-RPC defines an XML representation for program data. It does this for several basic data types, such as integers and strings, and for compound data structures, such as arrays.

Any data item in an XML-RPC request or response is contained within a `<value>` ... `</value>` element.

Simple Data Types

XML-RPC defines a set of simple data types, from which other, more complex, data structures can be built. These types are common to most programming languages.

Integers

XML-RPC has exactly one data type for integers. It is capable of representing a 32-bit signed integer: any integer between $-2,147,483,648$ (-2^{31}) and $2,147,483,647$ ($2^{31}-1$). It has two interchangeable representations:

```
<value><i4>n</i4></value>
```

or:

```
<value><int>n</int></value>
```

(Note that the **4** in **i4** is derived from the length of the integer: four octets, 32 bits.)

XML-RPC implementations must recognize both of these representations as input data. No recommendation is given as to which form they should use when generating output data, however. Because XML-RPC is strict about its limitations to 32-bit signed integers, it makes no difference which form is used: if larger integers (or *bignums*, arbitrarily large integers) are ever incorporated into the specification, another element name must be found anyway.

The character string representing the integer may contain no whitespace or other characters; that is, between `<int>` and `</int>` there may only occur the characters -, +, and the numerals 0 through 9. (A positive integer may optionally have the plus sign, +, as a prefix.)

Here are some integers encoded to the XML-RPC specification:

```
<value><int>42</int></value>
<value><i4>-32764</i4></value>
<value><int>0</int></value>
<value><int>+42</int></value>
```

Floating-point numbers

The XML-RPC specification expresses the range of the floating-point data type as "double-precision floating point." Conventionally,[*] this refers to the use of 64 bits for the representation of the number, giving an effective range of $\sim 10^{-323.3}$ to $\sim 10^{308.3}$. It has the following representation in XML-RPC:

```
<value><double>n</double></value>
```

As a consequence of its element name, the XML-RPC floating-point type is referred to as a *double*.

Although many computing platforms support abbreviated notations for floating-point numbers, XML-RPC restricts itself to one representation only. A double may be represented by a + or –, followed by digits and a decimal point, after which only further digits are permitted. Here are some double-precision floating-point numbers encoded to the XML-RPC specification:

```
<value><double>2.0</double></value>
<value><double>-0.32653</double></value>
<value><double>67234.45</double></value>
```

There are several caveats to using floating-point numbers in XML-RPC:

- You should be aware of rounding errors that occur with the use of floating-point numbers (due to the imprecise notation used inside computers). These errors can occur within your own programs or within the remote server.

- The decimal notation used may lead you to expect that arbitrarily precise (or large) decimals may be used in XML-RPC. This is not the case, and you should restrict yourself to what may be represented using an IEEE 754 double-precision integer.

- The special floating-point values *not-a-number* ("NaN"), *infinity*, and *indeterminate* have no representation in XML-RPC and may not be sent or received. This has consequences if your methods are performing floating-point operations and yield one of these values. These cases may be best handled using fault codes (see later in this chapter).

---

[*] The most common standard for defining floating-point numbers is IEEE 754, which defines single-precision (32 bits) and double-precision (64 bits) representations for floating-point numbers. A good overview of IEEE 754 floating-point numbers may be found at *http://www.research.microsoft.com/~hollasch/cgindex/coding/ieeefloat.html*.

Boolean values

XML-RPC defines a type used to encode Boolean logical values. The type has a range of two permissible values: 1 or 0. The value 1 corresponds to the Boolean value *true*, and 0 to the Boolean value *false*. The type is indicated by the element boolean:

```
<value><boolean>b</boolean></value>
```

Here are all the possible representations of Boolean values in XML-RPC:

```
<value><boolean>1</boolean></value>
<value><boolean>0</boolean></value>
```

Strings

String values within XML-RPC may use one of two alternative representations. In the first form, the string type is assumed to be the default for any value enclosed in the `<value>` ... `</value>` element. Thus, the string "Hello, World!" is legally represented as:

```
<value>Hello, World!</value>
```

Additionally, an explicitly typed representation of strings is available:

```
<value><string>Hello, World!</string></value>
```

XML-RPC implementations must understand both representations.

Whitespace is significant within strings. Furthermore, any XML character is permissible within a string. If you wish to include characters special to XML, such as & and <, in a string value, you must use their predefined entity references (e.g., `&amp;` (for &) and `&lt;` (for <)).

The XML-RPC specification clearly says that the string type is restricted to ASCII strings. This strategy works well with many programming environments that can only handle ASCII strings; however, it can become a substantial problem in cases when string content includes characters outside the ASCII set. Not even the accented characters of Latin-1 sets are available.

In theory, if every XML-RPC processor you use conforms to the XML 1.0 specification, the use of Unicode, ISO-8859-1, or other non-ASCII character sets will cause you no problem. However, the reality is somewhat different. Not every implementation of XML-RPC is built on top of a conformant XML 1.0 parser, for example, so you may find that character encoding issues arise. It is safe to assume that ASCII strings will always be passed unmolested, but you ought to conduct tests on the platforms of your choice to determine whether it is possible to use Unicode or another non-ASCII character encoding. You may encounter similar problems if you use XML character references, which are not explicitly supported by the XML-RPC specification.

Here are some valid representations of XML-RPC strings:

```
<value>Tom &amp; Jerry</value>
<value><string>Once upon a time</string></value>
<value><string>"Twelve apples please," she said.</string></value>
<value><string>3 &lt; 5</string></value>
```

Programs that process XML-RPC calls see the first string as Tom & Jerry and the fourth as 3 < 5 because they use the XML encoding for the special characters & and <.

When we examine a complete XML-RPC request later in the chapter, we will see that the specification's default position is to omit any declaration of character encoding. As per the XML 1.0 specification, this means that processors should assume that the incoming message is encoded in UTF-8. Because ASCII is a subset of UTF-8, this should work perfectly well for messages that conform to the XML-RPC's requirement of ASCII text.

Date-times

Dates and times are encoded in XML-RPC using the dateTime.iso8601 element type. This type permits the absolute specification of a combined date and time, according to the ISO 8601 standard.* To be more precise, XML-RPC uses a *profile* of ISO 8601 dates because ISO 8601 allows many different representations. A date-time is represented in XML-RPC as follows:

```
<value><dateTime.iso8601>CCYYMMDDTHH:MM:SS</dateTime.iso8601>
```

Some example date-times will make this clearer:

```
<value><dateTime.iso8601>19030223T00:30:00</dateTime.iso8601></value>
```

The above time means "thirty-minutes after midnight on the twenty-third of February, 1903" (using the 24-hour clock).

```
<value><dateTime.iso8601>20001231T12:30:25</dateTime.iso8601></value>
```

This time means "thirty-minutes and twenty-five seconds after midday on the thirty-first of December, 2000."

Conventionally, with ISO 8601 date-times, a time zone indicator follows the time part of the date-time string. However, date-times in XML-RPC are represented without any time zone information. The specification says that server owners should indicate their time zone by means of documentation. Unfortunately, this is not a satisfactory situation of which the client has no prior knowledge. For this

---

* The standard is available at *http://www.iso.ch/markete/8601.pdf*. You can also find an easy-to-read introduction to ISO 8601 dates at *http://www.hut.fi/u/jkorpela/iso8601.html*.

reason, we recommend that GMT (Greenwich Mean Time) be used within XML-RPC applications when possible. Because most programming languages commonly have functions that translate from GMT into the local time zone, this should simplify interoperability between systems in different time zones.

Binary

Certain characters are forbidden in XML (as explained in Appendix A). XML prohibits any character with an ordinal value lower than that of the space character (32), commonly called control characters. How, then, can data items, such as binary files, that may contain these characters be transported in an XML-RPC request? The solution is to use an ASCII-based encoding of the binary object. XML-RPC uses *base-64 encoding*, commonly found in Internet applications (email clients, for example, often use base-64 to encode attachments).

The `<base64> ... </base64>` element is used to enclose a binary object. Here's an example encoding of the string "Hello, World!":

```
<value><base64>SGVsbG8sIFdvcmxkIQ==</base64></value>
```

Implementations should ideally shield the base-64 encoding from the user and make the transport of binary items transparent. In other words, you provide binary data to the XML-RPC implementation and expect to receive binary data back. In the case that an implementation does not handle binary data transparently, decoding base-64 is easy, and most programming languages already have libraries to perform this decoding. The encoding is defined in RFC 2045, available at *http://www.ietf.org/rfc/rfc2045.txt*.

Compound Data Types

Although these basic types are sufficient for small applications, most programs compose simple types into more complex data structures, either in arrays or record-like structures (e.g., the *struct* in C). XML-RPC supports compound types that allow the combination of the basic types into more complex data structures. These types are arrays and structs.

Arrays

The array in XML-RPC allows synthesis of data items into a sequence. XML-RPC arrays are best thought of as untyped lists because their members are not forced to be of the same type, and their members are not numbered in any way you might expect in a conventional array.

Array values take the following form:

```
<value>
  <array>
    <data>
      <value> an XML-RPC value </value>
        ...
      <value> an XML-RPC value </value>
    </data>
  </array>
</value>
```

A data item within an array may be of any type, simple or compound. Thus, it is possible to represent multidimensional arrays by embedding an array within an array. The following example shows a representation of a tic-tac-toe board, which might reasonably be represented in a program as a two-dimensional array:

```
<value>
  <array>
    <data>
      <value><array><data>
        <value><string>-</string></value>
        <value><string>0</string></value>
        <value><string>X</string></value>
      </data></array></value>
      <value><array><data>
        <value><string>-</string></value>
        <value><string>X</string></value>
        <value><string>0</string></value>
      </data></array></value>
      <value><array><data>
        <value><string>0</string></value>
        <value><string>X</string></value>
        <value><string>-</string></value>
      </data></array></value>
    </data>
  </array>
</value>
```

The resulting array, of course, is a typical tic-tac-toe dead heat:

```
-OX
-XO
OX-
```

Structs

Whereas the array type allows representation of linear arrays, the struct type in XML-RPC allows encoding of another common type of array, the associative array, or dictionary.

A struct is represented as a series of *members*. Each member is a pair: a name and a value. The name must be an ASCII string, and the value may be any XML-RPC value, including an array or another struct. Structs take the following form:

```
<value>
  <struct>
    <member>
       <name>Name-1</name>
       <value>Value-1</value>
    </member>

       ...
    <member>
       <name>Name-n</name>
       <value>Value-n</value>
    </member>
  </struct>
</value>
```

Typically, an XML-RPC implementation converts between XML-RPC structs and the dictionary types of the host programming language. Here is an example XML-RPC struct that describes "Fred":

```
<value>
  <struct>
    <member><name>age</name><value><int>45</int></value></member>
    <member><name>name</name><value><string>Fred</string></value></member>
    <member><name>smoker</name><value><boolean>0</boolean></value></member>
    <member><name>children</name><value>
      <array><data>
        <value><string>Maisie</string></value>
        <value><string>Jeremy</string></value>
      </data></array>
    </value></member>
  </struct>
</value>
```

And here is an equivalent representation in Perl:

```
%fred = ( 'age' => 45,
          'name' => "Fred",
          'smoker' => 0,
          'children' => [ "Maisie", "Jeremy" ] );
```

The XML-RPC specification does not explicitly constrain name elements of the struct members to be unique, though they normally should be in practice. It does specify, however, that the list of members be considered unordered. Thus, the two structs shown in Example 2-1 are equivalent.

From this circumstance and the practical consideration that all XML-RPC implementations to date use standard hash-like data structures for XML-RPC structs, we can imply the constraint that member names must indeed be unique.[*]

---

[*] The only way duplicate names might be feasible would be if the order of members in an array were significant. Because members are unordered, we may conclude that duplicate names are not permitted, because otherwise there is no deterministic means of interpretation for a struct with a duplicate name.

Example 2-1. Two equivalent structs

```
<struct>                                  <struct>
  <member><name>a</name>                    <member><name>b</name>
    <value>                                   <value>
      <string>A</string>                        <string>B</string>
    </value>                                   </value>
  </member>                                  </member>
  <member><name>b</name>                    <member><name>a</name>
    <value>                                   <value>
      <string>B</string>                        <string>A</string>
    </value>                                   </value>
  </member>                                  </member>
</struct>                                  </struct>
```

Most XML-RPC implementations accept an illegal struct with duplicate member names, but apply the naïve behavior of overwriting previously processed members with the same name. You shouldn't, of course, rely on this behavior.

Request Format

XML-RPC defines an HTTP and XML request sent to a server to cause the server to perform an action. This request has two parts: the HTTP headers, which identify the server; and the XML payload, which contains information about which method to invoke.

XML Payload

The XML section of an XML-RPC request carries the name of the remote method to be invoked, along with all necessary parameters. The entire message is enclosed within `<methodCall>` `</methodCall>` tags. The method name is then given in the `<methodName>` ... `</methodName>` element. This is followed by a list of parameters, enclosed within `<params>` ... `</params>`. Each parameter is an XML-RPC value, as defined in the data types section earlier in this chapter, and must also be enclosed in `<param>` ... `</param>` tags.

The following example shows the encoding of a method call analogous to the C-style function call `print("Hello, World!")`:

```
<?xml version="1.0"?>
<methodCall>
  <methodName>print</methodName>
  <params>
    <param>
      <value><string>Hello, World!</string></value>
    </param>
  </params>
</methodCall>
```

Parameters

The parameter list enclosed by the **<params>** element may contain zero or more **<param>** elements. Even if the method requires no parameters, the **<params>** element must still be present.

Note that parameters take the form of a simple list. Several programming environments provide the ability to pass parameters referenced by name. For example, in Python you might write **updateDetails(name="Fred", age=43)**. This has no equivalent in XML-RPC, which means you cannot create methods that take a variable number of parameters.

If you need a method that accepts a variable number of parameters, the simplest way around this problem is to use a single struct as the parameter, as follows:

```
<?xml version="1.0"?>
<methodCall>
  <methodName>updateDetails</methodName>
  <params>
    <param>
      <value><struct>
          <member><name>name</name>
            <value><string>Fred</string></value>
          </member>
          <member><name>age</name>
            <value><int>43</int></value>
          </member>
        </struct></value>
    </param>
  </params>
</methodCall>
```

Method naming

Method names may contain only alphanumeric characters (A-Z, a-z, 0-9) and the dot (.), colon (:), underscore (_), or slash (/) characters. XML-RPC imposes no meaning on the method name at all; it is simply a way of communicating to the server the name of the functionality the client wishes to invoke.

However, a large unmanaged namespace can quickly become unwieldy, and an informal convention for dividing up the namespace of methods has arisen among XML-RPC implementers. This convention uses the dot as a separator to indicate functional units.

For example, if you wrote several methods to perform arithmetic operation on incoming data, you might name them as follows:

```
math.add
math.subtract
math.multiply
```

The dot in the name makes no difference as far as the XML-RPC specification is concerned, but it makes it easier to organize methods into logical blocks in your server. Some XML-RPC implementations actually make the dotted name meaningful by mapping it into their host environment (for instance, Zope maps the dotted name into its object hierarchy), but this is a detail you only need to consider if you are implementing an XML-RPC server. Later chapters in this book outline the peculiarities of each language's implementation. A client of the server need only know the correct name of the method; it does not need to be aware of how that method name is resolved to functionality inside the server.

HTTP Headers

XML-RPC requires a minimal number of HTTP headers to be sent along with the XML method request. As shown in the following complete example HTTP request, the `User-Agent`, `Content-Length`, `Content-Type`, and `Host` headers are used:

```
POST /myservice.php HTTP/1.0
User-Agent: PHP XMLRPC 1.0
Host: xmlrpc.usefulinc.com
Content-Type: text/xml
Content-Length: 216
```

POST

In the first line of the request, the HTTP `POST` method indicates to the host server that we are sending it data. The path (*/myservice.php*) following the `POST` method indicates the URL, relative to the server, of the script that should receive the data.

If your XML-RPC server is based on a regular web server, the path is likely to point to a program or script that will service the XML-RPC request, as in our example. If your server is solely dedicated to serving XML-RPC, the path may have some significance to the server, dependent on implementation. You may see a path of */RPC2* used commonly in various XML-RPC implementations, but there is no special need for a server to be placed at any particular path.*

Host

The `Host` header specifies the name of the server that should service this XML-RPC request. Borrowed from HTTP 1.1, the `Host` header allows the use of a virtual server that shares the same IP address as other servers. The value of the header must be a valid hostname. Here are some typical `Host` specifications:

```
Host: betty.userland.com
Host: xmlrpc.usefulinc.com
```

---

* This path choice is based on the path conventionally used in the Frontier implementation of XML-RPC and has also been adopted by the Zope and the Perl XML-RPC implementations.

If you are creating an XML-RPC server and intend to use a virtual server that shares an IP address with other server programs, there are two situations in which you need to take the Host header into account:

- If you use an existing web server, such as Apache, to handle the HTTP part of servicing an XML-RPC request, you need to configure a virtual server to ensure that the web server can find your XML-RPC server script when it receives the corresponding Host header.

  For the commonly used Apache web server, the relevant entries might look something like this:

  ```
  <VirtualHost xmlrpc.example.com>
  ServerName xmlrpc.example.com
  ServerAdmin webmaster@example.com
  DocumentRoot /usr/local/etc/httpd/htdocs/xmlrpc
  </VirtualHost>
  ```

  This example uses the hostname *xmlrpc.example.com* for the server host, and a particular portion of the file system (the directory */usr/local/etc/httpd/htdocs/ xmlrpc*) has been reserved for XML-RPC serving. The path details from the POST are then treated by the web server as relative to the DocumentRoot path.

- Alternatively, if you create your own server process instead of using a web server, you may want to perform custom processing of the Host header yourself, to differentiate incoming requests.

There are several useful applications of virtual XML-RPC hosts. For example, you may want to provide tighter security on one set of XML-RPC methods than another. This could be done by setting up two aliases for your server IP address, say *public-serv.example.com* and *private-serv.example.com*. By checking the Host header, either the web server or your own server program can direct servicing of an XML-RPC request to different programs or parts of a program; the public part offers fewer methods and lower security than the private part, which would enforce much stricter security policies. The use of the virtual named servers also allows you to separate these services onto two different physical machines at a later date, if you wish, by altering the DNS records for the hostnames.

The Host header, along with the POST path and the method name, allows even more flexibility for carving up the namespace of your XML-RPC servers. For a small XML-RPC setup, this is probably overkill. If you start deploying XML-RPC in a larger setting, however, you would be well advised to plan your server namespace carefully to allow you the maximum flexibility to implement security and failsafe mechanisms and to cope with the future growth of your serving platform.

Content-Type

The value of the `Content-Type` header is constant within XML-RPC; it is the Internet media type for XML, `text/xml`. XML-RPC appeared before RFC 3023 (*http://www.ietf.org/rfc/rfc3023.txt*), which specifies a mechanism for creating more specific identifiers for XML types. If you build XML-RPC implementations that accept other flavors of XML identified as `text/xml` (as well as XML-RPC over the same port), you'll need to identify XML-RPC messages by the `methodCall root` element.

Content-Length

The `Content-Length` header must contain the number of octets in the XML-RPC message body; that is, everything after the blank line separating the HTTP headers and the XML payload. Note that with ASCII payloads, one character is the same length as one octet. However, if you start dealing with non-8-bit character sets, be aware that it is the number of octets you must place in this header, not the number of characters.

User-Agent

The `User-Agent` header carries an identifier corresponding to the XML-RPC implementation that you use. It is normally of little significance and will never be observed if you use ready-made XML-RPC libraries for your platform of choice.

However, there are several interesting applications to which this header might be put. These come into play when you create an XML-RPC server and wish to have some extra levels of control or information. Note that neither of these suggestions is commonly implemented in today's XML-RPC services, but both could be integrated easily.

Conveying administrative information

If you run XML-RPC services available to a large number of users, it would be helpful to have contact details for a user accessing your service. This convention has often been employed in user agent strings incorporated in web crawlers for search engines. An email address is placed in parentheses at the end of the user agent string. Here are a couple of hypothetical examples:

```
User-Agent: PHP XMLRPC 1.0 (fred@example.com)
User-Agent: Frontier/5.1.2 (WinNT) (webmaster@example.org)
```

Obviously, this user agent extension would have to be implemented in the XML-RPC client code. Because most XML-RPC implementations available today are open source, making such a modification should be easy.

User-Agent negotiation

The XML-RPC specification includes a large amount of functionality for providing remote web services. However, there may be a situation in which you need to extend the protocol to provide functionality peculiar to your platform or application (for a discussion of one such extension, see the section "The Nil Value" later in this chapter). One difficulty in extending implementations in such a way is discovering whether XML-RPC clients and servers support these extended facilities.

For servers, it is not hard to imagine implementing a method that returns an array of all the extensions it supports; however, for clients, this is more difficult to achieve. One way of solving the problem would be to include a list of client capabilities in the user agent string. Here's a sample string that supports the "nil" extension for a client and is also capable of compressing its payloads using *gzip*:

```
User-Agent: Acme XML-RPC (extensions; nil, gzip)
```

On a more mundane level, it is unfortunately the case that sometimes implementations have bugs. By checking the user agent string of a client, a server may be able to bring workarounds into place or simply reject a request from a buggy client. (This technique is commonly used by web servers to work around browser bugs.)

Using other headers

No other headers are mandated by the XML-RPC specification, but there are cases when they may be useful. The most obvious of these cases is authentication. XML-RPC's basic model offers no authentication services, not even the basic authentication one can use with HTTP. Of course, HTTP basic authentication offers a very low level of security, but it does prevent casual intrusion and can be useful. Basic authentication, as per RFC 1945, uses the `WWW-Authenticate` and `Authorization` headers. Several XML-RPC implementations support user/password authentication using this procedure.

Other HTTP headers might be used for passing session data between client and server. As mentioned earlier in this chapter, XML-RPC has no way to connect one request with another. Headers could be used to pass session identifiers, much like the `Cookie` header is used in browser technology to create some kind of state persistence. However, it is probably best to avoid such methods and bring session identifiers explicitly into the parameter list of methods to maintain the interoperability and flexibility of your XML-RPC services.

If you do augment XML-RPC messages with your own non-HTTP headers, be sure to use the "X-" prefix as defined in RFC 1521 (*http://www.ietf.org/rfc/rfc1521.txt*) to indicate their nonofficial nature (e.g., `X-Foo: bar`).

A Complete Request

Here's an example that joins the headers and XML payload to form a complete XML-RPC request:

```
POST /rpchandler HTTP/1.0
User-Agent: AcmeXMLRPC/1.0
Host: xmlrpc.example.com
Content-Type: text/xml
Content-Length: 165

<?xml version="1.0"?>
<methodCall>
<methodName>getCapitalCity</methodName>
<params>
<param>
<value><string>England</string></value>
</param>
</params>
</methodCall>
```

Response Format

Upon receiving an XML-RPC request, an XML-RPC server must deliver a response to the client. The response may take one of two forms: the result of processing the method or a fault report, indicating that something has gone awry in handling the request from the client. As with an XML-RPC request, the response consists of HTTP headers and an XML payload (either the method result or a fault report).

Method Result

The successful invocation of a method on the server must return exactly one result—in contrast to the request payload, which may contain many parameters. Of course, with the ability to use either arrays or structs in the return value, this is no real restriction.

A response message is enclosed in `<methodResponse>` ... `</methodResponse>` tags and contains a `<params>` list (with only one `<param>`) in much the same format as the method request payload. Here's a response to a hypothetical method that asks for the capital city of England:

```
<?xml version="1.0"?>
<methodResponse>
  <params>
    <param>
      <value><string>London</string></value>
    </param>
  </params>
</methodResponse>
```

Sometimes a remote method does not need to return any response value: the equivalent of a void function in C. However, XML-RPC mandates that exactly one parameter must be returned from a method invocation. This conflict means that if you want to use valueless methods with XML-RPC, you must use some kind of workaround. Here are some possible finesses:

- Use a success value: return a Boolean value to indicate the success of the function. This will likely mean hardwiring the return value to true!

- Return any value that suits you, but document your method to let a user know that the return value is meaningless.

- Use the proposed nil value as a return value (see "The Nil Value" later in this chapter).

None of these solutions is the most elegant, but they will all work. Whatever route you take, the most important thing is that what to do is obvious to users of your methods.

Fault Reporting

Many modern programming languages, such as Java and Python, have the concept of *exceptions*. Throwing an exception causes a change in the flow of the program, skipping normal program execution and invoking an exception handler, which can deal with the exceptional situation that has arisen. The advantage of this mechanism is that error handling can be partitioned cleanly from the normal path of flow in the program, making it easier to see (and debug) what is going on.

Other languages, such as C, have no such mechanisms, and error conditions are generally handled by means of the return value of a function. This situation then requires more checking of values, normally resulting in plenty of if/then constructs in the resulting code.

XML-RPC provides a close analog to exceptions in its fault reporting framework. If a processing error occurs while handling a request, a <fault> ... </fault> structure, rather than the result of processing the method, is placed inside the method response.

A fault structure contains a single XML-RPC value, which is a struct with two members. In a fault condition, no other data besides the fault construct is allowed in the XML-RPC response. The members faultCode and faultString convey a numeric indicator of the fault that occurred, along with a human readable explanation. The following example shows a fault that might result if the server does not know about the method the client requested:

```
<?xml version="1.0"?>
<methodResponse>
```

```
<fault>
  <value>
    <struct>
      <member>
        <name>faultCode</name>
        <value><int>3</int></value>
      </member>
      <member>
        <name>faultString</name>
        <value><string>No such method.</string></value>
      </member>
    </struct>
  </value>
</fault>
</methodResponse>
```

Unfortunately, there are no guidelines on any standard codes and errors, so imple-menters have largely been left to their own devices on them. In effect, this means that unless you always know which XML-RPC implementation you will call, you rely on the human readable fault explanation rather than the fault code. For instance, the code 3 shown in the previous example corresponds to "No such method" in the Perl implementation of XML-RPC, but in the PHP implementation it means "Incorrect parameters passed to method."

Most XML-RPC implementations use faults to convey to the client an error in han-dling their request. If you write server methods (i.e., utilize an XML-RPC implemen-tation), using faults is a good way to convey errors in your processing, too. Since XML-RPC stacks generally seem to use the lower-numbered fault codes for their own purposes, it is advisable to start numbering your errors at a reasonably high number. (The PHP implementation, for instance, requires user fault codes to start at 800).

Here's a fault that might be returned in response to such a user-level error (the client has misspelled "England"):

```
<?xml version="1.0"?>
<methodResponse>
  <fault>
    <value>
      <struct>
        <member>
          <name>faultCode</name>
          <value><int>802</int></value>
        </member>
        <member>
          <name>faultString</name>
          <value><string>Unknown country, 'Engand'.</string></value>
        </member>
      </struct>
    </value>
  </fault>
</methodResponse>
```

In languages that support them, faults can be mapped to exceptions. For instance, the Python XML-RPC implementation uses the `xmlrpclib.Fault` exception to handle XML-RPC errors. In languages that don't support exceptions, a conditional construct must be used to check the return value (to verify that it doesn't represent a fault condition).

HTTP Headers

The HTTP headers sent by a server are mostly similar to those required from the client. Here's a sample set of headers from a server:

```
HTTP/1.1 200 OK
Date: Sun, 29 Apr 2001 11:21:37 GMT
Server: Apache/1.3.12 (Unix) Debian/GNU PHP/4.0.2
Connection: close
Content-Type: text/xml
Content-Length: 818
```

In this instance, the response has been delivered by the Apache web server, through which the XML-RPC request has been processed. The two headers critical to, and mandated by, XML-RPC are `Content-Type` and `Content-Length`. The others are normally generated by the host server software.

HTTP response code

The response code must always be 200 OK for XML-RPC. This is because XML-RPC layers on top of HTTP, rather than extending the HTTP protocol itself. However, although an XML-RPC server must always deliver 200 OK in response to an XML-RPC request, an XML-RPC client should be able to cope with the usual gamut of HTTP response codes.

Why is this? If the XML-RPC server is hosted on a normal web server and an incorrect path is given by the client, the server delivers a `404 Not Found` response. Or, for example, if basic authentication is being used, the client must be able to cope with `302 Forbidden` messages. The client need not "recognize" all these codes, but it should be able to provide reasonable behavior when it does not receive a 200 OK code, such as when returning a fault condition.

Server

The `Server` header is the equivalent of the `User-Agent` header for the client. It identifies which software provides the HTTP serving facility with which the client interacts. However, because XML-RPC servers are commonly layered on top of web servers, it does not have the potential for extension use that the `User-Agent` string has. It is merely an interesting piece of information to know and may occasionally come in handy in debugging.

Content-Type

As with the request, the `Content-Type` header of an XML-RPC response must always be `text/xml`. If you write your own XML-RPC serving code, rather than use an available XML-RPC library, be aware that you may need to take special action to generate this header.

Content-Length

The `Content-Length` header must contain the number of octets in the returned payload, in the same way as it is computed for a request. `Content-Length` is not optional and is mandated by the XML-RPC specification.

This requirement has an interesting consequence for XML-RPC implementations. It means that an entire response must be computed before it can be delivered to a client because the content length must be known in order to insert it in the HTTP response header. Consequently, it is not possible to create a streaming response (in which the client starts reading before the server finishes writing). It has been pointed out that this limits the use of XML-RPC in low-memory situations when constructing the entire response before commencing its output may be prohibitive.*

Although the specification requires the `Content-Length` header on a response, it is possible to create a nonstandard implementation that omits this, by using HTTP 1.1 (see section 4.4 of RFC 2616). If you do this, however, you must be willing to bear the risks of interoperability with arbitrary, specification-conformant XML-RPC clients.

A Complete Response

Here's a complete response from an XML-RPC server, including both the HTTP headers and the XML payload:

```
HTTP/1.1 200 OK
Date: Sun, 29 Apr 2001 12:08:58 GMT
Server: Apache/1.3.12 (Unix) Debian/GNU PHP/4.0.2
Connection: close
Content-Type: text/xml
Content-length: 133

<?xml version="1.0"?>
<methodResponse>
<params>
<param>
```

---

* See a message from John Wilson, a developer using XML-RPC on embedded systems, to the XML-RPC mailing list, archived at *http://www.egroups.com/message/xml-rpc/979*.

```
<value><string>Michigan</string></value>
</param>
</params>
</methodResponse>
```

The response is provided to a sample call to the method `getUSAStateByOrder`, which returns the name of the 26th state to join the United States: Michigan.

The Nil Value

As observed earlier, XML-RPC has no way to express a null value; that is, an absence of value. This value is commonly found in programming languages (Java's null, Python's None, Perl's undef, as well as in databases, such as NULL). Consequently, many users of XML-RPC have requested its inclusion.

Although there has been no movement to officially incorporate a null value into the XML-RPC specification, there is some experimental support for it in the Java XML-RPC implementation. A small definition of it is available on the Web at *http://www.ontosys.com/xml-rpc/extensions.html.*

The null value, called nil, has only one expression in XML-RPC:

```
<value><nil/></value>
```

Implementations that choose to support it should treat `<nil/>` as the equivalent of the host language's empty value.

A DTD for XML-RPC

This section provides a simple Document Type Definition (commonly referred to as a DTD, as explained in Appendix A) for XML-RPC. It is provided for interest only and is not sufficient for the implementation of an XML-RPC processor. In particular, DTDs are not expressive enough to convey the restrictions on elements such as int, which may only contain specific character sequences. Additionally, the introduction of a validating XML parser into an XML-RPC stack (as opposed to hard-coding the validation) may be more overhead than it is worth, especially since the DTD alone is not sufficient to verify an incoming request.

That being said, in systems where XML validation is already used, use of this DTD may aid the integration of XML-RPC:

```
<!ELEMENT i4 (#PCDATA)>
<!ELEMENT int (#PCDATA)>
<!ELEMENT boolean (#PCDATA)>
<!ELEMENT string (#PCDATA)>
<!ELEMENT double (#PCDATA)>
<!ELEMENT dateTime.iso8601 (#PCDATA)>
<!ELEMENT base64 (#PCDATA)>
```

```
<!ELEMENT data (value*)>
<!ELEMENT array (data)>
<!ELEMENT name (#PCDATA)>
<!ELEMENT member (name, value)>
<!ELEMENT struct (member*)>
<!ELEMENT value ( i4 | int | boolean | string | dateTime.iso8601
                 | double | base64 | struct | array )>

<!ELEMENT param (value)>
<!ELEMENT params (param*)>

<!ELEMENT methodName (#PCDATA)>
<!ELEMENT methodCall (methodName, params)>

<!-- note that the content model for fault is underspecified here -->
<!ELEMENT fault (value)>
<!ELEMENT methodResponse (params|fault)>
```

A more verbose DTD, with more explanation and support for the `nil` element type, can be found online at *http://www.ontosys.com/xml-rpc/xml-rpc.dtd.*

3

Client-Server Communication: XML-RPC in Java

Java was built from the ground up as a network-centric development environment. As a Java developer, XML-RPC offers you an opportunity to extend that foundation in a structured way. Adding XML-RPC to your toolkit makes it easier to integrate a Java application with an application built using another environment or simply to establish lightweight point-to-point communication between Java programs running on different computers. Although XML-RPC goes against the grain of much Java network programming (and even against some of the fundamental principles of object-oriented development), its alternative approach can be useful in many relatively common scenarios.

You already have a wide variety of Java-based XML and HTTP tools to choose from, but you can also take advantage of a prepackaged set of XML-RPC tools. Although understanding the foundations of XML-RPC is very useful for debugging and for establishing connections between systems in different environments, you can treat XML-RPC much like you do any other Java feature. There's some setup work to do, especially for XML-RPC servers, but most of this work is simple and needs to be done only once in the course of a program.

This chapter looks at how XML-RPC fits into Java's many network options. It demonstrates how to build a variety of different XML-RPC clients, servers, and handlers. Some of these examples take advantage of built-in functionality for setting up simple XML-RPC servers and handlers; others explore the possibilities opened up by handling more of the processing directly. The examples cover different styles of XML-RPC programming, from simple library function calls to more complex calls that manipulate information on the server.

Why XML-RPC for Java?

Java is already an extremely network-aware environment, complete with its own mechanisms for remote communication and coordination of objects on multiple systems. Remote Method Invocation (RMI) and RMI's support for the broader world of CORBA-based systems provide built-in support for distributing applications across multiple systems.* In many ways, Java is well ahead of its competitors, and its network support extends far beyond the simple request-response cycle of XML-RPC.

Despite Java's built-in network computing prowess, XML-RPC offers a few kinds of functionality that Java can't match. XML-RPC is far more lightweight than Java's built in RMI support, passing only parameters rather than objects. Java programs can use XML-RPC to connect directly to any other system supporting XML-RPC, rather than limiting connections to fellow RMI systems or having to use complex (and expensive) CORBA object request brokers.

As illustrated in Figure 3-1, XML-RPC can bring the direct connections RMI makes possible for strictly Java applications to applications that integrate multiple environmentsXML-RPC's use of HTTP as a transport substrate makes it relatively simple to integrate XML-RPC with the web-enabled applications that are already spreading across the computing landscape. At the same time, XML-RPC uses such a tiny subset of HTTP that Java applications can easily avoid the overhead of full-scale HTTP processing, working with a more minimal—and more efficient—driver that takes advantage of Java's built-in understanding of TCP/IP.

XML-RPC also offers you a shorter compilation and testing cycle. Unlike RMI, which requires recompilation of interfaces to register method signatures, XML-RPC allows the client to specify which method it wants to use and then looks for a handler. Because the reference is done by name, there aren't any stubs to manage or include, and changes can be made much more easily at runtime.

On the other hand, XML-RPC is definitely not appropriate in plenty of Java application situations. Much of the Enterprise JavaBeans (EJB) work already relies on RMI, and rewriting it to use XML-RPC would be a remarkable waste of time. Although a snippet of XML-RPC code might be useful as a simple bridge between an EJB-based application and code written for other environments, XML-RPC isn't designed explicitly to support the many demands of complex enterprise-scale design. Similarly, if you need to pass objects, rather than parameters, between-systems, you should look into a more sophisticated set of tools than XML-RPC.

---

* The Common Object Request Broker Architecture (CORBA), is designed to facilitate large-scale exchanges of object information and processing between systems that may or may not use similar environments or languages.

XML-RPC lets you pass sets of parameters, not complex nested structures with associated method information, back and forth. As explained later in this chapter, XML-RPC's approach doesn't match cleanly with JavaBeans, either.

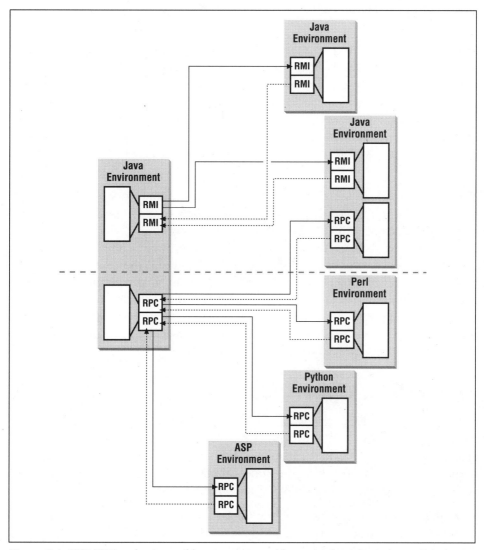

Figure 3-1. XML-RPC makes it possible to connect a wide array of programming environments

Although most Java programs aren't designed for use in the procedural framework that XML-RPC uses, an enormous amount of code in the typical Java program could conceivably be exposed as an XML-RPC procedure, with or without some degree of modification. Although Java is very object-focused, it retains enough links with procedural environments for developers to take advantage of "traditional" features, such as function calls, in the midst of complex object interactions. Although some of XML-RPC's rules, like its lack of support for void return values, make integrating XML-RPC with Java difficult, most of the integration process is pretty simple, limited only by the narrow range of data types and structures XML-RPC supports.

The XML-RPC library for Java does not require the methods it uses be static, but in some ways static methods fit the basic architecture of XML-RPC very well. Static methods are the closest things Java offers to procedural function calls, commonly used for utility functions (such as those in the **Math** class) for which the function itself is important, but there may not be any surrounding context. If you've built libraries of these kinds of methods, implementing key algorithms for processing arguments, you may find it especially easy to convert your old work to XML-RPC handlers.

You can also use XML-RPC servers in a larger Java framework to answer client requests while using those requests to modify their own information set. Rather than thinking about XML-RPC handlers as "mere" procedures, you can treat XML-RPC handlers as regular Java methods, limited only by difficulties in transferring objects between the routine making the method call and the routine performing processing. In every other way, XML-RPC can become a natural part of Java programming, providing yet another way to get information into and out of Java environments. Using XML-RPC can make connecting Java programs to programs written in other environments much simpler, and may be appropriate for some simple Java-to-Java cases, as well.

The XML-RPC Java Library

Although you could use the wide variety of XML resources available in Java to create your own XML-RPC package, Hannes Wallnöfer has already built a set of classes that provide XML-RPC capabilities for both clients and servers, including a small XML-RPC server that lets you work without the overhead of a full-scale Web server. Most examples in this chapter rely on his package.

As of this writing, the XML-RPC library for Java in still in beta, at Version 1.0 beta 4. Although it is unlikely that there will be major changes to the API, you should check the *index.html* file and documentation that come with the library if you encounter problems.

The XML-RPC Library for Java web site is *http://classic.helma.at/hannes/xmlrpc/*, and additional resources (including a mailing list with archives) are also available there. The examples in the current chapter use the **helma.xmlrpc** library, which is available at that site.

In addition to core XML-RPC functionality, the `helma.xmlrpc` package includes:

- Classes for quick XML-RPC client and server creation

- A micro-web server useful for setting up XML-RPC on systems that don't already have a web server running or don't want to use the existing server

- A sample of Java servlet integration

- A standalone set of classes used for building lightweight XML-RPC applets

The components included in the XML-RPC library include client- and server-specific classes used for creating requests and responses, as well as a more generic core that controls how the library handles HTTP processing and XML parsing.

Installing the helma.xmlrpc Library

The `helma.xmlrpc` library is available for free download as a zip archive at *http://classic.helma.at/hannes/xmlrpc/*. You'll need an unzipping utility to open the archive, which contains documentation, examples, source code, and three Java archive (*jar*) files. The files provide the executables you'll need to put XML-RPC into your Java environment.

The most critical of the *jar* files (all of which are stored in the *lib* directory) is *xmlrpc.jar*, which contains the core logic for implementing XML-RPC. The library also includes a jar file for the OpenXML parser, which is supported by default. You don't have to use the OpenXML parser, but it's very helpful if you install XML-RPC on a system without its own XML parser already installed. The last *jar* file, *xmlrpc-applet.jar*, includes code that lets you build applets that handle XML-RPC client transactions inside a browser and that can be controlled by JavaScript.

If you already have an XML parser installed, you only need to add *xmlrpc.jar* to your Java CLASSPATH environment variable, though you'll need to specify which parser you want to use in your XML-RPC client and server initialization code. If you don't have an XML parser already installed, or you just want to rely on the choice of `helma.xmlrpc`'s creator, add the *openxml-1.2.jar* file to your CLASSPATH in addition to *xmlrpc.jar*. Although you may want to add *xmlrpc-applet.jar* to your CLASSPATH for development convenience, it's designed to be used in a browser and doesn't have to be installed on client computers.

You can distribute the `helma.xmlrpc` package with your own code, though the author requests that the license be distributed with the package and that any modifications be clearly documented.

General XML-RPC Library Configuration

The `helma.xmlrpc` class includes a set of static methods used to configure your XML-RPC processing. Because they are static methods, they affect all XML-RPC processing. You can't specify that some groups of XML-RPC methods should use a different parser from others, nor can you specify that debugging information should only be reported for certain groups of methods. This isn't normally a liability, however—it's very difficult to imagine a situation in which using different parsers for different methods might be justified, for example.

The `setDriver()` method lets you choose an XML parser for processing XML-RPC requests as they arrive. By default, the XML-RPC library uses the OpenXML parser, but developers can change that to any SAX-compliant parser. If your application uses a different XML parser for some other aspect of processing, it probably makes sense to use a single parser—it's easier to manage and cuts down on the size of the distribution.

The `setDriver()` method takes a single argument, the name of the parser to be used. It's probably best to enclose this method in a **try/catch** exception handler to handle the **ClassNotFoundException** the method will throw if the Java environment can't find the class:

```
try {
    // Use the Microstar AElfred parser for XML-RPC processing

    XmlRpc.setDriver("com.microstar.xml.SAXDriver");
} catch (ClassNotFoundException e) {
    // If no AElfred, provide an intelligible error message

    System.out.println("Could not locate AElfred.  Please check your
classpath for com.microstar.xml.SAXDriver.");
}
```

The XML-RPC package also provides shortcut names for some commonly used parsers. For the most current list of shortcuts, see "Choosing the XML parser" in the documentation that comes with the distribution. In this case, we could have used **aelfred** instead of **com.microstar.xml.SAXDriver** as the argument to **XmlRpc.setDriver()**.

By default, all XML-RPC messages are sent using the ISO-8859-1 character encoding, but the **setEncoding()** method allows you to choose alternate encodings. Encodings must be specified from the list of available Java encodings, available at *http://java.sun.com/j2se/1.3/docs/guide/intl/encoding.doc.html*.

To send out requests using the UTF-8 character set, you can write:

```
XmlRpc.setEncoding("UTF8");  //Java identifies UTF-8 as UTF8 without dash
```

The setDebug() method lets you watch your XML-RPC method registrations and request processing much more closely, providing information to the system console about the structure of the document received, the parameters extracted, and the result returned. To start debugging output, you'll need to pass a value of **true** to the setDebug() method:

```
XmlRpc.setDebug(true);  //turn on verbose debugging output
```

When you no longer need debugging information (which can pile up very quickly), pass a value of **false** to setDebug():

```
XmlRpc.setDebug(false);  //turn off verbose debugging output
```

The helma.xmlrpc package provides a lot of information about what happens inside a transaction. The following output, for example, describes a server-side transaction involving the **anyArea** handler that is created later in this chapter. Content marked in bold was generated by the code used to build the XML-RPC server, but all the rest was generated by the helma.xmlrpc package itself:

```
Attempting to start XML-RPC Server...
Started successfully.
Target object is class AreaHandler
Registered AreaHandler class to area.
Now accepting requests. (Halt program to stop.)
POST / HTTP/1.0
User-Agent: helma XML-RPC 1.0
Host: localhost:8899
Content-Type: text/xml
Content-Length: 296

startElement: methodCall
startElement: methodName
endElement: methodName
startElement: params
startElement: param
startElement: value
startElement: struct
startElement: member
startElement: name
endElement: name
startElement: value
startElement: double
endElement: double
endElement: value
endElement: member
startElement: member
startElement: name
endElement: name
startElement: value
endElement: value
endElement: member
endElement: struct
endElement: value
```

```
endElement: param
endElement: params
endElement: methodCall
Spent 211 millis parsing
method name is area.anyArea
inparams = [{radius=3.0, type=circle}]
Searching for method: anyArea
Parameter 0: class java.util.Hashtable = {radius=3.0, type=circle}
outparam = 28.274333882308138
Spent 231 millis in request
```

In this case, the client requested a calculation of the area of a circle with a radius of 3, and received a response of 28.274.... after 231 milliseconds of processing on my 233MHz system. (This was an initial request, adding about 200 milliseconds while the classes loaded. Caching reduces the time per request significantly.)

The **version** field of the **XmlRpc** class may be useful for developers writing code that depends on version-specific features. At this point, the interface of the class appears to be stable, and developers should have control over the code they deploy, but this might be worth checking in situations when **CLASSPATH** conflicts and other hazards of shared systems could come into play.

Data Types and Java XML-RPC

The **helma.xmlrpc** package supports all XML-RPC data types (plus an extra, **nil**), representing them as built-in Java types. Because Java supports, and sometimes requires, object wrappers around its primitive types, the XML-RPC package can be flexible with XML-RPC clients and sometime with XML-RPC servers.

The **helma.xmlrpc** package can automatically map XML-RPC types to Java types, as shown in Table 3-1.

Table 3-1. XML-RPC versus Java data types

XML-RPC type	Simplest Java type	More complex Java type
i4	int	java.lang.Integer
int	int	java.lang.Integer
boolean	boolean	java.lang.Boolean
string	java.lang.String	java.lang.String
double	double	java.lang.Double
dateTime.iso8601	java.util.Date	java.util.Date
struct	java.util.Hashtable	java.util.Hashtable
array	java.util.Vector	java.util.Vector
base64	byte[]	byte[]
nil (extension)	null	null

XML-RPC clients may pass arguments to the `helma.xmlrpc` package using either of the choices above, when there is a choice. (Because Java won't accept primitives inside `Vectors` and `Hashtables`, the wrapper classes are sometimes necessary.) Similarly, XML-RPC handlers may use either choice for their return values. Because `i4` and `int` are considered identical by the XML-RPC specification, the `helma.xmlrpc` package accepts either of them in incoming requests. The `helma.xmlrpc` package handles all encoding and decoding needed by the `dateTime.iso8601` and `base64` types.

On the other hand, XML-RPC handlers that use the automatic registration feature of `helma.xmlrpc` *must* use the simplest Java type available to describe the parameters they accept. The examples in the next few sections detail how this works and show some of the occasional extra work required to map complex types to simpler types.

If you're reusing existing code that takes the wrapper class, rather than the primitive, as an argument, it is possible to create an XML-RPC processor that supports the wrapper argument. However, you either have to write extra code that manages the conversion of the primitives to the wrappers before calling the existing code or build your own set of tools for handling XML-RPC requests. Writing a middleware handler might seem ungainly, but it's probably the easier route and isn't that difficult with the `helma.xmlrpc.XmlRpcHandler` interface.

Building XML-RPC Clients

Building XML-RPC clients with the `helma.xmlrpc` package is a relatively simple operation, involving the creation of an `XmlRpcClient` object, assigning parameters, and making a call to the `XmlRpcClient`'s execute method. There are a number of exceptions that can be thrown, and there may be delays in getting a response, but for the most part, calling XML-RPC routines requires only a small amount of extra coding, much of which actually deals with exception handling.

The constructor and the `execute()` methods are the core of the `XmlRpcClient` class. The easiest way to handle them is in a `try`/`catch` structure, though you can encapsulate them in methods that throw the exceptions to a higher-level handler. The constructor may throw a `MalformedURLException`, a subclass of `IOException`; the `execute()` method may throw either `IOException` (when connections are refused, impossible, etc.) or `XmlRpcException`, which is issued when the XML-RPC server reports an error. The constructor accepts a `String` object representing a URL, a URL object, or the combination of a `String` for the hostname and an `int` for the port.

XmlRpcClient objects are reusable, though they only connect to the server originally specified when they were constructed. Applications that establish repeated connections to the same server may want to reuse the objects, but many applications just create the client, call a method, and disappear. In these cases, the constructor and execute() method may appear inside a single try/catch statement. When the constructor and execute() method appear together, the MalformedURLException may be treated as just another IOException, making it one fewer exception to catch.

The following example creates a client that can connect to port 8899 on the computer with the IP address 192.168.126.42. It sends a **double** (retrieved from user input through the **args**[] array) to a method identified as **area.circleArea**, expecting to get back the area of a circle whose radius is the double sent as the parameter. This code doesn't do anything with the result; it just sends the request and handles any exceptions that might be thrown.

```
try {
    // Create the client, identifying the server
    XmlRpcClient client =
        new XmlRpcClient("http://192.168.126.42:8899/");

    // Create the request parameters using user input
    Vector params = new Vector();
    params.addElement(new Double(args[0]));

    // Issue a request
    Object result =
        client.execute("area.circleArea", params);

} catch (IOException e) {
    System.out.println("IO Exception: " + e.getMessage());
} catch (XmlRpcException e) {
    System.out.println("Exception within XML-RPC: " + e.getMessage());
}
//Continue processing using result object...
    //result object will contain one of the XML-RPC data types
```

Depending on the response sent by the XML-RPC server, the result object may be any of the types described previously in the section "Data Types." In many cases, it is just a single typed value, but the **helma.xmlrpc** classes return **Vector** or **Hashtable** objects for XML-RPC responses that return arrays or structs.

As of Version 1.0 Beta 4, the **XmlRpcClient** class provides support for basic HTTP authentication. To use basic authentication, developers need to add only one method call to their client setup. The **setBasicAuthentication()** method takes two strings as arguments. The first is a username, the second is the password.

To add a username and password to the previous request, you simply need to add the code shown in bold in the following example:

```
try {
    // Create the client, identifying the server
    XmlRpcClient client =
        new XmlRpcClient("http://192.168.126.42:8899/");

            XmlRpcClient.setBasicAuthentication("myUsername", "myPassword");
    // Create the request parameters using user input
    Vector params = new Vector();
    params.addElement(new Double(args[0]));

    // Issue a request
    Object result =
        client.execute("area.circleArea", params);

} catch (IOException e) {
    System.out.println("IO Exception: " + e.getMessage());
} catch (XmlRpcException e) {
    System.out.println("Exception within XML-RPC: " + e.getMessage());
}
//Continue processing using result object...
    //result object will contain one of the XML-RPC data types
```

Although HTTP basic authentication isn't especially secure, code containing usernames and passwords in plain text is also a serious security risk. If you use this feature, you should consider combining it with other security tools (like the "paranoid" mode described for the XML-RPC server, later in this chapter) and protecting your code from distribution beyond the group of people authorized to work with those passwords.

The XmlRpcClient class uses Java's built-in support (java.net.URLConnection) for HTTP requests, giving it the ability to handle proxies automatically and to deal with a variety of server situations. Developers who need a lighter-weight XML-RPC client can use the XmlRpcClientLite class, which implements more minimal HTTP support. The two classes are identical, except in XmlRpcClient's support for more advanced HTTP functionality, including basic HTTP authentication.

Building XML-RPC Servers

Building XML-RPC servers is a bit more complex than building clients. In addition to building the core logic of your application, you need to publish your services to the XML-RPC library so it can manage requests. Your application may do this in the context of a servlet running within a larger Web server, or it may use the library's built-in WebServer class to create a minimal server handling only XML-RPC requests.

The simplest way to build an XML-RPC server relies on the `WebServer` class and uses the `XmlRpcServer` class's built-in ability to recognize Java classes and methods during the registration process. If you just need to publish methods whose parameters conform to the XML-RPC data types described earlier in this chapter, this is usually straightforward.

Using the WebServer Class

The `helma.xmlrpc` package includes a simple `WebServer` class that makes it easy to set up XML-RPC on systems that don't have a web server installed previously or to add an extra server listening on a nonstandard port. The `WebServer` class provides only the core of HTTP functionality used by XML-RPC, not the full set of functionality used to distribute web pages. This limitation should reduce the fears of network administrators who don't want to install internal web sites, while giving Java developers a small-footprint approach to adding XML-RPC to computers that aren't intended to be web servers.

Creating a new web server that uses the built-in `WebServer` class requires calling its constructor with a port number. For example, to create a web server that listens for XML-RPC requests on port 9876, you can call its constructor as follows:

```
WebServer server = new WebServer(9876);
```

If the `WebServer` can't start on the specified port, it throws a `java.io.IOException`. Depending on how you structure the program, you may want to enclose the constructor (and subsequent registrations) in a `try`/`catch` statement, or you may want the method managing the XML-RPC interface to pass the exception on to another handler.

Once you've set up the `WebServer` object, you can add and remove XML-RPC handlers to it using the functionality described in the section "Creating Handlers," later in this chapter. `WebServer` itself is a fairly small wrapper of functionality around the `XmlRpcServer` class, so you can use it the same way. The `WebServer` class does support HTTP Basic Authentication, but you'll need to create and register classes that implement the `AuthenticatedXmlRpcHandler` interface.

In addition to registering and processing XML-RPC handlers, the `WebServer` class provides a basic security model in the form of a "paranoid" mode. By default, WebServer accepts requests from all IP addresses. In paranoid mode, the server only accepts requests from specified IP addresses. It provides two methods, `acceptClient()` and `denyClient()`, for building lists of approved and rejected clients. By default, no client connections are accepted when `setParanoid()` has been called with an argument of `true`. You'll need to use the `acceptClient()` method to add approved IP addresses, and can use `denyClient()` to trim that list. Once an IP address has been put on the denied list, `acceptClient()` can't bring it back—denials are more permanent than acceptances. (You'll have to restart the XML-RPC sever to reopen it.) Both methods accept the asterisk (*) for wildcarding, a feature convenient for dealing with groups of addresses without resorting to loops.

If your Java XML-RPC server is only communicating with clients on the same computer—to bridge Java and another environment, most likely—you may want to shut down all IP addresses except localhost, `127.0.0.1`. The server won't even consider requests made from other systems if you take the following approach:

```
WebServer server = new WebServer(9876);
server.setParanoid(true);
server.addClient("127.0.0.1");
```

Using this setup, only requests directed to *http://127.0.0.1:9876* will be considered, and because of the unique nature of the *localhost* address, they'll have to originate from the same machine as the XML-RPC server.

Another common setup permits an entire IP subnet to access the XML-RPC server, but exclude a few systems, perhaps gateways to other networks that might be hijacked. If an XML-RPC server was in the 192.168.137.*x* private network and the gateway router was 192.168.137.55, that server could be made available to all hosts on the local network *except* the gateway using the following code snippet:

```
WebServer server = new WebServer(9876);
server.setParanoid(true);
server.addClient("192.168.137.*");
server.denyClient("192.168.137.55");
```

Although filtering messages based on IP addresses isn't a complete security model by any means, it may be enough to make XML-RPC usable in a wide variety of contexts. If you need more security than this, you should consider using the `XmlRpcServer` class in a richer web server context, using the HTTPS and certificates facilities available on larger-scale web servers.

Using XmlRpcServer Without WebServer

If you integrate XML-RPC with existing web servers or you need more security than the IP filtering model of the `WebServer` class, you should use the `XmlRpcServer` class. Although the `WebServer` class accepts HTTP POST requests and feeds them directly to handlers, `XmlRpcServer` acts as an intermediary, accepting request information from servlets or other sources. Although `XmlRpcServer` doesn't handle the connection management end of HTTP, it does process all textual information sent over HTTP.

XmlRpcServer is simpler than WebServer because it leaves network details and security to its surrounding environment. The two classes use identical approaches for registering and unregistering classes containing XML-RPC methods, but XmlRpcServer requires more assistance than WebServer. The WebServer class listens for requests and processes them automatically; XmlRpcServer needs another class to listen for requests.

The XmlRpcServer class uses an XML-in, XML-out model for handling requests, leaving the rest to the supporting environment. Servlets can process the header information of XML-RPC requests, but they pass those requests' XML content to the XmlRpcServer's execute() method as InputStreams. (Optionally, they can include a username and password derived from basic authentication.) The execute() method returns a String containing the response, which the supporting environment then wraps with appropriate HTTP header information.

For example, the WebServer class wraps its calls to the XmlRpcServer's execute method as follows:

```
ServerInputStream sin = new ServerInputStream (input, contentLength);
byte result[] = xmlrpc.execute (sin, user, password);
output.write (httpversion.getBytes());
output.write (ok);
output.write (server);
output.write (conclose);
output.write (ctype);
output.write (clength);
output.write (Integer.toString (result.length).getBytes());
output.write (doubleNewline);
output.write (result);
output.flush ();
```

WebServer takes a very basic approach, reading and writing the HTTP requests as streams of textual bytes. Within a servlet, developers can take advantage of a slightly higher level of abstraction, as shown in the Servlet that comes in the XML-RPC package:

```
public void doPost(HttpServletRequest req, HttpServletResponse res)
            throws ServletException, IOException  {
        byte[] result = xmlrpc.execute (req.getInputStream ());
        res.setContentType("text/xml");
        res.setContentLength (result.length);
        OutputStream output = res.getOutputStream();
        output.write (result);
        output.flush ();
}
```

In either case, XmlRpcServer accepts an XML-RPC request as an XML document and returns an XML-RPC response document. The supporting environment has to handle the rest of the transaction.

The `XmlRpcServer` class also provides support for the `Authenti-catedXmlRpcHandler` interface. You can also pass information using a three-argument version of execute, which allows the `XmlRpcServer` class to send authentication information to the handler. In addition to the `InputStream`, you'll need to add the username and password strings. Because the authentication header, which includes both the username and password, is sent using `base64` encoding and the servlet package doesn't provide a simple means of reaching the password, extracting the username and password requires a few extra steps. These steps are highlighted in bold in the following example:

```
public void doPost(HttpServletRequest req, HttpServletResponse res)
            throws ServletException, IOException  {

    //get authorization header from request
    String auth=req.getHeader("Authorization");
    if (!auth.toUpperCase().startsWith("BASIC")) {
        throw ServletException("wrong kind of authorization!");
    }

    //get encoded username and password
    String userPassEncoded=auth.substring(6);

    //create a base64 decoder using Sun utility class
    sun.misc.BASE64Decoder dec=new sun.misc.BASE64Decoder();
    String userPassDecoded=new String(dec.decodeBuffer(userPassEncoded));

    //split decoded username and password
    StringTokenizer userAndPass=new StringTokenizer(userPassDecoded,":");
    String username=userAndPass.nextToken();
    String password=userAndPass.nextToken();

    //send input stream, username, and password to xmlrpc.execute
        String result = xmlrpc.execute (req.getInputStream (), username, password);
        res.setContentType("text/xml");
        res.setContentLength (result.length ());
        PrintWriter writer = res.getWriter();
        writer.write (result);
        writer.flush ();
}
```

The `WebServer` class already includes this decoding, providing a more transparent means of handling authenticated transactions.

Creating XML-RPC Handlers

Both `WebServer` and `XmlRpcServer` employ the same set of methods for registering and unregistering classes whose methods can be used through XML-RPC. Java classes whose methods accept the standard data types (described earlier in this chapter) can use the `WebServer` and `XmlRpcServer` classes' built-in logic for mapping XML-RPC calls to Java methods; other classes can be extended with a single `execute()` method for mapping XML-RPC requests to Java methods. In both cases, the `addHandler()` and `removeHandler()` methods are used the same way to add and remove classes that can handle XML-RPC methods.

Creating Handlers Using Automatic Registration

If the methods you want to use for processing XML-RPC requests are written so that they only accept and return the data types described, you can use the automatic registration process. The following code sample demonstrates these methods using a simple testing procedure that accepts two strings and returns a new string that concatenates the strings in the reverse order of how they were received:

```
public class testHandler {

        public String nameTester(String first, String last) {
                return "Reversed: " + last + ", " + first;
        }
    }
```

Making the `nameTester()` method available as an XML-RPC procedure requires two steps. First, set up a web server to handle the HTTP transactions. Second, register this method with that server to make it available via XML-RPC. Once the server object has been created, the `testHandler` can be registered with the server using the `addHandler()` method. The server then accepts and processes requests for the method:

```
WebServer server = new WebServer(9876);
server.addHandler("test", new testHandler());
```

The server examines the `testHandler` class and extracts its method signatures for mapping to XML-RPC requests. XML-RPC clients may now send requests for the `test.nameTester` method, sending two strings as parameters. They'll receive a single string back, which begins with the text "Reversed:" and then concatenates the strings in reverse order.

If that method needs to be disengaged at some later point, the `removeHandler()` method can be called:

```
server.removeHandler("test");
```

Now the `test.nameTester()` method is no longer available. Although turning XML-RPC methods on and off dynamically might create serious chaos for a lot of stable service-oriented applications, it can be very useful for managing XML-RPC methods in conjunction with some kind of control panel. Among other things, it lets you update the classes used to handle an XML-RPC request without having to stop and restart the XML-RPC server or servlet.

Creating Handlers Using Explicit Registration

If you prefer to manage the mappings between classes and methods more directly, you can register classes that implement the `helma.xmlrpc.XmlRpcHandler` interface. When the server encounters these classes, it defers to their mapping from XML-RPC method names and parameters to Java methods. Instead of trying to pass arguments directly to Java methods inside a class, the XML-RPC server passes the method name and parameters (as a `Vector`) to the execute method, the single method required by the `XmlRpcHandler` interface.

The default behavior of `helma.xmlrpc` handles most situations, but mapping methods directly is appropriate in a number of cases. You may have a set of classes you're retrofitting to XML-RPC that expect their arguments to arrive as objects rather than primitives. You would prefer to handle that packaging in a single method rather than by creating method-by-method front ends. You may want to hide the internal structures of your processing, a reasonable strategy when exchanging information with potential competitors. Finally, you may be creating methods that are minor variations on a theme, where the method name differentiates only a small change, such as the expected return value type.

Implementing the `XmlRpcHandler` interface requires only one method, `execute()`. If a class implements the `XmlRpcHandler` interface, all XML-RPC calls are directed to the execute method, short-circuiting the automatic method mapping of the `XmlRpcServer` class. The `execute()` method takes a `String` and a `Vector` as arguments and returns an `Object`. The `String` is the method named by the XML-RPC request; the `Vector` contains all parameters that were sent with that request.

The `execute()` method can be used in several different ways. The logic inside the `execute()` method may just ship the Vector containing the parameters to other methods, leaving them to unpackage and process the parameters. Some `execute()` methods may emulate the `helma.xmlrpc.XmlRpc` package's own processing, mapping the method name and parameter set to appropriate handlers. More sophisticated `execute()` methods might read the parameters inside the `Vector` and create objects based on those parameters, which are then shipped to the appropriate target method. In any of these cases, the `execute()` method acts as a gateway.

Example 3-1 uses the `execute()` method to pass information to the `nameTester()` method used in the automatic registration example. Note that the `nameTester()` method is now private, accessible only through the `execute()` method. This isn't required, but it illustrates that the `execute()` method has taken over from the XML-RPC package's native registration.

Example 3-1. Creating an XML-RPC handler

```
import java.util.Vector;
import helma.xmlrpc.XmlRpcHandler;

public class testHandler implements XmlRpcHandler {

        public Object execute(String methodName, Vector parameters) throws java.lang.
Exception {
                if (methodName=="nameTester") {
                        String first=(String) parameters.elementAt(0);
                        String last=(String) parameters.elementAt(1);
                        return nameTester(first, last);
                } else {
                        throw new Exception("No such method!");
                }
        }

        private String nameTester(String first, String last) {
                return "Reversed: " + last + ", " + first;
        }

}
```

Classes that implement the `AuthenticatedXmlRpcHandler` interface instead of `XmlRpcHandler` can process the username and password pairs from basic authentication as well as the method names and parameters, giving them additional gateway functionality. You'll want to implement a more sophisticated password checking mechanism—and perhaps move it to a separate class to be shared among various handlers. The `testHandler` class in Example 3-2, however, demonstrates how a handler supporting authentication might work.

Example 3-2. Creating an XML-RPC handler with authentication

```
import java.util.Vector;
import helma.xmlrpc.*;

public class testHandler implements AuthenticatedXmlRpcHandler {

//authenticated execute
        public Object execute(String methodName, Vector parameters,
                        String username, String password) throws Exception {
                if (checkPassword(username, password)) {
                        return execute(methodName, parameters);
                } else {
                        throw new Exception("Unauthorized user");
                }
        }
//unauthenticated execute - called by authenticated
        protected Object execute(String methodName, Vector parameters)
                        throws Exception {
                if (methodName=="nameTester") {
                        String first=(String) parameters.elementAt(0);
```

Example 3-2. Creating an XML-RPC handler with authentication (continued)

```
                String last=(String) parameters.elementAt(1);
                return nameTester(first, last);
        } else {
                throw new Exception("No such method!");
        }
    }

    private boolean checkPassword(String username, String password) {
    //password checking logic should be more sophisticated!
        if (username.equals(password)) {
                return true;
        } else {
                return false;
        }
    }

    private String nameTester(String first, String last) {
        return "Reversed: " + last + ", " + first;
    }
}
```

The `XmlRpcServer` class checks the type of class it works with and passes the correct set of parameters to the `execute()` method. Classes that implement `XmlRpcHandler` receive two parameters—method name and the `Vector` containing the parameters—while classes that implement `Authenticated-XmlRpcHandler` receive four parameters: method name, the `Vector` containing parameters, username, and password.

Three Practical Examples

Although XML-RPC itself is very simple, it can be applied to a number of programming styles. The approach that most directly fits "remote procedure calls" is one that calls procedures across a network, as shown in the library function example in the next section. Procedure calls can also be used easily for client-to-server reporting, shown in an example that logs error reports from clients. Finally, just as Java itself uses get and set methods to manipulate the properties of objects, XML-RPC can extend that functionality to expose those methods to other systems on the network.

Library Functions

This example creates a simple Java library that performs mathematical calculations without any side effects on the server. The calculations performed—determining the areas of circles and squares—aren't very complex, but this same approach could be used for much more intensive algorithms. Although the average applet is certainly capable of calculating the area of a square on its own, many fields of computing rely on mathematical tools that demand extraordinary amounts of processing power.

As shown in Example 3-3, the `AreaHandler` class has two methods and no properties. The first method takes two arguments, `length` and `width`, and returns the area of a rectangle; the second method takes a single argument, `radius`, and returns the area of a circle.

Example 3-3. Library function implemented as XML-RPC handler

```
public class AreaHandler {

    public Double rectArea(double length, double width) {
    return new Double(length*width);
    }

    public Double circleArea(double radius) {
        double value=(radius*radius*Math.PI);
        return new Double (value);
    }

}
```

This code is run as an XML-RPC client on the server, with a simple client to pass it values. The code for the server builds on the generic code created in the previous section, using the `helma.xmlrpc` library's built-in `WebServer` class, as shown in Example 3-4.

Example 3-4. Hosting the area function

```
import java.io.IOException;
import helma.xmlrpc.WebServer;
import helma.xmlrpc.XmlRpc;

public class AreaServer {

    public static void main(String[] args) {
        if (args.length < 1) {
            System.out.println(
                "Usage: java AreaServer [port]");
            System.exit(-1);
        }

        try {

            // Start the server, using built-in version
            System.out.println("Attempting to start XML-RPC Server...");
            WebServer server = new WebServer(Integer.parseInt(args[0]));

            System.out.println("Started successfully.");

            // Register our handler class as area
            server.addHandler("area", new AreaHandler());
            System.out.println(
                "Registered AreaHandler class to area.");
```

Example 3-4. Hosting the area function (continued)

```
        System.out.println("Now accepting requests. (Halt program to stop.)");

    } catch (IOException e) {
        System.out.println("Could not start server: " +
            e.getMessage());
    }
  }

}
```

To start this server and the servers in the rest of the examples, call the Java runtime with the name of the class and an argument of 8899, in this case:

```
D:\xmlrpc\example1a>java AreaServer 8899
```

A simple client might call one of these methods and return its result. Most of the code in Example 3-5 provides an interface between the command line and the XML-RPC request itself, but it works well as test code.

Example 3-5. An XML-RPC client that calls the area function

```java
import java.io.IOException;
import java.util.Vector;
import helma.xmlrpc.XmlRpc;
import helma.xmlrpc.XmlRpcClient;
import helma.xmlrpc.XmlRpcException;

public class AreaClient {

    public static void main(String args[]) {
        if (args.length < 1) {
            System.out.println(
                "Usage: java AreaClient [radius]");
            System.exit(-1);
        }

        try {
            // Create the client, identifying the server
            XmlRpcClient client =
                new XmlRpcClient("http://localhost:8899/");

            // Create the request parameters using user input
            Vector params = new Vector();
            params.addElement(new Double(args[0]));

            // Issue a request
            Object result =
                client.execute("area.circleArea", params);

            // Report the results
            System.out.println("The area of the circle would be: " + result.toString());
```

Example 3-5. An XML-RPC client that calls the area function (continued)

```
        } catch (IOException e) {
            System.out.println("IO Exception: " + e.getMessage());
        } catch (XmlRpcException e) {
            System.out.println("Exception within XML-RPC: " + e.getMessage());
        }
    }

}
```

When this XML-RPC client is run from the command line, it's possible to send a
radius and receive back an area:

```
D:\xmlrpc\example1a>java AreaClient 3
The area of the circle would be: 28.274333882308138
```

Although this library works well in its current form, it's possible to add more flexibility to the way in which the arguments are sent by using a **struct** and named
parameters instead of the direct approach. To make this work, the **AreaHandler**
class needs a new method for processing the **Hashtable** used when structs are
sent, and then needs to route requests to the appropriate method based on a **type**
value in the struct. The new method is shown in Example 3-6.

Example 3-6. A method for routing XML-RPC requests

```
    public Double anyArea(Hashtable arguments) {
        Double value;
        value=new Double(0);
        String requestType=(String) arguments.get("type");
        if (requestType.equals("circle")) {
            Double radius=(Double) (arguments.get("radius"));
            value=circleArea(radius.doubleValue());
        }
        if (requestType.equals("rectangle")) {
            Double length=(Double) (arguments.get("length"));
            Double width=(Double) (arguments.get("width"));
            value=rectArea(length.doubleValue(), width.doubleValue());
        }

        return value;
    }
```

Most of the code handles conversions from the generic **Object** types stored in the
Hashtable to the primitive types needed by the actual **circleArea()** and
rectArea() methods. Although this code still returns the same results as the simpler methods it calls and adds an extra layer of processing overhead, you may find
this approach useful if you need to create libraries that produce different results
based on different types of named inputs.

Now the client code looks a little different because it has to assemble a `Hashtable`, not just simple parameters. Differences are highlighted in bold in Example 3-7.

Example 3-7. A client that calls the router

```
import java.io.IOException;
import java.util.Vector;
import java.util.Hashtable;
import helma.xmlrpc.XmlRpc;
import helma.xmlrpc.XmlRpcClient;
import helma.xmlrpc.XmlRpcException;

public class AreaClient {

    public static void main(String args[]) {
        if (args.length < 1) {
            System.out.println(
                "Usage: java AreaClient [radius]");
            System.exit(-1);
        }

        try {
            // Create the client, identifying the server
            XmlRpcClient client =
                new XmlRpcClient("http://localhost:8899/");

            // Create a double from the user argument
            Double radius=new Double(args[0]);

            // Create a hashtable and add a circle request
            Hashtable requestHash = new Hashtable();
            requestHash.put("type", "circle");
            requestHash.put("radius", radius);

            // Create the request parameters using user input
            Vector params = new Vector();
            params.addElement(requestHash);

            // Issue a request
            Object result =
                client.execute("area.anyArea", params);

            // Report the results
            System.out.println("The area of the circle would be: " + result.toString());

        } catch (IOException e) {
            System.out.println("IO Exception: " + e.getMessage());
        } catch (XmlRpcException e) {
            System.out.println("Exception within XML-RPC: " + e.getMessage());
        }
    }

}
```

The call and the results will look the same—users do not need to be aware of the extra flexibility they have available:

```
D:\xmlrpc\example1b>java AreaClient 5.6
The area of the circle would be: 98.5203456165759
```

Also, unless the `circleArea()` and `rectArea()` are changed to become private methods, direct XML-RPC requests for those methods will continue to work.

Although this `struct` approach is somewhat like implementing the `XmlRpc-Handler` interface and directing XML-RPC requests yourself, it isn't nearly as demanding because you control how much you use this approach. You can redirect some methods, but let `XmlRpcServer` figure out simpler methods. You could also implement something very similar using a Java `Vector`/XML-RPC array to send information between client and server, relying on order rather than labeling.

Reporting

The procedures called by XML-RPC requests don't have to be library routines used to retrieve information. Clients may just send servers information that they record—perhaps in a database, just in a file, or even on the system console. The example in this section builds a simple logging application that collects client exceptions and records them to the system console. This kind of tiny application can be very useful for debugging distributed applications, giving you an easy way to centralize information from multiple systems running concurrently.

This application first requires the design of a static method that captures exceptions and reports them via XML-RPC to a central server. As shown in Example 3-8, the first parameter is the IP address of the client sending the request (that information isn't passed to the XML-RPC handler), and the second is a `String` containing the message from the exception.

Note that methods that process Java exceptions have to be static methods. In addition, because the `report()` method itself has some possible exceptions due to the XML-RPC call, the entire body of the method is contained inside a `try`/`catch` statement.

Example 3-8. Exception reporting XML-RPC client

```
import java.io.IOException;
import java.net.*;
import java.util.Vector;
import helma.xmlrpc.XmlRpc;
import helma.xmlrpc.XmlRpcClient;
import helma.xmlrpc.XmlRpcException;

public class XLogClient {
```

Example 3-8. Exception reporting XML-RPC client (continued)

```java
public static void main(String args[]) {
    try {
        throw new Exception("help");
    } catch (Exception e) {
        report (e);
    }
}

public static void report(Exception eReport) {
    try {
        // Create the client, identifying the server
        XmlRpcClient client =
            new XmlRpcClient("http://192.168.124.14:8899/");

        //get local hostname and IP address
        InetAddress address=InetAddress.getLocalHost();
        String ipAddress=address.toString();

        // Create the request parameters using user input
        Vector params = new Vector();
        params.addElement(ipAddress);
        params.addElement(eReport.getMessage());
        // Issue a request
        Object result =
            client.execute("XLog.XLogReport", params);

        // Report the results - this is just for the example
        // In production, the 'ack' will be thrown away.
        // Alternatively, the log system could be more interactive
        // and the result might have meaning.
        System.out.println("Reponse was: " + result.toString());

        //If we can't report to server, report locally
    } catch (IOException e) {
        System.out.println("IO Exception: " + e.getMessage());
    } catch (XmlRpcException e) {
        System.out.println("Exception within XML-RPC: " + e.getMessage());
    }
}
}
```

The **main()** method in Example 3-8 is very short—it throws an exception with a message of "help" and then catches it, sending it to our **report()** method. The **report()** method sends the address of this system along with the exception message to the XML-RPC server. If something goes wrong with that transmission, the **report()** method prints its error messages to standard output.

The server that hosts this reporting system only needs to set up a web server and register one class for monitoring incoming exception reports. It builds on the same basic framework used for previous examples, as shown in Example 3-9.

Example 3-9. A host for the logging handler

```java
import java.io.IOException;
import helma.xmlrpc.WebServer;
import helma.xmlrpc.XmlRpc;

public class XLogServer {

    public static void main(String[] args) {
        if (args.length < 1) {
            System.out.println(
                "Usage: java AreaServer [port]");
            System.exit(-1);
        }

        try {
            // Start the server, using built-in version
            System.out.println("Attempting to start XML-RPC Server...");
            WebServer server = new WebServer(Integer.parseInt(args[0]));

            System.out.println("Started successfully.");

            // Register our handler class as area
            server.addHandler("XLog", new XLogHandler());
            System.out.println(
                "Registered XLogHandler class to XLog.");

            System.out.println("Now accepting requests. (Halt program to stop.)");

        } catch (IOException e) {
            System.out.println("Could not start server: " +
                e.getMessage());
        }
    }
}
```

For this demonstration, and often in practice, only a basic exception log handler is necessary. The handler defined in Example 3-10 just takes the addresses and messages and reports them to standard output.

Example 3-10. A simple XML-RPC handler for reporting messages

```java
public class XLogHandler {
    public String XLogReport(String address, String message) {
        System.out.println("From: " + address);
        System.out.println("Message: " + message);
        return "ack";
    }
}
```

The results of the test are simple, but could be effective if they represented real crises in need of attention:

```
D:\xmlrpc\example2>java XLogServer 8899
Attempting to start XML-RPC Server...
Started successfully.
Registered XLogHandler class to XLog.
Now accepting requests. (Halt program to stop.)
From: javalab1/192.168.124.12
Message: help
From: javalab5/192.168.124.17
Message: help
From: javalab6/192.168.124.19
Message: help
From: javalab27/192.168.124.141
Message: help
```

More sophisticated handling might filter through the messages to flag especially important alerts or save the messages to a file, but the basic `report()` method and the server already provide a strong foundation for future development. Building a more sophisticated log tracking facility would involve sending the information to something more permanent (and searchable) than screen output, like a database or even a file.

A get and set Approach

Although the previous example featured a relatively active client and a passive server, XML-RPC can be used to create more controlling clients, as well. XML-RPC's procedural approach fits fairly well with the common JavaBeans approach of `getProperty()` and `setProperty()` methods, though simple JavaBeans doesn't work in XML-RPC. Why? The set methods return `void`, and all XML-RPC methods have to return a value of some kind. On a relatively fundamental level, XML-RPC and JavaBeans are mismatched.

It isn't that difficult to write an `execute()` method that does the mapping, or even to modify `helma.xmlrpc` to return an empty value on methods that return `void`. However, the current section illustrates a simpler approach, building a controlling client and a server that maintains state between requests. Although this pattern isn't very sophisticated, it can be combined with other patterns to build more sophisticated applications. XML-RPC could be used throughout those applications, or it could just be one part of many.

To satisfy XML-RPC's need for return values, this example returns the current value of the property from the server to the client. This is duplicate information to some extent, but at least that information might be useful to verify that the change was made. Empty strings would be slightly more efficient, but would still incur overhead to no benefit.

The current example uses XML-RPC client requests to get and set a value on a Java object. Although the example used here is simple, it isn't difficult to extend it into more complex terrain using the same basic framework.

The key to this example lies in the handler class, shown in Example 3-11, which supports the get and set of its own value property.

Example 3-11. An XML-RPC handler that manipulates a variable

```
public class GetSetHandler {
    protected int value;

    public GetSetHandler(int initialValue) {
        value=initialValue;
    }

    public int getValue(String requester) {
        return value;
    }

    public int setValue(String requester, int newValue) {
        value=newValue;
        return value;
    }
}
```

The value property here is an integer, and the framework looks much like a Java-Beans component, but with the added return values and arguments noted earlier.

As shown in Example 3-12, the server code is much like that used by earlier examples—this is just another handler, and state management is up to the handler, not the server code wrapping it. You don't need to create a static variable to host the handler object because the GetSetHandler object is bound to the XML-RPC handling code.

Example 3-12. XML-RPC host for GetSetHandler

```
import java.io.IOException;
import helma.xmlrpc.WebServer;
import helma.xmlrpc.XmlRpc;

public class GetSetServer {

    public static void main(String[] args) {
        if (args.length < 1) {
            System.out.println(
                "Usage: java GetSetServer [port]");
            System.exit(-1);
        }
        try {
            // Start the server, using built-in version
            System.out.println("Attempting to start XML-RPC Server...");
```

Example 3-12. XML-RPC host for GetSetHandler (continued)

```
            WebServer server = new WebServer(Integer.parseInt(args[0]));

            System.out.println("Started successfully.");

            // Register our handler class as area
            server.addHandler("getSet", new GetSetHandler(20));
            System.out.println(
                "Registered GetSetHandler class to getSet.");

            System.out.println("Now accepting requests. (Halt program to stop.)");

        } catch (IOException e) {
            System.out.println("Could not start server: " +
                e.getMessage());
        }
    }
}
```

Example 3-13 shows the client used to test this code. It is more complex, largely because it needs to manage both get and set possibilities. In production code, most of this complexity can be ignored because programs calling functions are generally more predictable than human input. On the other hand, this interface can be very useful during the debugging cycle.

Example 3-13. Client for manipulating values on the server

```
import java.io.IOException;
import java.net.*;
import java.util.Vector;
import helma.xmlrpc.XmlRpc;
import helma.xmlrpc.XmlRpcClient;
import helma.xmlrpc.XmlRpcException;

public class GetSetClient {

    public static void main(String args[]) {
        if (args.length < 1) {
            System.out.println(
                "Usage: java GetSetClient [get | set] [value]");
            System.exit(-1);
        }

        String getOrSet=new String(args[0]);

        if (!((getOrSet.equals("get")) || (getOrSet.equals("set")))) {
            System.out.println(
                "First argument must be get or set");
            System.exit(-1);
        }
```

Example 3-13. Client for manipulating values on the server (continued)

```
    try {
        // Create the client, identifying the server
        XmlRpcClient client =
            new XmlRpcClient("http://localhost:8899/");

        //get local host IP address
    InetAddress address=InetAddress.getLocalHost();
    String ipAddress=address.toString();

        // Create the request parameters using user input
        Vector params = new Vector();
        params.addElement(ipAddress);
        if (getOrSet.equals("set")) {
        Integer newValue=new Integer(args[1]);
        params.addElement(newValue);
    }

        // Issue a request
    Object result=null;
        if (getOrSet.equals("set")) {
             result = client.execute("getSet.setValue", params);
    } else {
            result =  client.execute("getSet.getValue", params);
    }

        // Report the results
        System.out.println("The response was: " + result.toString());

    } catch (IOException e) {
        System.out.println("IO Exception: " + e.getMessage());
    } catch (XmlRpcException e) {
        System.out.println("Exception within XML-RPC: " + e.getMessage());
    }
    }
}
```

After you start the server, you can test the implementation from the command line:

```
D:\xmlrpc\example3>java GetSetClient get
The response was: 20
D:\xmlrpc\example3>java GetSetClient set 21
The response was: 21
D:\xmlrpc\example3>java GetSetClient get
The response was: 21
D:\xmlrpc\example3>java GetSetClient set 200
The response was: 200
D:\xmlrpc\example3>java GetSetClient get
The response was: 200
D:\xmlrpc\example3>java GetSetClient set 750
The response was: 750
D:\xmlrpc\example3>java GetSetClient get
The response was: 750
```

The `GetSetHandler` object retains the last value it was set for, starting with the initial value of 20 it received when first initialized. Although the command line here is testing the setting on a single system, multiple systems have access to both setting and retrieving that value, which could make such a drop-box useful as a central point for information distribution, provided that security isn't that important an issue.

This kind of get-set mechanism can be used for all kinds of programming tasks, allowing clients to control server properties and behavior. It's a common feature in interfaces used to administer a wide variety of systems and can be used both to tweak values occasionally and to send long lists of orders that must be carried out over time. This can be an easy way to control Java systems from programs running in other environments because XML-RPC provides the glue and the get-set mechanism is a common pattern in Java programming.

Moving Toward Cross-Platform Peer-to-Peer

The three preceding examples have moved from clients using servers as remote processors to clients reporting information to servers to clients actually controlling servers. XML-RPC's basic client-server foundation makes exchanging information in a wide variety of different ways possible, and its variable structures are flexible enough that single methods can have different behaviors, depending on the kinds of parameters they are sent.

The flexibility you need to move from client-server XML-RPC to a more peer-to-peer model is already there, thanks to arrays and structs. Clients can send any quantity of information that the application can then pick through, and servers can return any quantity of information for the client. Some clients may be capable of sending more information than others; servers can send extra information to clients, understanding that only some of their targets will use the entire set of information. There's no need for clients to play a purely client role or for servers to play purely server roles. Every program can be both a client and a server, if and when that seems appropriate.

As long as that flexibility is sufficient for your needs, the `helma.xmlrpc` package can provide you with a foundation for communication with non-Java systems with which you can define the roles of client and server as you find appropriate.

4

XML-RPC and Perl

XML-RPC and the Perl scripting language are a particularly powerful combination for creating flexible web services rapidly. Perl has long been the language of choice to obtain and manipulate data for the Web, and it is moving into the growing field of web services. One of Perl's guiding philosophies is "Easy things should be easy, and hard things should be possible." The Perl module for XML-RPC, `Frontier::RPC`, embodies this.

To show how easy Perl's XML-RPC library, `Frontier::RPC`, makes remote procedure calls, consider the following code snippet:

```
use Frontier::Client;
my $client = Frontier::Client->new
        ( url => "http://example.com:1080");
print "helloWorld('Bob') returned: ",
        $client->call('helloWorld', 'Bob'), "\n";
```

Assume that on a machine called *example.com*, there is an XML-RPC server running on port 1080 that has implemented a procedure named `helloWorld()`. Given these assumptions, these three lines of Perl code are all that's needed to make an XML-RPC call. Although this chapter explores the details of using this library more thoroughly, many XML-RPC Perl clients aren't any more complicated than this example.

This chapter begins with a discussion of the history, requirements, and architecture of Perl's XML-RPC library, `Frontier::RPC`. Then it covers how to create XML-RPC clients and servers using Perl, including instructions for running an XML-RPC server from a web server.

Perl's Implementation of XML-RPC

As of this writing, there's only one XML-RPC implementation on the Comprehensive Perl Archive Network (CPAN) (*http://www.cpan.org*). It's named `Frontier::RPC` and consists of several `Frontier` modules, a number of examples, and `Apache::XMLRPC`, which embeds an XML-RPC server in the Apache web server using `mod_perl`.

Why is this implementation tagged "Frontier" and not "XMLRPC"? Because way back in 1998, when Ken MacLeod was first putting `Frontier::RPC` together, the XML-RPC specification didn't exist. The protocol was merely "RPC over HTTP via XML," the one used at Dave Winer's UserLand site, implemented in the Frontier language. Ken's work was, in fact, the first third-party implementation of the protocol to be released. Note that this chapter is based on Version 0.07 of `Frontier::RPC`. There are significant changes from the previous version, including the introduction of a new module, `Responder`, so be sure to upgrade if you have an earlier version.

`Frontier::RPC` uses other modules for much of its work: `Data::Dumper`, `MIME::Base64`, `MD5`, `HTML::Parser`, `URI`, various `Net::` modules from the libnet distribution, various modules from the libwww-perl (LWP) suite, and `XML::Parser`. These are all available from CPAN.

All but one of these Perl modules should install without difficulty. However, the latest version of the `XML::Parser` module (a front end to the **expat** XML parser, written in C) does not include the expat C source. You must download this source from *http://sourceforge.net/projects/expat*. Fortunately, **expat** compiles cleanly on most versions of Unix, and Windows users of ActiveState Perl will find that `XML::Parser` is already installed.

A Perl script that wants to be an XML-RPC client uses the `Frontier::Client` module. An XML-RPC client script creates a `Frontier::Client` object and makes remote procedure calls through methods of that object.

A standalone Perl script that wants to be an XML-RPC server uses the `Frontier::Daemon` module. ("daemon" is the traditional Unix term for a long-running server process.) The script creates a long-lived `Frontier::Daemon` object that listens for XML-RPC method calls on a specific TCP/IP port. Unfortunately, `Frontier::Daemon` is not a particularly high-performance server. For web services that require better response time, consider using `Frontier::Responder`. This module lets a standard CGI process answer XML-RPC client calls. Used in conjunction with Apache and `mod_perl`, these kinds of XML-RPC listeners are more responsive than programs written using `Frontier::Daemon`.

Regardless of whether you're writing a client or server, you'll probably use some of the `Frontier::RPC2::*` modules to consistently translate between XML-RPC data types and Perl. Although the server and client classes can guess how to convert between Perl and XML-RPC data types, these objects provide a way to remove the guesswork.

Data Types

The interesting part of an XML-RPC call is how language-specific data types are turned into XML-RPC tagged data. Each XML-RPC parameter must have one of the data types documented in the XML-RPC specification and introduced in Chapter 2. For example, here's how the floating-point value 2.718 is encoded as a parameter:

```
<param><value><double>2.718</double></value></param>
```

Table 4-1 shows the correspondence (or lack thereof) between XML-RPC data types and Perl data types.

Table 4-1. Data types: XML-RPC versus Perl

XML-RPC data type (XML element)	Perl built-in data type	Frontier::RPC2 module
`<int>` (or `<i4>`)	scalar	`Frontier::RPC2::Integer`
`<double>`	scalar	`Frontier::RPC2::Double`
`<string>`	scalar	`Frontier::RPC2::String`
`<boolean>`	scalar	`Frontier::RPC2::Boolean`
`<dateTime.iso8601>`	scalar	`Frontier::RPC2::DateTime::ISO8601`
`<base64>`	scalar	`Frontier::RPC2::Base64`
`<array>`	array	`Array`
`<struct>`	hash	`Hash`

Translating Perl Values to XML-RPC Elements

Both clients and servers translate Perl values to XML elements as follows:

- When a Perl client's XML-RPC call includes an argument list that contains a set of Perl values, the client translates each value to XML for inclusion in the outgoing `<methodCall>` message.

- When a Perl server creates a return value, it translates a single Perl value to XML and includes the result in a `<methodResponse>` message.

Packaging Scalar Values

Although Perl has just the scalar data type, XML-RPC has many types: int, double, string, Boolean, and sometimes even dateTime and base64. You can either let the Frontier libraries make an educated guess as to the appropriate XML-RPC encoding for Perl data types, or you can use Frontier::RPC2::* objects to force explicit representations.

The data types of the parameters to an XML-RPC call are part of the exposed API. If a server expects an integer and you send it a string form of that integer, you've done something wrong. Similarly, if a server expects a string and you send it an integer, you're at fault. Although it may seem clumsy to use objects instead of simple scalars, they have a purpose: they formalize the encoding, and in doing so ensure that your code plays well with others.

If you are a Perl developer, you are used to working in an extremely flexible environment in which there is little worry about which data type applies to a particular variable. Does Perl consider "1" to be a number or a string? Actually, this detail depends on how the value is used. Unfortunately, XML-RPC doesn't offer the same flexibility.

When you include a scalar value (either as a literal or with a scalar variable) in the argument list of an XML-RPC call, a Frontier::Client object tries to interpret it as a numeric value—first as an integer, then as a floating-point number— before simply treating it as a string. To encode "37" as a string and not an integer, then you'd need to create a Frontier::RPC2::String object as a wrapper for the value.

For example, these two calls:

```
rpc-call(... , 1776, ...)
rpc-call(... , "1776", ...)
```

both produce an integer-valued parameter in the outgoing <methodCall> message:

```
<param><value><int>1776</int></value></param>
```

To explicitly encode the value as a string, you need to say:

```
$val = Frontier::RPC2::String->new("1776");
rpc-call(... , $val, ...)
```

or:

```
rpc-call(... , Frontier::RPC2::String->new("1776"), ...)
```

When writing an XML-RPC server, you have the same choice of either letting the Frontier library implicitly encode return values or explicitly encode them with the Frontier::RPC2 classes.

Preparing Date-Time Data

XML-RPC date-time parameters are passed as strings in ISO 8601 format.* Creating a date-time parameter involves two steps:

- Create a string in ISO 8601 format, specifying a particular date and time. Because this is a very simple format, you may find it practical to create the string yourself. For example, it doesn't take too much work to write "10/12/00 at 2:57 PM" as the string `20001012T14:57:00`. For a bit more automation, you may want to use the `strftime()` function in the standard Perl module POSIX. For example, here's how to turn the current time, provided by built-in Perl functions, into an ISO 8601 format string:

```
use POSIX "strftime";
    ...
$dt_string = strftime("%Y%m%dT%H:%M:%S", localtime(time()));
```

- Wrap the ISO 8601 format string in an `ISO 8601` object:

```
$date_obj = Frontier::RPC2::DateTime::ISO8601->new($dt_string);
```

    Note that the `Frontier::RPC2::DateTime::ISO8601` package name has an extra component (`ISO 8601`).

Including this `ISO 8601` object in the argument list of an XML-RPC call produces the appropriate date-time parameter in the outgoing `<methodCall>`. Thus, the call:

```
rpc-call(... , $date_obj, ...)
```

produces something like this:

```
<param><value>
<dateTime.iso8601>20001009T17:26:00</dateTime.iso8601>
</value></param>
```

Likewise, a server can specify an `ISO 8601` object as a return value to produce the appropriate date-time parameter in the outgoing `<methodResponse>`.

Preparing Encoded Binary Data

The strategy for handling string-encoded binary parameters closely parallels that for date-time parameters. XML-RPC binary parameters are passed as strings encoded in the `base64 content-transfer-encoding` scheme. Creating a binary argument involves two steps:

- Create a `base64` string that represents the binary data. You can do this using the `encode_base64()` function in the standard Perl module: `MIME::Base64`.

---

* For a brief discussion of this format, see *http://www.cl.cam.ac.uk/~mgk25/iso-time.html.*

For example, here's how to turn the contents of a small binary data file *mypicture.jpg* into a `base64` string:

```
use MIME::Base64;
    ...
open F, "mypicture.jpg" or die "Can't open file: $!";
read F, $bin_string, 10000;
$base64_string = encode_base64($bin_string);
```

- Then wrap the `base64` string in a `Base64` object. The package name is `Frontier::RPC2::Base64`:

```
$bin_obj = Frontier::RPC2::Base64->new($base64_string);
```

Including this `Base64` object in the argument list of an XML-RPC call produces the appropriate encoded-binary parameter in the outgoing `<methodCall>`. Thus, the call:

```
rpc-call(... , $bin_obj, ...)
```

produces something like this:

```
<param><value>
<base64>/9j/4AAQSkZJRgABAQEASABIAAD/2wBDAAUDBAQE
AwUEBAQFBQUGBwwIBwcHBw8LCwkMEQ8SEhEPERETFhwXExQ=</base64>
</value></param>
```

Likewise, a server can specify a `Base64` object as a return value to produce the appropriate encoded-binary parameter in the outgoing `<methodResponse>`.

Using Helper Methods to Create Objects

Instead of creating a `Frontier::RPC2::Integer` object directly, you can use your `Client` object's `int()` method:

```
$int_obj = $client->int(1776);
```

The `int()` "helper method" creates an `Integer` object and returns it. But first, it performs a very valuable job: it checks that the scalar value to be wrapped in an `Integer` object really is an integer. The argument to `int()` must consist of digits only, optionally preceded by a plus (`+`) or a minus sign (`-`); otherwise, a `die` error occurs. Invoke the `int()` method in an `eval` block to deal with the error case:

```
eval { $int_obj = $client->int($value) };
if ($@) {
    # oops: $value wasn't really an integer
} else {
    $response = $client->call(... , $int_obj, ...);
}
```

Similarly, helper methods create all other `Frontier::RPC` objects: `double()`, `string()`, `boolean()`, `date_time()`, and `base64()`. At the time of writing, only the `int()`, `double()`, and `boolean()` methods perform data validation.

Preparing Array and Hash Data

Each argument type described in the preceding sections is an individual value: a single number, a single string, or a single block of binary data. XML-RPC also defines two aggregate (or "collection") data types: `<array>` and `<struct>`. Happily, these XML-RPC types correspond exactly to Perl built-in data types:

- An XML-RPC `<array>` corresponds to a Perl array. It's a sequence of values, each of which can be either individual or aggregate (another `<array>` or `<struct>`).

- An XML-RPC `<struct>` corresponds to a Perl hash (associative array). It's a collection of name/value pairs; each name is a string, and each value can be either individual or aggregate.

To create an XML-RPC `<array>` or `<struct>` parameter, create a Perl array or hash with the appropriate values. Then specify a *reference* to the array or hash (not the aggregate data structure itself) as an argument to an XML-RPC call or as a server's return value.

For example, suppose you want to create an argument that's a three-item array: a string (employee name), an integer (employee ID), and a Boolean (is this a full-time employee?). Here's how you might create the required array reference:

```
$emp_name = "Mary Johnson";
$emp_id   = "019";
$emp_perm = Frontier::RPC2::Boolean->new(1);

$ary_ref = [$emp_name, $emp_id, $emp_perm];
```

You can include the array reference `$ary_ref` in the argument list of any XML-RPC call. This call:

```
rpc-call(... , $ary_ref, ...)
```

produces the following parameter in the outgoing `<methodCall>` message:

```
<param><value>
<array><data>
<value><string>Mary Johnson</string></value>
<value><int>019</int></value>
<value><boolean>1</boolean></value>
</data></array>
</value></param>
```

`Frontier::RPC` can encode nested hashes and arrays, just as you would in any other Perl script.

Translating XML-RPC Elements to Perl Values

Both clients and servers translate XML elements to Perl values as follows:

- When processing an XML-RPC method call, a Perl server translates the call's parameters, encoded as XML elements in the <methodCall> message, to Perl values.

- A Perl client translates the server's response, encoded as an XML element in the server's <methodResponse> message, to a Perl value.

Certain data types can be translated to either a Perl object or a scalar value. Frontier::RPC defines a use_objects mode for both Client objects, which make XML-RPC method calls, and for Daemon objects, which service those calls. In use_objects mode, the Client or Daemon translates an incoming XML-RPC <int>, <double>, or <string> value to a Frontier::RPC Integer, Double, or String object. When not in use_objects mode, the Client or Daemon translates an XML-RPC <int>, <double>, or <string> value to a Perl scalar. All other XML-RPC values are translated to the corresponding built-in Perl object (array or hash) or Frontier::RPC object.

Let's consider the viewpoint of a client receiving a response to its method call from the server. (The situation of a server processing the parameters of an XML-RPC method call is entirely similar.) The client code might be:

```
$response = rpc-call(...);
```

If the Client is in use_objects mode, $response is guaranteed to be a reference. For example:

- If the XML-RPC server responds with a <string> value, $response gets a reference to a Frontier::RPC2::String object.

- If the server sends a <boolean>, $response gets a reference to a Frontier::RPC2::Boolean object.

- If the server sends a <struct> or <array>, $response gets a reference to a Perl hash or array.

If the Client is not in use_objects mode, $response sometimes gets a regular Perl scalar—when the server's response is an <int>, <double>, or <string>. Incoming <int>, <double>, and <string> values embedded in an <array> or <struct> response are converted similarly: they become either Frontier::RPC objects (if in use_objects mode) or Perl scalars (if not). The resulting values are embedded within the array or hash that represents the overall response.

Extracting Values from Objects

In the previous section, we noted that an incoming XML-RPC data item is frequently translated to an object reference. There are a couple of methods for getting to the real data. If the reference is to a Perl array or hash, use the standard Perl arrow operator:

```
$response->[3]           # item at position 3 in a response array
$response->{"emp_name"}  # item with key emp_name in a response hash
```

If the reference is to one of the **Frontier::RPC** objects, use the object's **value()** method:

```
$response->value()    # value wrapped in a Frontier::RPC object
```

The **value()** method always returns a Perl scalar. The value extracted from a **Frontier::RPC2::Integer** object is an integer; the value extracted from a **Boolean** object is either 0 or 1; the value extracted from a **Base64** object is a block of binary data encoded as a Base64 string; and so on. (To turn a Base64 string back into a block of binary data, use the **decode_base64()** function in the standard Perl module **MIME::Base64**.)

Determining the Type of Object

When you have an object in hand, you may need to be able to find out what kind of object it is. Of course, in most cases, you should know in advance, because the XML-RPC server's API should be well documented. For example, the documentation may say that the response to a **GetExpirationDate** method should be an ISO 8601 object, the response to an **Expired** method should be a **Boolean** object, and a **SetSize** method should take a string argument and an integer argument. But maybe the API isn't well documented, or perhaps you don't want to trust the server to document its API. Or maybe you want to implement a method that accepts an argument of any data type.

The standard Perl tool for determining the type of a data item is the built-in **ref** function. If variable **$response** contains a Perl scalar value, the expression:

```
ref $response
```

yields the empty string. If **$response** contains an object reference returned by the **call()** method, this expression must yield one of the following strings:

```
ARRAY
HASH
Frontier::RPC2::Integer
Frontier::RPC2::Double
Frontier::RPC2::String
Frontier::RPC2::Boolean
Frontier::RPC2::DateTime::ISO8601
Frontier::RPC2::Base64
```

The following code skeleton shows how you can handle a "mystery" value:

```
$response = rpc-call( ... );
$objtype = ref $response;
if (not $objtype) {
    # response is a scalar value
} elsif ($objtype eq "ARRAY") {
    # response is an array
} elsif ($objtype eq "HASH") {
    # response is a hash
} elsif ($objtype eq "Frontier::RPC2::Integer") {
    # response in an Integer object
} elsif ...
```

XML-RPC Clients

Now that you understand how XML-RPC data types work in Perl, we can get to actually creating a Perl XML-RPC client—a script that makes calls to an XML-RPC server and gets responses back from it. We'll start with an overview of the method-call process and then describe how to create a client that does the job.

Client Architecture

To call one or more XML-RPC methods on a particular server, a Perl script creates a `Frontier::Client` object. This object represents a connection to that server. The script can then invoke the `Client` object's `call()` method as many times as desired to make XML-RPC calls. The `call()` method:

- Accepts a user-specified string as the method name
- Converts each user-specified argument from Perl format (scalar or object) to XML format
- Packages Perl data in an XML `<methodCall>` message and sends it to the server
- Decodes the `<methodResponse>` message returned by the XML-RPC server into Perl data

Invoking a Remote Procedure

Here are the steps involved in making an XML-RPC call:

1. Create a `Frontier::Client` object.

2. Call the method, passing arguments.

3. Get the response to the call.

Creating the client object

The only Perl module you need to import explicitly is the one that defines the `Frontier::Client` package:

```
use Frontier::Client;
```

Create an object in the `Frontier::Client` package in the regular way, using the package's **new()** method. You must specify a **url** argument, which sets the web address (URL) of the XML-RPC server host. For example:

```
$client = Frontier::Client->new(url => "http://www.rpc_wizard.net");
```

This line specifies that the (fictional) host *www.rpc_wizard.net* is the XML-RPC server. In specifying the host, keep these points in mind:

- You may need to include a port number in the URL. Some hosts run a regular web server on one port (port 80 is the industry standard) and an XML-RPC server on another port:

    ```
    http://www.rpc_wizard.net:8888
    ```

- You may need to specify the string RPC2 as *extra path information* in the URL, to identify it as an XML-RPC call:

    ```
    http://www.rpc_wizard.net/RPC2
    ```

    (In particular, servers implemented in Perl or `Frontier::RPC` impose this requirement.)

Each `Client` object you create is dedicated to a particular XML-RPC server. If you need to switch back and forth among several such servers, just create several clients. In addition to the required URL argument, the `Client` object-constructor method supports some optional arguments:

proxy
A URL that specifies a *proxy host* for the outgoing XML-RPC call to be routed through. You may need to use this option if your host is behind an Internet firewall.

debug
A flag (set its value to 1) that turns on display (using the **print** statement) of both the XML <methodName> message that represents the outgoing XML-RPC call and the <methodResponse> message returned by the server. This is a very valuable "training wheels" feature.

encoding
A string that specifies the character set encoding for the XML document (the <methodName> message) that contains the outgoing XML-RPC call. The string is inserted into the XML document header. For example, the following option:

```
encoding => "ISO-8859-4"
```

creates this XML declaration:

```
<?xml version="1.0" encoding="ISO-8859-4"?>
```

Be careful with this option. If the XML parser used by the XML-RPC server is unable to process the encoding you specify, an error occurs.

use_objects

A flag (set its value to 1) that enables use_objects mode in this Client. This enabling causes each scalar value in the <methodResponse> message returned by the server to be converted to an object of type Frontier::RPC2::Integer, Frontier::RPC2::Double, or Frontier::RPC2::String. (The use_objects mode is discussed further in the earlier section "Translating XML-RPC Elements to Perl Values.")

fault_as_object

A flag (set its value to 1) that changes the way in which the Client executes a die statement if it gets a <fault> response from the server. By default, the Client places a string value in variable $@ as it dies. If this flag is set, $@ gets a reference to a hash created from the <fault> structure.

You can list the argument-name/argument-value pairs in any order in the invocation of the new() method. For example, here's an invocation that specifies several options:

```
$client = Frontier::Client->new(
        url          => "http://www.rpc_wizard.net:8888",
        use_objects  => 1,
        debug        => 0,
        proxy        => "http://mylocalproxy.org");
```

Calling the XML-RPC method

As the preceding sections have suggested, you make an XML-RPC remote procedure call by invoking the call() method of a Client object:

```
$response = $client->call(method, parameter, ... );
```

The first—and only required—argument specifies the name of the remote procedure. Thus, a minimalist call might look like this (if $client is a Client object):

```
$client->call("hello_world");
```

Following the method-name argument, you can specify as many additional arguments as you like. Each such argument must be one of these data types:

- A Perl scalar value (integer, floating-point number, or string)

- A Frontier::RPC-defined object that represents some XML-RPC data type

- An array reference or a hash reference

The `call()` method packages all this data into a `<methodCall>` XML message and sends it to the XML-RPC server. See Example 4-1 for real `Frontier::Client` code in action.

Getting the response to the call

The `Client` object's `call()` method accepts a response from the XML-RPC server. This response is in the form of an XML `<methodResponse>` message that contains a single `<value>` element (or a `<fault>` element, in the case of an error). In many cases, it's a simple numeric value (for example, an `int` such as 47) or string value (such as "10-4 good buddy"). But the response can be any one of the XML-RPC data types, including the aggregate types `<array>` and `<struct>`, so that single response value might actually be a complex data hierarchy. Note that the `call()` method converts each XML-RPC data item in the response `<value>` back into the corresponding Perl value.

The response that comes back from the remote XML-RPC server becomes the return value of the `call()` method. So most of your calls will probably look like this:

```
$response = $client->call( ... );
```

Thus, the `$response` variable might get a scalar value, but it also might get an array reference, a hash reference, or an object.

Handling error responses

Sometimes the XML-RPC server cannot successfully execute a remote procedure call. Maybe you named a non-existent method; maybe you passed a bogus argument (such as a `<dateTime.iso8601>` value that is not a ISO 8601 format string); or maybe there was a bug in the method you called. When the server detects an error, it sends a special error response back across the wire. At the XML level, it's a `<fault>` element containing a `<struct>` whose members are named `faultCode` and `faultString`.

When the `Client`'s `call()` method gets the error response, it calls `die`, placing a string that incorporates the `faultCode` and `faultString` values in the scalar variable `$@`. If the `Client`'s `fault_as_object` option is enabled, the `$@` value is a reference to a hash created from the `<struct>` response:

```
$@->{"faultCode"}
$@->{"faultString"}
```

The previous description applies to error messages generated by the XML-RPC server. You can also experience errors in which a server host is never contacted at all: network unavailable, incorrect host name/address, or bogus port number.

In these cases, the `call()` method generates a simple error message (in clear text, not in XML format). For example:

```
500 Can't connect to www.boomer.com:8889 (Unknown error)
```

This particular error message comes from the `HTTP::Request` object embedded in the `Client` object.

A Client Script

Example 4-1 shows an XML-RPC client to a simplified punch-clock system. The server for this system is defined later in Example 4-2. Often, a manager needs to track the time each workgroup spends on a particular project. The API for this system defines five procedures:

punch_in(*$user*)
  Records that the specified user is beginning work now

punch_out(*$user*)
  Records that the specified user is ending work now

project_total_time()
  Returns the total time all workgroup members spent on this project

emp_total_time(*$user*)
  Returns the total time a given user has spent on this project

add_entry(*$user*, *$start*, *$end*)
  Takes the start and end times a user provides and creates a record of that information

In Example 4-1, there are only two users in the workgroup, "jjohn" and "bob." Although this script shows typical actions that would happen in a real system, it is more likely that these client calls would be made from a CGI script or other GUI that presented a friendlier interface to the punch-clock system.

Example 4-1. Punch-clock client

```perl
#!/usr/bin/perl --
# XML-RPC client for the punch-clock application

use strict;
use Frontier::Client;
use Time::Local;
use POSIX;

use constant SAT_MAY_5_2001_9AM => timelocal(0,0,9,5,4,101);
use constant SAT_MAY_5_2001_5PM => timelocal(0,0,17,5,4,101);
use constant XMLRPC_SERVER =>
                'http://marian.daisypark.net:8080/RPC2';
```

Example 4-1. Punch-clock client (continued)

```perl
# create client object
my $client = Frontier::Client->new( url   => XMLRPC_SERVER,
                                    debug => 0,
                                  );

# jjohn starts working on the project
print
  "Punching in 'jjohn': ",
  status( $client->call('punch_in', 'jjohn') ),
  "\n";

# bob stops working on the project
print
  "Punching out 'bob': ",
  status( $client->call('punch_out', 'bob') ),
  "\n";

# output the total time spent on the project
printf
  "Total time spent on this project by everyone: %s:%s:%s\n",
  @{$client->call('project_total_time')};

# output bob's time on the project
printf
  "Time 'bob' has spent on this project: %s:%s:%s\n",
  @{$client->call('emp_total_time', 'bob')};


# set up date-time values
my $iso8601_start = strftime("%Y%m%dT%H:%M:%S",
                        localtime(SAT_MAY_5_2001_9AM));

my $iso8601_end   = strftime("%Y%m%dT%H:%M:%S",
                        localtime(SAT_MAY_5_2001_5PM));

my $encoder = Frontier::RPC2->new;

my $start = $encoder->date_time($iso8601_start);
my $end   = $encoder->date_time($iso8601_end);

# log overtime hours for bob
print
  "Log weekend work for 'bob': ",
  status( $client->call('add_entry', 'bob', $start, $end) ),
  "\n";

sub status {
  return $_[0] ? 'succeeded' : 'failed';
}
```

As is typical of XML-RPC clients, a new `Frontier::Client` object needs to be created before invoking any remote procedures:

```
my $client = Frontier::Client->new( url   => XMLRPC_SERVER,
                                    debug => 0,
                                  );
```

By defining constants (such as **XMLRPC_SERVER**) at the top of the program, it becomes easier to change the URL of the XML-RPC server when neccessary. Including the debug parameter in the object initialization is a good idea, even if it's not needed right away. Although client-side debugging is turned off in this example, it would be simple to turn it on again, if needed.

When a users come to work, they punch in. In a production environment, this functionality would be wrapped inside a nice GUI, but the XML-RPC call would still look something like this:

```
print
  "Punching in 'jjohn': ",
  status( $client->call('punch_in', 'jjohn') ),
  "\n";
```

In this case, the user "jjohn" is starting to work on this project. Because **punch_ in()** returns a Boolean value indicating success, the call is wrapped in the **status()** subroutine to print out a result more understandable to humans. If a user tries to **punch_out()** without having successfully called **punch_in()**, the procedure returns a value of **false**.

To see how much time all users have spent on this project, the program calls **project_total_time()**. This function returns a three-element list that contains hours, minutes, and seconds, respectively. This list can be printed easily with **printf**:

```
printf
  "Total time spent on this project by everyone: %s:%s:%s\n",
  @{$client->call('project_total_time')};
```

It can be a little tricky to deal with date values in XML-RPC. To log Bob's weekend overtime using the **add_entry()** procedure, the Unix date values for the start and end times need to be converted into ISO 8601 format. Using the Perl module **Time::Local**, a Unix date can be determined and assigned to a constant:

```
use constant SAT_MAY_5_2001_9AM => timelocal(0,0,9,5,4,101);
```

Then, using the POSIX function **strftime**, that date can be converted into ISO 8601 format:

```
my $iso8601_start = strftime("%Y%m%dT%H:%M:%S",
                    localtime(SAT_MAY_5_2001_9AM));
```

Finally, this string can be used to create a `Frontier::RPC2::ISO8601` object, which the server expects to receive. In the code fragment that follows, both `$start` and `$end` are `Frontier::RPC2::ISO8601` objects:

```
$client->call('add_entry', 'bob', $start, $end) )
```

Note that although Example 4-1 does work, it is possible to take a lot more care in checking that each call succeeded and handled problems appropriately.

XML-RPC Servers

Now we can turn to the operation and construction of a Perl XML-RPC server—a script that receives calls from an XML-RPC client and sends responses back to it. After presenting an overview of server operation, we describe how to create a server.

Server Architecture

To set up a server to handle incoming XML-RPC calls, a Perl script creates a `Frontier::Daemon` object. This object implements a server process that listens for XML-RPC calls on a particular port. The server dispatches each call to a corresponding Perl subroutine, and then it sends the subroutine's return value back to the client as the response to the XML-RPC call.

The `Frontier::Daemon` object gets its knowledge of HTTP communications by being a specialization of the standard Perl `HTTP::Daemon` object. The `Daemon` object:

- Uses an XML parser to interpret the incoming XML-RPC `<methodCall>` message.

- Determines the method name (a string).

- Converts each parameter from XML format to a Perl scalar value or object.

- Invokes a Perl subroutine that corresponds to the specified method name. The `Daemon` passes the arguments (now in Perl format) to the subroutine in the standard manner, as the contents of the `@_` array.

- Packages the subroutine's return value in an XML `<methodResponse>` message and sends it back to the client.

Setting Up an XML-RPC Server

The most important part of creating an XML-RPC server is implementing the defined API. With the `Frontier::Daemon` library, remote procedures are implemented as simple Perl subroutines. As shown later in Example 4-2, there is a mapping between API procedure names and the Perl subroutines that implement them.

This is convenient when API names conflict with Perl reserved words. Here is an example of a server that implements a single procedure called `helloWorld` with an anonymous subroutine:

```
use Frontier::Daemon;
Frontier::Daemon->new( LocalPort => 8080,
                       method => {
                                  helloWorld =>
                                    sub {return "Hello, $_[0]"}
                                 },
                     );
```

`Frontier::Daemon` is a subclass of `HTTP::Daemon`, which is a subclass of `IO::Socket::INET`. This means that the object constructor for `Frontier::Daemon` uses the named parameter `LocalPort` to determine the port on which it should listen.

The next most important parameter in this object's constructor is called `methods`; it points to a hash reference that maps API procedure names to the subroutine references that implement them. (Note that different API procedure names can map to the same Perl subroutine.)

The Perl subroutine that implements an XML-RPC API procedure receives its argument list in the standard `@_` array. The data types of these arguments depend on whether the `Daemon` object was created in `use_objects` mode. The guidelines are as follows:

- If an argument is a Perl scalar, you can use it directly.

- If an argument is a `Frontier::RPC` object, invoke its `value()` method to determine its value (which is always a scalar).

Normally, the Perl subroutine that implements an XML-RPC procedure produces a return value. The `Daemon` object takes this value and it sends back across the wire, in the form of an XML `<methodResponse>` message, to the client. All subroutines must return at most one scalar value. This can be a simple scalar, like an integer or string; or it can be a reference to a complex value, such as a list of hashes of lists. The value's complexity is irrelevant. (Veteran Perl hackers shouldn't expect `wantarray()` to work in XML-RPC servers. Remember, the clients calling these servers may not have any notion of list versus scalar context.)

Sometimes the Perl subroutine that implements an XML-RPC method doesn't return a value. Perhaps the subroutine encounters a runtime error (e.g., division by zero, file not found, etc.); or maybe there is no subroutine because the client requested a nonexistent method. XML-RPC terms this situation a *fault*.

When any of these situations occurs, the **Daemon** automatically responds with a special <struct> value, containing two members:

- A <faultCode> element containing an integer value (<int> parameter).

- A <faultString> element containing a string value (<string> parameter).

A Server Script

Example 4-2 implements the punch-clock system described in the section "A Client Script." Refer to that section for a discussion of the API. This system stores its information in a MySQL database, accessed with standard DBI calls.

Example 4-2. Punch-clock server

```
#!/usr/bin/perl --
# XML-RPC server for the punch-clock application

use strict;
use Frontier::Daemon;
use DBI;

# create database handle
my $Dbh = DBI->connect('dbi:mysql:punch_clock', 'editor', 'editor') ||
        die "ERROR: Can't connect to the database";

END { $Dbh->disconnect; }

# initialize XML-RPC server
Frontier::Daemon->new(
                    methods   => {
                            punch_in            => \&punch_clock,
                            punch_out           => \&punch_clock,
                            project_total_time  => \&total_time,
                            emp_total_time      => \&total_time,
                            add_entry           => \&add_entry,,
                                 },
                      LocalPort => 8080,
                 );

# punch_clock API function
sub punch_clock {
  my ($user) = @_ or die "ERROR: No user given";

  $Dbh->do("Lock Tables punch_clock WRITE")
      or die "ERROR: Couldn't lock tables";

  if( is_punched_in($user) ){
    my $sth = $Dbh->prepare(<<EOT);
update punch_clock set end=NOW() where username = ?
and (end = "" or end is NULL)
EOT
    $sth->execute($user) || die "ERROR: SQL execute failed";
```

Example 4-2. Punch-clock server (continued)

```
  }else{
    my $sth = $Dbh->prepare(<<EOT);
insert into punch_clock (username, begin) values (?, NOW())
EOT
    $sth->execute($user) || die "ERROR: SQL execute failed";

  }

  $Dbh->do("Unlock Tables");

  my $encoder = Frontier::RPC2->new;
  return $encoder->boolean(1);
}

# total_time API function
sub total_time {
  my ($user) = @_;

  my $sth;
  if( $user ){
    $sth = $Dbh->prepare(<<EOT);
Select SEC_TO_TIME(SUM(UNIX_TIMESTAMP(end) - UNIX_TIMESTAMP(begin)))
from punch_clock where username = ?
EOT
  $sth->execute($user) || die "ERROR: SQL execute failed";

  }else{
    $sth = $Dbh->prepare(<<EOT);
Select SEC_TO_TIME(SUM(UNIX_TIMESTAMP(end) - UNIX_TIMESTAMP(begin)))
from punch_clock
EOT
    $sth->execute || die "ERROR: SQL execute failed";
  }

  my $total = $sth->fetchall_arrayref;
  # return an hour, minute, second list
  if( $total && $total->[0] ){
    return [ split ':', $total->[0]->[0], 3 ];
  }else{
    die "ERROR: Couldn't retrieve any data"
  }
}

# add_entry API function
sub add_entry {
  my ($user, $start, $end) = @_;

  if( !($user && $start && $end) ){
    die "ERROR: Need username and start and end dates";
  }
```

Example 4-2. Punch-clock server (continued)

```perl
  my $sth = $Dbh->prepare(<<EOT);
insert into punch_clock (username, begin, end) values (?,?,?)
EOT

  unless( $sth->execute($user,
                  iso2mysql($start->value),
                  iso2mysql($end->value))    ){
    die "ERROR: SQL execute failed";
  }

  my $encoder = Frontier::RPC2->new;
  return $encoder->boolean(1);

}


# helper functions

sub is_punched_in {
  my ($user) = @_;

  my $sth = $Dbh->prepare(<<EOT);
select begin from punch_clock where username = ?
and (end = "" or end is NULL)
EOT

  $sth->execute($user) || die "ERROR: SQL execute failed";
  my $result = $sth->fetchall_arrayref;
  if( $result && $result->[0]){
    if( $result->[0]->[0] ){
      return 1;
    }
  }
  return;
}

sub iso2mysql {
  my ($iso) = @_;

  $iso =~ s/T/ /;
  $iso =~ s/^(.{4})(.{2})(.{2})/$1-$2-$3/;
  return $iso;
}
```

Because this is a single process server, it creates one DBI handle as a file-scoped global variable that is visible to every subroutine that needs to get at the SQL tables. The DBI handle is created as follows:

```perl
    my $Dbh = DBI->connect('dbi:mysql:punch_clock', 'editor', 'editor') ||
            die "ERROR: Can't connect to the database";
```

If you are unfamiliar with Perl's DBI module, look at *Programming the Perl DBI*, by Alligator Descartes and Tim Bunce (also published by O'Reilly & Associates, 2000). For security reasons, you should certainly choose a better username ("editor") and password (ahem, "editor"). Because DBI complains to STDERR if DBI handles aren't explicitly closed, an END subroutine is used to make sure this is done whenever the process is killed:

```
END { $Dbh->disconnect; }
```

The object initialization of this **Frontier::Daemon** server should look familiar by now:

```
Frontier::Daemon->new(
              methods   => {
                     punch_in            => \&punch_clock,
                     punch_out           => \&punch_clock,
                     project_total_time  => \&total_time,
                     emp_total_time      => \&total_time,
                     add_entry           => \&add_entry,,
                           },
              LocalPort => 8080,
          );
```

Again, the mapping of API procedure names to Perl subroutines happens here. Notice that the five API procedures map to only three Perl subroutines.

Here is the SQL needed to define the tables this punch-clock system uses. The first table, **users**, simply maps usernames to first and last names:

```
create table users (
  username  varchar(12) auto_increment not null primary key,
  firstname varchar(25),
  lastname  varchar(25)
);
```

The second table, **punch_clock**, maps usernames to start and end times:

```
create table punch_clock (
  username varchar(12) not null,
  begin    datetime not null,
  end      datetime,
  primary key (username, begin)
);
```

When a user tries to punch in or out, the subroutine **punch_clock()** is called. By looking at the **punch_clock** table, this routine can figure out if the user needs to punch out (if there's a row in the table without a defined "end" column) or punch in. To prevent another process from updating the table, the **lock tables** MySQL directive is issued. This isn't strictly necessary here, but in a larger system, selecting from a table and then updating it are not atomic actions. In other words, another process could alter the table between the `select` and `update`. Upon successful completion, `punch_clock()` returns a Boolean object to the client:

```
my $encoder = Frontier::RPC2->new;
return $encoder->boolean(1);
```

When either `project_total_time()` or `emp_total_time()` is called, `total_time()` is invoked in the server. Some fancy MySQL-specific code here converts from the MySQL date-time type to a Unix timestamp to figure out the interval between the start and end times:

```
$sth = $Dbh->prepare(<<EOT);
Select SEC_TO_TIME(SUM(UNIX_TIMESTAMP(end) -
                      UNIX_TIMESTAMP(begin)))
from punch_clock where username = ?
EOT
```

The `SUM()` function takes all rows that have the given username and adds the difference of every row's end and start times (calculating the user's total work time). The result is a number of seconds, which is then converted back into hours, minutes, and seconds by `SEC_TO_TIME()`. When `fetchall_arrayref fetches the result`, it contains only one row with one field, which is a colon-separated string of hours, minutes, and seconds:

```
return [ split ':', $total->[0]->[0], 3 ];
```

This can be split into a three-element list easily. Recall that only single values can be returned to XML-RPC clients, so this list needs to be enclosed in an anonymous array.

The last subroutine that implements an API procedure is `add_entry()`. While the helper function `iso2mysql` doesn't do anything tricky, it does use regular expressions to turn ISO 8601 date values into something MySQL can use to populate its date-time fields.

Integrating XML-RPC into a Web Server

The preceding section describes a standalone server—a process dedicated to handling XML-RPC method calls that listens for those calls on a dedicated TCP/IP port. But this approach ignores (or, at least, minimizes) one of XML-RPC's main design points: its use of the HTTP protocol. In many situations, the machine designated to handle XML-RPC method calls is already running a process that accepts HTTP requests—a standard web server.

So why not let the web server handle all the HTTP-level communications? A browser might retrieve a regular web page at one location on the server (for example, *http://MyStore.com/catalog/mittens.html*), while an XML-RPC client might make method calls at another location (for example, *http://MyStore.com/ catalogAPI*). Same server, same port—different web-based information services.*

This section describes how to implement an XML-RPC server as part of a web server, using CGI to have a Perl script handle an incoming XML-RPC method call. Note that your code is invoked only when a method call arrives; the web server itself is the long-lived listener process. Note also that the CGI script runs in a separate OS-level process (or thread) than the web server.

An XML-RPC client just needs to know which URL to specify; it doesn't need to know whether it's communicating with a standalone server, a CGI script, or an Apache virtual document.

This discussion assumes that you already have a CGI-enabled web server running. A good resource in this area is *CGI Programming with Perl, 2nd Edition* by Scott Guelich, Shishir Gundavaram, and Gunther Birznieks (published by O'Reilly, 2000).

Here's a procedure for taking an existing Perl script that implements a standalone XML-RPC server and turning it into a CGI script:

1. In a directory configured to hold executable CGI programs, create a Perl script file that uses the **Frontier::Responder** module.

2. Copy the subroutines that implement the XML-RPC API into the new script.

3. Create a mapping of the XML-RPC API procedure names to the subroutines copied from the existing script.

4. Initialize a new **Frontier::Responder** object with this mapping.

To map the XML-RPC API procedure names to real Perl subroutines, simply create a hash whose keys are the API procedure names and whose values are references to the implementing subroutines. In this instance, that hash looks like this:

```
$map = (
            punch_in            => \&punch_clock,
            punch_out           => \&punch_clock,
            project_total_time  => \&total_time,
            emp_total_time      => \&total_time,
            add_entry           => \&add_entry,
        );
```

---

* As we discussed in Chapter 1, there is a lot of controversy on the subject of using the same TCP/IP port to provide multiple services with different performance requirements, security requirements, etc. We'll duck those issues here and just tell you how to get the job done.

The next step is to create a new `Frontier::Responder` object that is constructed with this hash. The hash variable, $map, refers to the previous code:

```
use Frontier::Responder;

# process the call, using Responder object to
# translate to/from XML
my $response = Frontier::Responder->new( methods => $map );
print $response->answer;
```

One important difference between standalone servers and CGI servers is how they respond to `print` statements. In a standalone server, `print` output goes to the server's console; but in a CGI script, `print` output goes into the HTTP response and will most likely garble it. So, don't use `print` in a CGI-based XML-RPC server.

Clients that talked to a `Frontier::Daemon` server need to change the URL parameter in the `Frontier::Client` object initialization when the server is ported to a CGI environment. Fortunately, this change is small and isolated:

```
$client = Frontier::Client->new(
        url => "http://somewhere.com/cgi-bin/xmlrpc.pl");
```

`Frontier::Responder` can also be used in mod_perl environments. Use of it can help improve the performance of an XML-RPC server. Using *mod_perl*, code is invoked only when a client call arrives; the web server itself is the long-lived listener process. Unlike traditional CGI scripts, however, your program is cached in the web server and doesn't run in a separate process. Besides providing a big performance boost, this lets you do things like maintain persistent data, cache connections, and take advantage of Apache features such as authentication and logging. For more information on **mod_perl**, see the book *Writing Apache Modules with Perl and C*, by Lincoln Stein and Doug MacEachern (published by O'Reilly, 1999).

5

Integrating Web Applications:
XML-RPC in PHP

PHP is a popular open-source scripting language used to create web pages. Growing originally from a Perl application, PHP is now a fully fledged language that is most commonly used as a module for the Apache and IIS web servers, but is also available as a standalone interpreter. When PHP is embedded in a web server, standard HTML tags and PHP code can be mixed together freely in much same the way as other "server side include" technologies, such as Microsoft's Active Server Pages or Allaire's Cold Fusion can.

When a PHP-enabled web server serves a page, any PHP code found there is executed. The results of the PHP code and any HTML tags on that page are sent to the requesting browser. This arrangement can greatly simplify the lives of web designers and programmers. Once the programmers create PHP code that performs some required function, the web designers can make sure that the output of that code matches the rest of the web site. PHP has the capability to allow programs embedded in web pages to easily present data stored in databases, mail servers, and directory servers. With the addition of the XML-RPC library described in this chapter, PHP programmers can now participate in the emerging world of web services. The second half of this chapter presents a PHP application that uses XML-RPC to enhance an existing web service.

Although the examples in this chapter are largely self-explanatory, some small knowledge of PHP is expected of the reader. Good resources for learning more about PHP include Rasmus Lerdorf's *PHP Pocket Reference* (O'Reilly, 2000), the PHP home page (*http://www.php.net/*), and the O'Reilly Network PHP development center (*http://www.oreillynet.com/php/*).

Getting the XML-RPC Library for PHP

The XML-RPC classes for PHP may be downloaded from *http://xmlrpc.usefulinc. com/php.html* as either ZIP or *tar.gz* archives. The classes themselves take the form of PHP code, which may be included by other PHP scripts to provide XML-RPC functionality. The main two files in the distribution are:

xmlrpc.inc

 The code in this file provides XML-RPC client functionality.

xmlrpcs.inc

 When used in addition to *xmlrpc.inc*, this file provides server functionality.

All that is needed to use the XML-RPC classes is a simple include() instruction. For testing, it is adequate to place the *.inc* files in the same directory as your PHP code. However, for maintainability it would be wise to place the XML-RPC class files in a directory set apart for reusable code. Your own code can then include the XML-RPC files by using an explicit pathname; or, if you want to keep your code pathname-independent, you must add the directory where they reside into the PHP include search path.* Note that the distribution also includes comprehensive documentation and various test and example programs.

Understanding the Client Classes

Before going deeply into the details of the PHP XML-RPC implementation, let's look at a short example that gives a good idea of what a simple client XML-RPC method invocation looks like. Example 5-1 shows an invocation of the method `examples.getStateName` that takes an `int` value and returns a `string` that contains the name of the corresponding U.S. state.

Example 5-1. Using UserLand's state name server

```
include("xmlrpc.inc");

$thestate=32;

$c=new xmlrpc_client("/RPC2", "betty.userland.com", 80);
$f=new xmlrpcmsg('examples.getStateName',
                array(new xmlrpcval($thestate, "int")));
$r=$c->send($f);
$v=$r->value();

if (!$r->faultCode()) {
    print "State number ". $thestate . " is " .
        $v->scalarval() . "<br />";
```

---

* See the explanation of the `include_path` directive in the online PHP documentation at *http://www. php.net/manual/configuration.php*.

Example 5-1. Using UserLand's state name server (continued)

```
        print "<hr />I got this value back<br /><pre>" .
        htmlentities($r->serialize()). "</pre><hr />\n";
} else {
   print "Fault: ";
   print "Code: " . $r->faultCode() .
   " Reason '" .$r->faultString()."'<br />";
}
```

The text marked in bold within this example highlights all the information needed to invoke the method. This code performs the following operations:

1. The `xmlrpc_client` constructor prepares a client object that accesses a specific server.

2. The `xmlrpcmsg` constructor prepares for the remote procedure invocation, using the `xmlrpcval` object to package up the parameters.

3. `send()` invokes the remote procedure.

4. The `$v` object encapsulates the return value and `$v->scalarval()` extracts the result.

5. `fault_code()` is used to check for error conditions.

Mapping Data Between PHP and XML-RPC

The primary task of every XML-RPC library is to map XML-RPC's data types, described in Chapter 2, to the native data types of the library's implementation language. Many scripting languages, such as Python, Perl, and PHP, are *weakly typed* languages. This simply means that these languages hide from the programmer the details of data type coercion, like turning the string "5" into the integer 5 when adding that data to another integer. Other languages, such as C and Java, are *strongly typed*, so that you must explicitly convert data into a type accepted by a particular function. Most languages provide some way for you to define your own data types. In PHP, classes are provided, in part, to allow some data type checking.

The XML-RPC data types that have a direct mapping in PHP are int, `string`, and `double`. To preserve further type information, the XML-RPC type must be encapsulated in a class, which can carry the necessary type in addition to the data value. It can be argued that this is unnecessary overhead and that using those three basic types is sufficient because the knowledge of the context of method calls can be used to help further manipulation. However, PHP is again restricted when it comes to packaging up arrays because it has no means of distinguishing between a conventional serial array and an associative array.

For this reason, XML-RPC for PHP takes the route of creating its own type system—along with the consequent increase in awkwardness for the programmer. Many scripting languages also use this trick (see Chapters 4 and 6 for how Perl and Python do it, respectively). Recall that because an XML-RPC client written in a strongly typed language can connect to a server written in a weakly typed language, it is often necessary to ensure that the server encodes the outgoing data according to the agreed-upon application programming interface (API) for that web service.

Getting PHP Data into XML-RPC Tags

The `xmlrpcval` class provides a type wrapper for a value. The easiest value to construct with this class is an XML-RPC string, which is presumed to be the default type. The following lines show two possible ways to construct a "Hello, World!" string:

```
$xstr=new xmlrpcval("Hello, World!")
$xstr=new xmlrpcval("Hello, World!", "string")    // more verbosely
```

By explicitly asking the `xmlrpcval` class to encode the data as a string, the second way ensures that even arbitrary strings, such as "255", are sent across the network as a string. You can construct the remaining simple scalar types in a similar fashion. The following three lines construct an integer, a floating-point value, and a Boolean value, respectively:

```
$xint=new xmlrpcval(34, "int");        // an integer, 34
$xfloat=new xmlrpcval(23.435, "double"); // a floating-point value, 23.435
$xbool=new xmlrpcval(1, "boolean");      // a boolean true value
```

Constructing XML-RPC date-times is also simple, as illustrated by the following line of code:

```
$xdate=new xmlrpcval("2000-11-18T20:30:05", "dateTime.iso8601");
```

Constructing date-times can be made even easier if you use functions that convert from Unix timestamps (representing the number of seconds since the start of 1970).* One such function, `iso801_encode()`, is used in the following two examples, to return the local time and Greenwich Mean Time, respectively:

```
$xdate=new xmlrpcval(iso801_encode(time()));    // local time
$xdate=new xmlrpcval(iso801_encode(time(), 1)); //specifies GMT
```

The construction of a binary object (the **base64** type) follows the same pattern:

```
$xbinary=new xmlrpcval($binaryData, "base64");
```

---

* See *http://xmlrpc.usefulinc.com/doc/helpers.html#ISO8601ENCODE* for full documentation on these conversion functions. Because these functions use Unix timestamps, they only work for dates for which there exists a Unix timestamp.

Note that `$binaryData` doesn't have to be pre-encoded. The `xmlrpcval` class does this for you.

The array types **array** and **struct** are only slightly more complex to create. The creation of an array requires you to pass a PHP array of `xmlrpcval` objects. For example, to create an XML-RPC array containing the numbers 1, 2 and 3, you can use the following code:

```
$xarr=new xmlrpcval(array(
    new xmlrpcval(1, "int"),
    new xmlrpcval(2, "int"),
    new xmlrpcval(3, "int")), "array");
```

Creating structs follows a similar pattern. However, instead of passing a linear array to the `xmlrpcval` constructor, you pass an associative array in which the keys are the member names, as in the following code:

```
$xstruct=new xmlrpcval(array(
    "one"   => new xmlrpcval(1, "int"),
    "two"   => new xmlrpcval(2, "int"),
    "three" => new xmlrpcval(3, "int")), "struct");
```

You may have noticed that in each of these examples, the type is specified by a literal string ("int", "struct", etc.). To avoid spelling and casing mistakes, consider using the following predefined global variables in place of string literals as the second argument to the `xmlrpcval` constructor:

```
$xmlrpcI4       = "i4";
$xmlrpcInt      = "int";
$xmlrpcBoolean  = "boolean";
$xmlrpcDouble   = "double";
$xmlrpcString   = "string";
$xmlrpcDateTime = "dateTime.iso8601";
$xmlrpcBase64   = "base64";
$xmlrpcArray    = "array";
$xmlrpcStruct   = "struct";
```

It is good practice to use these variable names instead of the literal type names because it should help you pick up on errors more easily.

Turning XML-RPC Data Back into PHP

Once you have packaged up an `xmlrpcval` object or received one as the result of a method call, you need to access the corresponding values again. To do this, you need to know if your value represents a scalar, an array, or a struct type. If you cannot be certain of the return data type, you can use the `kindOf()` method of the object to find this out. This method returns a string value of **scalar**, **array**, or **struct**.

If your value is a scalar, then you can access it with the **scalarval()** method. If you need to know the type of the scalar, use the **scalartyp()** method. The following example performs both of these operations:

```
// $xv is an XML-RPC value
if ($xv->kindOf=="scalar") {
    print "I got a scalar, value " . $xv->scalarval() .
        ", of type " . $xv->scalartyp() . "<br />\n";
}
```

If your value is an XML-RPC array, you can access its members by using the **arraymem()** method, which takes one parameter, the array index. The number of members in the array can be determined with the **arraysize()** method. Remember that each member of the array is an **xmlrpcval** object. The following example demonstrates unpacking an array of scalar values:

```
// $xv is an array of integers
for($a=0; $a<$xv->arraysize(); $a++) {
    $v=$xv->arraymem($a);
    print "Got this number: " . $v->scalarval() . "<br />\n";
}
```

For handling structs, XML-RPC for PHP offers two access methods. If the members of the struct are known in advance, the **structmem()** method allows direct access to the member values. The following example demonstrates accessing known members of a struct:

```
// $p is a struct representing someone's personal details
$age=$p->structmem("age");
$name=$p->structmem("name");
print $name->scalarval() . " is " . $age->scalarval() .
    " years old.<br />\n";
```

If the member names are not known in advance, **xmlrpcval** has methods similar to the **reset()** and **each()** functions that PHP uses for navigating associative arrays. The following example demonstrates iterating through a struct in which the members are unknown:

```
// $xs is an example struct
$xs->structreset();
while(list($key, $xval)=$xs->structeach()) {
    print "Member '${key}' ";
    switch($xval->kindOf()) {
    case "scalar":
        print "is a scalar, type: " .
            $xval->scalartyp() . "<br />\n";
        break;
    default:
        print "is complex, type: " .
            $xval->kindOf() . "<br />\n";
    }
}
```

Shortcuts to Encoding and Decoding XML-RPC Values

Using the `xmlrpcval` class constructor in the manner described previously is somewhat cumbersome. In particular, the indirection through the `xmlrpcval` wrapper always adds an extra step. The XML-RPC for PHP library includes two helper routines to speed the conversion to PHP variables. However, there is a trade-off: although you gain convenience, you lose a certain amount of type control.

The `xmlrpc_encode()` function creates an `xmlrpcval` object from a native PHP value. To demonstrate, the following example shows three normally constructed `xmlrpcval` scalar objects and their `xmlrpc_encode()` shortcut equivalents:

```
// integers
$xa=new xmlrpcval(23, "int");
$xa=xmlrpc_encode(23);

// doubles
$xb=new xmlrpcval(56.234, "double");
$xb=xmlrpc_encode(56.234);

// strings
$xc=new xmlrpval("Fred Smith");
$xc=xmlrpc_encode("Fred Smith");
```

The shortcut methods do not support the Boolean, date, or binary (base64) types because PHP has no native types that correspond to them. Neither are arrays supported, as PHP cannot tell the difference between an array and an associative array with the linear indices (0, 1, 2, etc.) as keys. However, because there is relatively little syntactic overhead for constructing arrays, this is not such a problem. Probably the best use of the shortcut encoding method is when structs are involved because `xmlrpc_encode()` transforms them into `xmlrpcval` structs. The following code shows a comparison between the shortcut and normal methods:

```
// verbose construction
$person=new xmlrpcval(array(
        "name"   => new xmlrpcval("Fred Smith"),
        "age"    => new xmlrpcval(45, "int"),
        "height" => new xmlrpcval(1.84, "double")), "struct");

// shortcut construction
$person=xmlrpc_encode(array(
        "name"   => "Fred Smith",
        "age"    => 45,
        "height" => 1.84));
```

Decode XML-RPC values into native PHP types with the `xmlrpc_decode()` function. Because XML-RPC values have full type information, all types are supported. The only caveat is that you lose the ability to determine what their original types were: everything is coerced into a PHP string, integer, or floating-point variable.

The next example shows `xmlrpc_decode()` used to output the contents of a struct, such as that defined by the previous example; note that this code assumes that all the members are scalar values:

```
// $xv is an xmlrpcval struct
$s=xmlrpc_decode($xv);
reset($s);
while(list($key, $val)=each($s)) {
    print "${key} is ${val}<br />\n";
}
```

Notice that the indirection through the `xmlrpval` wrapper has been removed.

Invoking Methods

Now that we've covered encapsulating values (a process generally known as *marshaling*), we can move on and cover the steps necessary to complete an entire call to an XML-RPC server. This section covers the `xmlrpc_client` class, which holds the URL of the XML-RPC server; the `xmlrpcmsg` class, which holds the XML-RPC payload; and the `xmlrpcres` class, which holds the data returned by the remote procedure call.

Preparing a Client Object

The first step in invoking a method involves initializing an `xmlrpc_client` object for the target XML-RPC server you wish to use. The `xmlrpc_client` constructor takes the following form:

```
$client=new xmlrpc_client($server_path, $server_hostname, $server_port);
```

So, for example, a client object targeted at the server at the URL *http://xmlrpc.usefulinc.com:80/demo/server.php* can be invoked like this:

```
$client=new xmlrpc_client("/demo/server.php", "xmlrpc.usefulinc.com", 80);
```

Calling the constructor simply initializes the client object; it does not perform any communication at this point. Two further initialization methods are useful at this stage. The first is the `setDebug()` method, which causes the XML-RPC libraries to output extra information about what the client receives from the server. This information is invaluable in debugging. Debugging is turned on by the following code, called after construction of the client object:

```
$client->setDebug(1);
```

The second post-construction initialization step you may need to make is to set authentication credentials. The XML-RPC for PHP libraries offer support for HTTP

Basic Authentication. In order to enable authentication, it is necessary to make a call to the **setCredentials()** method:[*]

```
$client->setCredentials($username, $password);
```

The username and password must both be in plain text.

Preparing a Method Invocation and Its Parameters

Once a client object is created, it must be passed a message object, which it then sends to the target server. The message encapsulates the name of the method to be invoked, along with its parameters. The object used for this purpose is **xmlrpcmsg**, and it is constructed in the following manner:

```
$msg=new xmlrpcmsg($methodName, array($p1, $p2 ... ));
```

The method name is a string (e.g., **examples.getStateName**), and each member of the array of parameters must be an **xmlrpcval** object. An alternative form of the constructor, for which there are no parameters given, is also possible:

```
$msg=new xmlrpcmsg($methodName);
```

Subsequent parameters can also be added in order to the message by use of the **addParam()** method, which takes exactly one **xmlrpcval** object as its argument.

For debugging purposes, you may wish to see what the XML encoding of your XML-RPC method call looks like. This can be done with the **serialize()** method. The following example shows code for the construction of an XML-RPC method invocation:

```
$msg=new xmlrpcmsg("examples.getStateName",
                   array(new xmlrpcval(23, "int")));
print "<pre>" . htmlentities($msg->serialize()) . "</pre>";
```

Here's the output from the **serialize()** method, showing the message's XML encoding:

```
<?xml version="1.0"?>
<methodCall>
<methodName>examples.getStateName</methodName>
<params>
<param>
<value><int>23</int></value>
</param>
</params>
</methodCall>
```

---

[*] Note that although the XML-RPC libraries currently support only an HTTP transport, architectural scope is available for other protocols to transport the XML-RPC packets. In this case, the credentials would be used for whatever authentication mechanisms exist within that protocol.

Invoking the Method

Once an `xmlrpcmsg` object has been created, it can be passed to the `send()` method of the client object to exercise it on the remote server. The `send()` method may be invoked in one of two ways. The usual way is to simply pass the message as a parameter, as in the following example:

```
$result=$client->send($msg);
```

The result of the method invocation is an `xmlrpcresp` object. Note that program execution blocks until a result is retrieved: this could be an unreasonable length of time. If you wish to set a timeout after which a message send will fail, use the second form of the `send()` method and pass a timeout in seconds as the second parameter:

```
$result=$client->send($msg, 60); // timeout after 60 seconds
```

Checking the Result

Sending an XML-RPC message to a remote server can result in any one of the following conditions:

* A low-level I/O error

* A valid XML-RPC response

* An XML-RPC error condition

Low-level I/O errors include such things as not being able to resolve the host-name for the destination server or not being able to connect to the remote machine. Before attempting to unpack a returned value, you must check that no low-level error has occurred. If an error has occurred, error information can be accessed via the `errstr` and `errno` member variables of the client object. The following example shows one way to handle low-level errors:

```
$result=$client->send($msg);
if (!$result) { // a low-level error has occurred
    print "Help! A low-level error occurred. Error # " .
        $client->errno . ": " . $client->errstr . "<br />\n";
    exit(0); // stop the script executing
}
```

`$client->errno` and `$client->errstr` normally correspond to the low-level errors defined by the underlying I/O libraries from PHP. You can find a list of these errors on a Unix machine by typing **man errno**. However, you will find the text explanation in `$client->errstr` sufficient in most cases.

Presuming no low-level errors occur, the result of the remote method invocation can be obtained. This result is either an XML-RPC value or an XML-RPC error condition. To retrieve the value, the response object has a `value()` method that returns an **xmlrpcval** object. All methods outlined in the section "Turning XML-RPC Data Back into PHP" (earlier in this chapter) can be used to manipulate the return value. The following code shows how a scalar return value might be unpacked:

```
$result=$client->send($msg);
if ($result) { // no low-level error has occurred
    if ($result->value()) { // no error has occurred
        // use a shortcut function to lazily decode a scalar
        $val=xmlrpc_decode($result->value());
        print "Got this result: ${val}<br />\n";
    } else {
        // deal with XML-RPC level error
    }
} else {
    // deal with low-level error
}
```

If the method invocation was unsuccessful, the result of the **value()** method is null. The next section deals with handling and interpreting such errors.

Handling XML-RPC Error Conditions

If a null return value is contained in the XML-RPC response object, an error condition (fault) has been experienced. (An in-depth discussion of fault conditions can be found in Chapter 2.) Faults are returned to the user with both a number- and human-readable explanation. The following example shows how the number and text description are accessed using the **faultCode()** and **faultString()** methods of the **xmlrpcresp** object:

```
$result=$client->send($msg);
if ($result) {
    if (!$result->value()) { // a fault has occurred
        print "A fault occurred, code number: " .
            $result->faultCode() . ", explanation: " .
            $result->faultString() . "<br />\n";
    }
}
```

Because the XML-RPC specification lays down no guidelines for the allocation of fault codes, a program can do little automated processing of faults, apart from indicating that there has indeed been a fault and outputting a textual error. If, however, you know that both XML-RPC client and server use the PHP implementation, you can rely to a larger extent on the fault codes.

Table 5-1 shows the fault codes reserved for use by the PHP for XML-RPC classes. Note that user-level fault codes—those provided by the server implementer—start at 800 (decimal).

Table 5-1. Predefined fault codes

Fault code	Fault string and reason for error
1	*Unknown method* The caller has specified a method name unknown to this server.
2	*Invalid return payload: enabling debugging to examine incoming payload* This error is generated by the client code when what it receives from the server is not a valid XML-RPC response message. Turning on debugging with setDebug() allows you to see the incoming data and debug the error. Client XML parsing errors will be logged to PHP's error channel (usually the web server error log).
3	*Incorrect parameters passed to method* The caller has not passed the correct number and/or type of parameters to a remote method.
4	*Can't introspect: method unknown* Introspection failed because the server doesn't know the method requested. More about introspection is explained later in this chapter.
5	*Didn't receive 200 OK from remote server* An HTTP transport error has occurred. Again, turn on debugging with setDebug() to discover more about the cause of this error.

Whereas client XML-parsing errors (i.e., the server sent invalid XML) are handled via PHP's error channel, server XML parsing errors (i.e., the client has sent invalid XML) are handled via the XML-RPC fault reporting structures. Error codes from 100 are reserved for XML parser errors. See the PHP documentation of the XML module for more details on these errors. (Note that 100 is added to the PHP XML parser error number to generate the fault code.)

Building XML-RPC Servers in PHP

A PHP XML-RPC server is simply another PHP script, in the same way an XML-RPC client is. If the server resides on a normal web server, the port number for the request is 80, the default for HTTP. If you wish to make your server available on another port, consult the configuration instructions for your web server.

The most important task of writing an XML-RPC server is to define the procedures of its web service. The PHP library goes beyond those of other languages in allowing the server to be self documenting. Through a facility called *introspection*, any client can ask the PHP server for the list of remote procedures it implements.

Methods

The heart and soul of an XML-RPC server is the set of procedures it makes available as a web service. Remember that the procedure names that clients use are not necessarily the names of functions on the server. The PHP library provides a mechanism for mapping between the web service API procedure names and the names of the PHP functions that implement those procedures on the server.

An XML-RPC method in PHP takes the form shown in the following example:

```
function myMethod($xmlrpcMessage) {
    $errorHappened=0;
    $param0=$xmlrpcMessage->getParam(0);
    $param1=$xmlrpcMessage->getParam(1);
    // .. computation
    if ($errorHappened) {
        $r=new xmlrpcresp(0, $errno, $errmsg);
    } else {
        $r=new xmlrpcresp(new xmlrpcval("Return value"));
    }
    return $r;
}
```

The method takes an **xmlrpcmsg** object as its single argument. The parameters to the XML-RPC method can then be accessed as **xmlrpcval** objects using the **getParam()** accessor method of the **xmlrpcmsg**. The **getNumParams()** method can be used to determine the number of parameters, enabling the function to accept a varying number.

Values are returned to the caller by means of an **xmlrpcresp** object. The method must return exactly one of these objects, whether it is successful in its execution or not. There are two ways of constructing an **xmlrpcresp** object:

new xmlrpcresp(0, *$errno*, *$errmsg*)

This first form contains a 0 as its first argument, indicating that the returned value is a fault condition. The second argument gives the fault number, and the third gives the human readable explanation of that error. PHP XML-RPC defines a global constant, **$xmlrpcerruser**, the base number of user-generated fault conditions. All reported error numbers should be this value or greater.

new xmlrpcresp(*$xmlrpcValue*)

This second form is used to return the value of a successful computation. An XML-RPC method call may only return exactly one value, which must be an **xmlrpcval** object. If several return values are desired, create an array return value to contain them.

Place your computation code in between the lines of code that access the parameters and the lines that create the return value. Remember that if an error occurs, it must still result in an **xmlrpcresp** being returned from your function; using PHP routines like **die()** or **warn()** will result in a non-XML return to the client. Syntax errors or other faults in your server code will also result in a malformed return payload sent to the client. Turn debugging on in the client to see the PHP error report. If you want to provide diagnostic information to aid the development of your service, there are two options:

- Use the PHP error logging facilities to send errors to your web server's log. For more information on this option, see *http://www.php.net/manual/features. error-handling.php*. PHP allows you to do fancy things like install your own error handler, send diagnostics to email, and log to a file.

- Call the global function **xmlrpc_debugmsg()**. This function takes one string argument and appends a message inside a comment field in the XML that is returned to the client. XML-RPC clients ignore text inside comments, but if you enable debugging on the client, you will be able to read the debugging information. The comment will appear at the very start of the returned XML payload.

The remaining part of the puzzle is to connect the PHP functions you have defined to the XML-RPC method names exposed by the server.

Service Descriptions

PHP for XML-RPC stores the description of all methods it supports in the *dispatch map*. The dispatch map is an associative array mapping the XML-RPC method name to the PHP definition of that method, a list of permissible parameters, and a pointer to documentation for that method. The following example shows a typical dispatch map:

```
$findstate_sig=array(array($xmlrpcString, $xmlrpcInt));

$findstate_doc='When passed an integer between 1 and 51 returns the
name of a US state, where the integer is the index of that state name
in an alphabetic order.';

$echoback_sig=array(array($xmlrpcString, $xmlrpcString));

$echoback_doc='When passed a string, returns the same string.';

$disp_map=array(    "examples.getStateName" =>
                        array("function" => "findstate",
                        "signature" => $findstate_sig,
                        "docstring" => $findstate_doc),
                    "examples.echoString" =>
                        array("function" => "echoback",
                        "signature" => $echoback_sig,
                        "docstring" => $echoback_doc));
```

Note the use of the period in the example to provide XML-RPC method namespaces. XML-RPC for PHP reserves the **system.*** namespace for its own uses; see "Introspection" later in this chapter for more details. The righthand side of each array element is actually another associative array. Three keys are required in each instance of this array:

function

> The value assigned to the function must be a string that is the exact name of the PHP function that defines the behavior for the XML-RPC method.

signature

> The value assigned to the signature must be an array of possible method signatures. The signature specifies the return type and parameters required by the XML-RPC method. An individual signature is an array of at least two items: the first item is the name of the return type ("string" in the definitions in the previous example), and the remaining items are the types of parameters expected by the method. You can specify multiple signatures to allow methods to have different numbers and types of parameters. On method invocation, the server class checks to see if the types passed by the client match any of the signatures provided by the dispatch map. If they do not, then a fault condition is generated.

docstring

> The value assigned to the docstring must be a string containing documentation for this method. XML-RPC for PHP allows a remote client to discover the documentation, as described in the section "Introspection" later in this chapter.

The dispatch map is then passed to the server object upon its construction, as described in the next section.

Servicing a Request

Once the methods have been defined and a dispatch map is created, servicing an incoming XML-RPC request is simple. First, your PHP script must include *xmlrpcs. inc* in addition to the normal *xmlrpc.inc* file. Second, it must construct an **xmlrpc_server** object, passing the dispatch map as the argument. The following code performs the necessary steps:

```
include("xmlrpc.inc");
include("xmlrpc.inc");

// definition of functions

// definition of dispatch map

$s=new xmlrpc_server($dispatchMap);
```

The constructor for **xmlrpc_server** then services the request, so no other code is required. It may be the case that for some reason you wish to perform computation in between creating the server object and servicing the request. One such reason might be to perform custom security validation, for instance. In this case, a zero can be passed as the second argument to the constructor to suppress execution, as shown in the following example:

```
$s=new xmlrpc_server($dispatchMap, 0);

// computation

$s->service();
```

Your script must not generate any output before it reaches the point of servicing the XML-RPC request. Further computation may be performed after servicing the request, but it must not generate any other output; otherwise, the client will not receive a well-formed XML response.

Introspection

XML-RPC for PHP has a facility, commonly known as introspection, that enables a client to interrogate the server in order to discover the methods it supports. The server class does this by reserving method names in the **system.*** namespace. Three methods are defined to support introspection:

system.listMethods()
> This method takes no parameters. It returns an array of strings, the names of the methods that the server supports (i.e., the keys from the dispatch map plus the built-in system methods).

system.methodSignature(*methodname*)
> This method has one string parameter, the name of a method supported by the server. It returns an array of signatures for that method—each signature being a struct with keys, as described in the section "Service Descriptions" earlier in this chapter.

system.methodHelp(*methodName*)
> This method provides access to the documentation strings attached to each method. It takes one string parameter, a method name, and returns a string.

These three methods enable a certain amount of "late binding" to take place; that is, you can write programs that do not need to know the interface presented by an XML-RPC server until runtime. For more information, visit *http://xmlrpc.usefulinc. com/demo/introspect.php.*

Connecting Web Applications

The following sections explore using PHP to integrate two web applications into one interface. The first section demonstrates how to create a complete PHP XML-RPC server application, in this case a discussion server. The web application to which this server will be connected is a database called Meerkat, the brainchild of Rael Dornfest and O'Reilly & Associates, Inc. (who also happen to be the publishers of this book). Meerkat is a storehouse of news about technological developments. After a subsequent section that gives an overview of Meerkat, the chapter demonstrates how to integrate the database with the custom XML-RPC discussion server.

Creating a Discussion Server

A feature of many successful web sites and online applications is the ability to annotate, or provide comments regarding, on-site content. Unfortunately, it can be hard to obtain software supporting this feature that will integrate in the way you wish, often due to rigid user-interface constraints.

In this section, we attempt to solve this problem by creating an XML-RPC discussion/comment server. Because the interface is XML-RPC, you will be able to integrate it into your own applications without sacrificing the feel of your user interface.

The first task is to design the API. In the spirit of doing the simplest thing that works, this example application uses a straightforward interface. All items that can be commented on are identified by a string ID—this might be a URL, for example, or just a number corresponding to a database record identifier. Here is the API:

`discuss.addComment(`*item_id, person_name, comment*`)`
> This method adds a comment to the item specified by the item ID. It also records the name of the commenter against that comment. All three arguments are strings.

`discuss.getComments(`*item_id*`)`
> This method returns an array of structs; each struct corresponds to an individual comment and has two members: "person" and "comment."

This minimal interface allows a basic form of annotation to be added to web applications. Example 5-2 shows the listing of the server script that implements the interface. A simple file-based database is used to store the comments.

Note that the server uses Berkeley DB2 databases, so your installation of PHP must be compiled with support for this.* The web server must have write access to the directory where the database is stored. Windows users also have to change this directory to something like *C:\TEMP*.

Example 5-2. Discussion server

```php
<?php
// $Id: ch05,v 1.19 2001/06/11 16:28:51 aschirmer Exp aschirmer $
// A basic comment server. Given an ID it will store
// a list of names and comment texts against it.

include("xmlrpc.inc");
include("xmlrpcs.inc");

// implement discuss.addComment

$addcomment_sig=array(array($xmlrpcInt, $xmlrpcString,
    $xmlrpcString, $xmlrpcString));

$addcomment_doc='Adds a comment to an item. The first parameter
is the item ID, the second the name of the commenter, and the third
is the comment itself. Returns the number of comments against that
ID.';

function addcomment($m) {
     global $xmlrpcerruser;
     $err="";

   // decode the three string parameters
     $msgID=xmlrpc_decode($m->getParam(0));
   $name=xmlrpc_decode($m->getParam(1));
   $comment=xmlrpc_decode($m->getParam(2));

   // open up our comment store
   // (adjust the path for your own machine)
   $dbh=dba_open("/tmp/comments.db", "c", "db2");

   if ($dbh) {

       // look for the number of messages against
       // this ID
       $countID="${msgID}_count";
       if (dba_exists($countID, $dbh))
           $count=dba_fetch($countID, $dbh);
       else
           $count=0;

       // add the new comment in
       dba_insert($msgID . "_comment_${count}", $comment, $dbh);
```

---

* Berkeley DB is now known as SleepyCat DB; see *http://www.sleepycat.com/* for more information.

Example 5-2. Discussion server (continued)

```
            dba_insert($msgID . "_name_${count}", $name, $dbh);
            $count++;
            dba_replace($countID, $count, $dbh);
            dba_close($dbh);
    } else {
            // set an error that will be returned
            // as a fault
            $err="Unable to open comments database.";
    }

  // if we generated an error, create an error return response
  if ($err) {
            return new xmlrpcresp(0, $xmlrpcerruser, $err);
  } else {
            // otherwise, we return the new number of total
            // comments against the ID
            return new xmlrpcresp(new xmlrpcval($count, "int"));
  }
}

// implement discuss.getComments

$getcomments_sig=array(array($xmlrpcArray, $xmlrpcString));

$getcomments_doc='Returns an array of comments for a given ID, which
is the sole argument. Each array item is a struct containing name
and comment text.';

function getcomments($m) {
  global $xmlrpcerruser;
  $err="";
    $ra=array();

    // get the ID for which comments are required
    $msgID=xmlrpc_decode($m->getParam(0));

    // open up the comments database
    $dbh=dba_open("/tmp/comments.db", "r", "db2");

    if ($dbh) {
            // look for the number of comments for this ID
            $countID="${msgID}_count";
            if (dba_exists($countID, $dbh)) {
                $count=dba_fetch($countID, $dbh);

                // fetch each comment
                for($i=0; $i<count; $i++) {
                    $name=dba_fetch("${msgID}_name_${i}", $dbh);
                    $comment=dba_fetch("${msgID}_comment_${i}", $dbh);

                    // bundle the name and comment into a struct
                    $ra[]=new xmlrpcval(array(
                            "name" => new xmlrpcval($name),
```

Example 5-2. Discussion server (continued)

```
                        "comment" => new xmlrpcval($comment)
                        ), "struct");
            }
        }
    }

    // if we generated an error, create an error return response
    if ($err) {
        return new xmlrpcresp(0, $xmlrpcerruser, $err);
    } else {
        // otherwise, return the list of comment structs
        return new xmlrpcresp(new xmlrpcval($ra, "array"));
    }
}

// instantiate the server and get it to process the request
$s=new xmlrpc_server( array( "discuss.addComment" =>
                array("function" => "addcomment",
                    "signature" => $addcomment_sig,
                    "docstring" => $addcomment_doc),
              "discuss.getComments" =>
                array("function" => "getcomments",
                    "signature" => $getcomments_sig,
                    "docstring" => $getcomments_doc))
            );
?>
```

Meerkat: O'Reilly's Technology Database

The Meerkat web application (*http://meerkat.oreillynet.com/*) is O'Reilly & Associates' database of headlines from technology sites around the Web. (O'Reilly & Associates is known, among other things, for the animal-themed cover designs of the books they publish. Meerkat's name carries on this tradition among O'Reilly's online offerings.) The Meerkat database aggregates the title, description, and URL of technology news stories and other resources from XML files, using the RDF Site Summary (RSS) format.* Each site creates an RSS file, which Meerkat retrieves and adds to its database. Meerkat organizes the web sites ("channels") into categories, according to the subject matter they cover. Figure 5-1 shows a screenshot of Meerkat, displaying stories in its "XML" category

In addition to its web interface, Meerkat provides an XML-RPC interface that gives access to its content. A well-structured PHP program normally abstracts its functionality into classes, which contain the program logic and separate activation of those classes in conjunction with HTML markup. XML-RPC for PHP can take advantage of that structuring, enabling you to add a web application interface

---

* Resources and tutorials for RSS can be found on the O'Reilly Network Syndication DevCenter at *http://www.oreillynet.com/rss/*.

easily by writing simple wrappers for your existing program logic. Meerkat is an example of an application that has done just that.

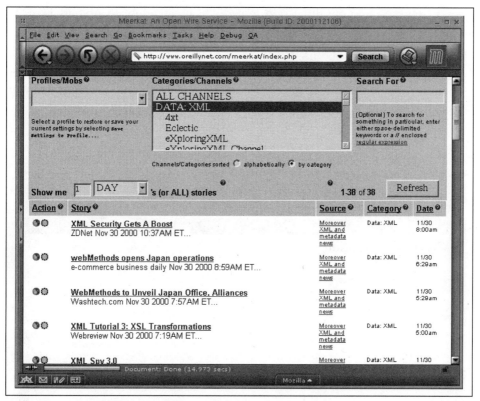

Figure 5-1. Meerkat showing stories from its "XML" category

Meerkat's interface offers the following methods, three of which are used in Example 5-3:

`meerkat.getCategories()`

Returns an array of structs of available Meerkat categories (member "title"), each with its associated category ID (member "id").

`meerkat.getChannels()`

Returns an array of structs of available RSS channels (member "title"), each with its associated channel ID (member "id").

`meerkat.getChannelsByCategory(category_id)`

Returns an array of structs of RSS channels in a particular category (specified by integer category ID), each with its associated channel ID.

`meerkat.getItems(recipe)`

Returns an array of RSS item structs, given a "recipe" struct. See *http://www.oreillynet.com/pub/a/rss/2000/11/14/meerkat_xmlrpc.html* for Meerkat info.

Joining Meerkat and the Discussion Server

Now we have two XML-RPC applications at our disposal: Meerkat, to explore stories on web sites, and our discussion server, which can annotate arbitrary items as long as they can be given a string identifier.

PHP and XML-RPC can be used to synthesize these two applications into a new one, allowing spontaneous discussions to take place around news stories. Figures 5-2 and 5-3 show the user interface for such an application. Users can browser Meerkat's database, and whenever stories that have comments are found, the comments are displayed against them. A link gives the option to add a comment to a story.

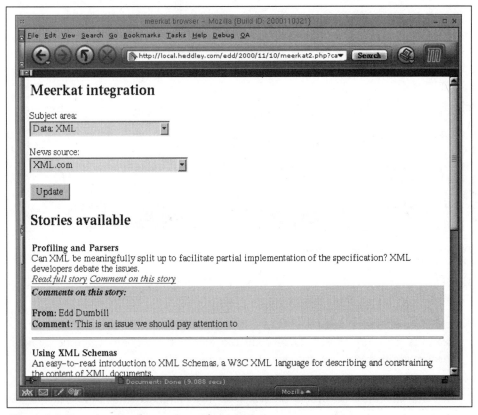

Figure 5-2. Browsing Meerkat stories with comments

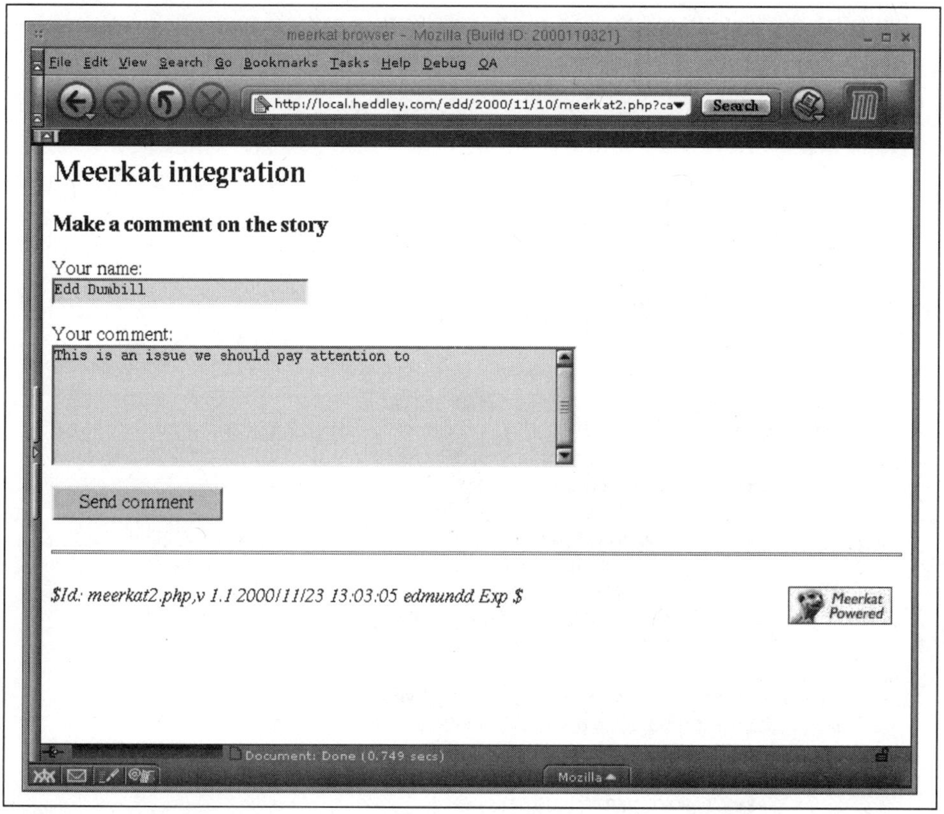

Figure 5-3. Comment form

Example 5-3 gives a complete listing of the code required to build this application.

Example 5-3. Meerkat discussion application

```php
<?php
// $Id: ch05,v 1.19 2001/06/11 16:28:51 aschirmer Exp aschirmer $
// A program that browses Meerkat's story store and allows
// users to append spontaneous discussions to the story
// in question.

include("xmlrpc.inc");

$mydir="/demo";

// bomb() just finishes off the page before quitting
function bomb() { print "</body></html>"; exit(); }

// dispatch() ensures error handling for XML-RPC calls
function dispatch($client, $method, $args) {
    $msg=new xmlrpcmsg($method, $args);
    $resp=$client->send($msg);
```

Example 5-3. Meerkat discussion application (continued)

```php
    if (!$resp) { print "<p>IO error: ".$client->errstr ."</p>"; bomb(); }
    if ($resp->faultCode()) {
        print "<p>There was an error: " . $resp->faultCode() . " " .
            $resp->faultString() . "</p>";
        bomb();
    }
    return xmlrpc_decode($resp->value());
}

// create client for discussion server
$dclient=new xmlrpc_client("${mydir}/discuss.php",
                    "xmlrpc.usefulinc.com", 80);

// check if we're posting a comment, and send it if so
$storyid=$HTTP_POST_VARS["storyid"];
if ($storyid) {
    // send the comment to the comment server
    $res=dispatch($dclient, "discuss.addComment",
            array(new xmlrpcval($storyid),
                new xmlrpcval(stripslashes
                    ($HTTP_POST_VARS["name"])),
                new xmlrpcval(stripslashes
                    ($HTTP_POST_VARS["commenttext"])))));

    // send the browser back to the originating page
    Header("Location: ${mydir}/comment.php?catid=" .
                $HTTP_POST_VARS["catid"] . "&chanid=" .
                $HTTP_POST_VARS["chanid"] . "&oc=" .
                $HTTP_POST_VARS["catid"]);
    exit(0);
}

?><html><head><title>meerkat browser</title></head>
<body bgcolor="#ffffff">
<h2>Meerkat integration</h2>
<?php
// handle incoming parameters
$catid=$HTTP_GET_VARS["catid"];
if ($HTTP_GET_VARS["oc"]==$catid)
    $chanid=$HTTP_GET_VARS["chanid"];
else
    $chanid=0;

// create the Meerkat client
$client=new xmlrpc_client("/meerkat/xml-rpc/server.php",
                        "www.oreillynet.com", 80);

if ($HTTP_GET_VARS["comment"]) {
    // we're making a comment on a story,
    // so display a comment form.
    // TODO: retrieve the story headline & abstract
?>
```

Example 5-3. Meerkat discussion application (continued)

```
<h3>Make a comment on the story</h3>
<form method="post">
<p>Your name:<br /><input type="text" size="30" name="name" /></p>
<p>Your comment:<br /><textarea rows="5" cols="60"
    name="commenttext"></textarea></p>
<input type="submit" value="Send comment" />
<input type="hidden" name="storyid"
    value="<?php echo $HTTP_GET_VARS["comment"];?>" />
<input type="hidden" name="chanid"
    value="<?php echo $chanid; ?>" />
<input type="hidden" name="catid"
    value="<?php echo $catid; ?>" />

</form>
<?php
} else {
    // we're exploring the story store
    // first, get the list of top-level categories
    $categories=dispatch($client, "meerkat.getCategories", array());

    // if we've chosen a category, get list of
    // web sites in that category
    if ($catid)
        $sources = dispatch($client, "meerkat.getChannelsByCategory",

     array(new xmlrpcval($catid, "int")));

    // if we've chosen a web site, get list of
    // most recent 5 stories from that web site
    if ($chanid) {
        $stories = dispatch($client, "meerkat.getItems",
            array(new xmlrpcval(
                array(
                    "channel" => new xmlrpcval($chanid, "int"),
                    "ids" => new xmlrpcval(1, "int"),
                    "descriptions" => new xmlrpcval(200, "int"),
                    "num_items" => new xmlrpcval(5, "int"),
                    "dates" => new xmlrpcval(0, "int")
                    ), "struct")));
    }
    // data is fetched, now render the page
?>
<form>
<p>Subject area:<br />
<select name="catid">
<?php
    // category chooser
    if (!$catid)
            print "<option value=\"0\">Choose a category</option>\n";
        while(list($k,$v) = each($categories)) {
            print "<option value=\"" . $v['id'] ."\"";
            if ($v['id']==$catid) print " selected=\"selected\"";
```

Example 5-3. Meerkat discussion application (continued)

```php
            print ">". $v['title'] . "</option>\n";
        }
?>
</select></p>
<?php
    if ($catid) {
?>
<p>News source:<br />
<select name="chanid">
<?php
    // web site chooser
    if (!$chanid)
        print "<option value=\"0\">Choose a source</option>\n";
    while(list($k,$v) = each($sources)) {
        print "<option value=\"" . $v['id'] ."\"";
        if ($v['id']==$chanid) print "\" selected=\"selected\"";
        print ">". $v['title'] . "</option>\n";
    }
?>
</select>
</p>

<?php
    } // end if ($catid)
?>

<p><input type="submit" value="Update" /></p>
<input type="hidden" name="oc" value="<?php echo $catid; ?>" />
</form>

<?php
    if ($chanid) {
?>

<h2>Stories available</h2>
<table>
<?php
    // story chooser
    while(list($k,$v) = each($stories)) {
        print "<tr>";
        print "<td><b>" . $v['title'] . "</b><br />";
        print $v['description'] . "<br />";
        print "<em><a target=\"_blank\" href=\"" .
            $v['link'] . "\">Read full story</a> ";
        print "<a href=\"comment.php?catid=${catid}&chanid=${chanid}&" .
            "oc=${oc}&comment=" . $v['id'] . "\">Comment on this story</a>";
        print "</em>";
        print "</td>";
        print "</tr>\n";

        // now look for existing comments that the
        // comment server knows about.
```

Example 5-3. Meerkat discussion application (continued)

```
        $res=dispatch($dclient, "discuss.getComments",
            array(new xmlrpcval($v['id'])));

        if (sizeof($res)>0) {
            // $res is an array of associative arrays
            // -- the result of an xmlrpc_decode() call

            print "<tr><td bgcolor=\"#dddddd\"><p><b><i>" .
                "Comments on this story:</i></b></p>";
            for($i=0; $i<sizeof($res); $i++) {
                $s=$res[$i];
                print "<p><b>From:</b> " .
                    htmlentities($s['name']) . "<br />";
                print "<b>Comment:</b> " .
                    htmlentities($s['comment']) . "</p>";
            }
            print "</td></tr>\n";
        }
        print "<tr><td><hr /></td></tr>\n";
    }
?>
</table>

<?php
    } // end if ($chanid)
} // end if ($HTTP_GET_VARS["comment"])
?>

<!-- page footer -->
<hr />
<p>
<a href="http://meerkat.oreillynet.com"><img align="right"
    src="http://meerkat.oreillynet.com/icons/meerkat-powered.jpg"
    height="31" width="88" alt="Meerkat powered, yeah!"
    border="0" hspace="8" /></a>
<em>$Id: ch05,v 1.19 2001/06/11 16:28:51 aschirmer Exp aschirmer $</em></p>
</body>
</html>
```

A Closer Look at the Meerkat Discussion Server

After reading this chapter, there should hopefully be no surprises for you in the Meerkat discussion application. It is a purely client-based application, creating two **xmlrpc_client** objects: one for Meerkat and one for our discussion server. However, there are some features worth noting:

- The **dispatch()** function wraps all the common error handling required in processing XML-RPC method calls. It may prove useful in your own programs.

- The application uses a naïve implementation. Within one invocation of this script, many XML-RPC method calls are generated. HTTP connections are slow to create, and thus it is advisable to make as few method calls as possible within one script. Several tactics could be used to reduce this overhead, such as:

— Redesigning the server API to return more data per method call. The discussion server might be redesigned so that `discuss.getComments()` accepts an array of IDs as its argument and returns an array of arrays holding the comments for each ID.

— Caching returned results. In our application, the entire list of categories is retrieved each time, regardless of whether it has changed or not. For data that changes infrequently it may be acceptable to cache data, once retrieved, for the rest of the user session. One way to do this in the discussion application would be to use frames to separate the category, channel, and story lists, and to add some JavaScript to enable the frames to interact with each other. This would entail reorganization of the PHP script to support this new architecture.

In general, it is not wise to include many XML-RPC calls in applications that require rapid user feedback—although many factors, such as server load and network conditions, obviously affect this decision.

What PHP and XML-RPC Can Do

This chapter demonstrates the use of PHP in creating XML-RPC client and server applications. PHP is ideal for creating XML-RPC web services in an environment that already has a running web server, and thus for adding XML-RPC interfaces to existing web applications. This chapter also shows the strengths of PHP used as a web integration language, bringing together disparate applications under one user interface.

Although normally thought of as a frontend application tool, PHP can now be a viable choice for creating backend systems by using XML-RPC as a middleware language. Consider the advantages of hiding access to a database behind an XML-RPC service. You could use PHP's native database routines to tightly control access to the underlying data store. CGI applications written in any language can then retrieve information from the database without actually knowing anything about the particular Relational Database Management System (RDBMS) used.

The possibilities for web services are only now being explored. PHP makes that exploration both easy and fun.

6

XML-RPC and Python

By combining the rapid development of scripting languages with a carefully designed object-oriented interface, Python is becoming the tool of choice for many programmers on both Windows and Unix platforms. Like Perl, Python has strong string handling and networking tools that make it a good fit for building web applications. Not surprisingly, Python also supports XML-RPC, a no-nonsense web service protocol. Here's an example of a Python client's calling a remote procedure, `getStateName()` on UserLand's server:

```
import xmlrpclib
client = xmlrpclib.Server("http://betty.userland.com")
print "The second state listed on betty is " + \
      client.examples.getStateName(2)
```

Although the answer, "Alaska," is irrelevant, notice that this script needs no additional information to use this service. Not only is the operating system of the server unimportant here, but the implementation language of this service is reduced to the point of trivia.

This chapter shows the details of making XML-RPC client calls in Python and describing the process for setting up standalone XML-RPC servers.

Python Implementations of XML-RPC

As of this writing, only one XML-RPC implementation is archived at the Vaults of Parnassus, the unofficial repository of third-party Python modules (found at *http://www.vex.net/parnassus* or through a link at *http://www.python.org*). First released in January 1999, this XML-RPC library is part of the PythonWare software suite produced by Secret Labs in Sweden. The writer and maintainer of the implementation is Fredrik Lundh (*fredrik@pythonware.com*). PythonWare XML-RPC includes:

- A module named `xmlrpclib`

- A simple XML-RPC server implementation named *xmlrpcserver.py*

This chapter covers the latest stable version of PythonWare's library, Version 0.9.8. The adventurous may want to try the experimental 0.9.9 version. This chapter's code was written with the stable version, but has not been verified with any previous ones. To follow along with this material, consider upgrading from an older version.

Installing PythonWare XML-RPC

Because `xmlrpclib` consists of a single Python module, installation is simple:

1. Download the distribution—a ZIP archive—from *http://www.pythonware.com/ products/xmlrpc/* (or by searching for "xmlrpc" in the Vaults of Parnassus).

2. Unpack the ZIP archive, which contains a *README* file and three *.py* files.

3. Place the *xmlrpclib.py* file in a directory within your Python module search path. (To determine the module search path, start an interactive Python session, import the `sys` module, and check the value of the `sys.path` variable.)

4. Place the *xmlrpcserver.py* file in a directory in which you do Python development work. This isn't a class, but a template for making your own XML-RPC servers.

To use PythonWare XML-RPC, your Python programs need to import just a single module, `xmlrpclib`. This module relies, in turn, on the following standard Python library modules:

Basic modules
    `time`, `StringIO`, and `string`

Network-related and web-related modules
    `SocketServer`, `BaseHTTPServer`, `httplib`, `urllib`, `cgi`, and `base64`

XML parser module
    `xmllib` or `sgmlop`. Python normally installs with `xmllib`, but `sgmlop`, a compiled extension, is faster. Check out the PythonWare page for more details.

Data Types

Many data types defined in the XML-RPC specification correspond to Python's built-in data types. For the other XML-RPC data types, the `xmlrpclib` module defines corresponding classes. For example, the XML-RPC `dateTime.iso8601` data type corresponds to the Python class `DateTime`. Table 6-1 shows the mapping between XML-RPC and Python data types.

Table 6-1. Data types: XML-RPC versus Python

XML-RPC data type (XML element)	Python built-in data type	Class defined in xmlrpclib module
`<int>` (or `<i4>`)	`int`	–
`<double>`	`float`	–
`<string>`	`string`	–
`<boolean>`	–	`Boolean`
`<dateTime.iso8601>`	–	`DateTime`
`<base64>`	–	`Binary`
`<array>`	`list` or `tuple`	–
`<struct>`	`dictionary` or class instance	–

Python Data and XML Elements

Although the Python library often makes smart decisions about packing variables, some care is needed to encode Python data into some of the more esoteric XML-RPC tags. XML-RPC client calls usually return data in a form immediately usable by Python. Again, for the less-often used XML-RPC types, you'll need a little extra effort to extract the return values.

Data types that require no extra work

When a Python script makes an XML-RPC call whose parameters are of the XML-RPC type `<int>`, `<float>`, `<string>`, `<array>`, or `<struct>`, you can use normal Python variables. Similarly, when a XML-RPC server returns those types, the client Python script gets back simple Python data. Python data of type `list` or `tuple` becomes XML-RPC arrays, and Python's dictionaries become structures. User-defined objects (that is, `instances` of a user-defined `class`) are very similar to dictionaries.

Aggregate data items are handled recursively: each member value can be either individual (e.g., `string`) or aggregate (e.g., `instance`). Some restrictions apply to using an aggregate value as an argument or return value:

- You can't specify a `class` object itself, only an instance of the class.

- The keys of a dictionary must all be strings. (Python itself allows integers and tuples to be keys.)

- Each attribute of an instance must have one of the data types discussed above or be one of the objects discussed in the next section. No function objects allowed!

Data types that must be wrapped in an object

The preceding sections covered the built-in Python data types that translate directly to XML-RPC data types. But there are several XML-RPC data types that don't correspond to any built-in Python data type. The `xmlrpclib` module remedies this situation with classes that serve as user-defined data types: `Boolean`, `DateTime`, and `Binary`; they correspond to the XML-RPC data types `<boolean>`, `<dateTime.iso8601>`, and `<base64>`.

A client script can use instances of these classes as arguments to XML-RPC calls. Likewise, a server script can use any of these objects as a return value.

Boolean data. To specify a true/false argument or return value, use an instance of the `xmlrpclib.Boolean` class. For convenience, there are two prefabricated `Boolean` objects, named `xmlrpclib.True` and `xmlrpclib.False`:

```
rpc-call("complete", xmlrpclib.True)     # argument
return xmlrpclib.False                    # return value
```

When receiving a Boolean object back from an XML-RPC call, use the `value` attribute to get data Python can use:

```
response = client.isPrime(7)
if response.value == 1:
    print "7 is a prime number"
else:
    print "7 is not a prime number"
```

You can also create a `Boolean` object in the standard Python manner, but we don't recommend it. Potential bugs lurk because the `Boolean` constructor (`__init__` method) doesn't have the same notion of truth as Python's `if` function. For example:

```
if "": ...              # condition is false
xmlrpclib.Boolean("")   # creates a True object
```

Similarly, the `None` object is false to the `if` function, but true to the `Boolean` constructor. For the curious, *xmlrpclib* uses the standard Python class `operator`'s method `truth` to determine how to encode the argument to `Boolean`.

Date-time data. To specify an ISO 8601 date-time value as an argument or return value, use an instance of the `xmlrpclib.DateTime` class:

```
timestamp = xmlrpclib.DateTime( ... )
rpc-call("update_complete", timestamp)
```

The `DateTime` object constructor accepts several kinds of arguments, specifying a point in time:

- A string in ISO 8601 format:

```
timestamp = xmlrpclib.DateTime("20001023T10:48:26")
```

The object constructor does not verify that the string is actually in ISO 8601 format. This allows you to create a value that is correct at the XML-syntax level, but is meaningless as a representation of time. Consult the documentation for POSIX `strftime` for details on how strings are converted into the ISO 8601 format.

- A date-time tuple (such as that produced by the `time.localtime()`) function:

```
timestamp = xmlrpclib.DateTime((2000, 10, 23, 10, 48, 26, 0, 297, 1))
```

The final three items in the tuple are ignored by the constructor.

- An integer specifying the number of seconds since the Epoch (such as that produced by the `time.time()` function):

```
import time
...
timestamp = xmlrpclib.DateTime(time.time())
```

The constructor automatically converts the time value to local time.

The previous example shows the canonical way to create a `DateTime` object that represents the current time. When getting a `DateTime` object from an XML-RPC call, use the attribute **value** to extract the string in ISO 8601 format. A script might parse out the year, month, and day from a date-time argument like this:

```
timestamp = code-that-extracts-DateTime-argument-from-arg-list
year = timestamp.value[0:4]
month = timestamp.value[4:6]
day = timestamp.value[6:8]
```

Note that **year**, **month**, and **day** all get string values. You can convert them to integers using the built-in `int()` function.

Binary data. To specify binary data—encoded as a `Base64` string—as an argument or return value, use an instance of the `xmlrpclib.Binary` class:

```
b64_obj = xmlrpclib.Binary( ... )
rpc-call(b64_obj)
```

The `Binary` object constructor takes a string containing binary data. You might create such a string by reading the contents of a binary file. Thus, it's simple to transfer a binary file to a remote host in the form of an XML-RPC argument:

```
binary_string = open( filename ).read()
b64_obj = xmlrpclib.Binary(binary_string)
rpc-call(b64_obj)
```

When getting a `Binary` object back from a server, extract the data with the `data` attribute:

```
response = rpc-call( ... )
binary_string = response.data
f = open("myicon.gif", "w")
f.write(binary_string)
f.close()
```

For small binary files, such as images, an XML-RPC service could replace FTP.

XML-RPC Clients

This section describes the operation and construction of a Python XML-RPC client—a script that makes calls to an XML-RPC server and gets responses back from it. We start with an overview of the method-call process, and then we describe how to create a client to do the job.

Client Architecture

A client Python script must import the `xmlrpclib` module. Most of the script's XML-RPC-level work is performed by an instance of the class `xmlrpclib.Server`. This object provides a connection to a particular XML-RPC server. (The selection of "Server" as the class name wasn't ideal. It may help to think "client's-connection-to-server" when you read the section "XML-RPC Servers" later in this chapter.)

Here's the basic recipe for making a call:

1. Create an `xmlrpclib.Server` object. Be sure to import the XML-RPC library first.

2. Prepare one or more arguments to be passed to the XML-RPC method.

3. Call the method.

4. Get the response to the call.

In the following example, an XML-RPC call is made to a remote procedure, `getTickets()`, that requires an integer and ISO 8601 date and that returns a Boolean value to indicate success. This code attempts to buy four tickets for an event 30 days in the future:

```
import xmlrpc, time
client = xmlrpclib.Server("http://i.writethesongs.com:1080")
ts = xmlrpclib.DateTime( time.time() + 60 * 60 * 24 * 30 )
resp = client.getTickets(4, ts)
if resp.value :
    print "We're on for Manilow!"
else:
    print "Shucks! No Barry for us!"
```

Checking for errors is simple with Python. Both XML-RPC and standard Python exceptions can be handled by wrapping the XML-RPC call in a try-except construct:

```
try:
    response = rpc-call( ... )
except xmlrpclib.Fault, faultobj:
    # exception caused by <fault> response from server
    print "XML-RPC fault code:", faultobj.faultCode
    print ">>> %s <<<" % faultobj.faultString
except:
    # exception caused other problem,
    # including failure to contact server at all
    print "Problem of type:", sys.exc_type
    print ">>> %s <<<" % sys.exc_value
else:
    # call succeeded, interpret "response"
```

A Client Script

Example 6-1 shows a complete XML-RPC client script that calls two methods: `SetColor()` and `Describe()`. (The XML-RPC server script in Example 6-2 implements this API.) Note that these functions don't perform any useful operation; they just serve to demonstrate XML-RPC calls in Python. In its structure, the client script follows the recipe presented in the preceding section.

Like all Python XML-RPC scripts, this one needs to create a new **Server** object that connects to a particular XML-RPC server. If a server is not specified on the command line, it is assumed to be local. To demonstrate the PythonWare XML-RPC library's ability to map native data into XML-RPC, the script creates several variables of various Python types that are passed to the remote procedures.

All client calls happen in the **try** block. Recall that many accidents can happen to an XML-RPC message during transmission. When a problem occurs, it raises an exception that can be dealt with in a controlled manner. The calls to **SetColor()** and **Describe()** succeed, but the spurious call to **ThisMethodDoesNotExist()** throws an exception.

Example 6-1. Python XML-RPC client script

```
# ora_client.py

"""
ora_client: test Python client for XML-RPC
"""

import sys, xmlrpclib

##### create xmlrpclib.Server object

# XML-RPC server host might be specified on command line
```

Example 6-1. Python XML-RPC client script (continued)

```python
if len(sys.argv) > 1:
    host = sys.argv[1]
else:
    host = "http://localhost:8000"

# create object representing connection to server host
conn = xmlrpclib.Server(host)

###### prepare arguments

i1 = 37          # integer datatype
s1 = "37"        # string that looks like a number
s2 = "hi, mom"   # string that looks like a string
f1 = 3.1416      # floating-point number
s3 = "3.1416"    # string that looks like a floating-point number

a1 = range(3)    # list
a2 = (0, 1, 2)   # tuple
d1 = {'alpha':1, 'beta':2}   # dictionary

# user-defined object
class MyClass:
    """
    simple class, with some instance attributes
    """
    def __init__(self):
        """
        initialize instance data attributes
        """
        self.alpha = 1
        self.beta = 2

o1 = MyClass()    # must use object (instance), not class itself

### special XML-RPC datatypes

# boolean data
obj_bool = xmlrpclib.False

# date-time data: current time
import time
obj_dtime = xmlrpclib.DateTime(time.time())

# base64 data
# Binary object constructor takes a stream of binary data
binary_file = r'0.gif'
obj_bin = xmlrpclib.Binary(open(binary_file).read())

##### call the remote procedures

try:
    ### 1st call
    print "\n*** Calling SetColor() ..."
```

Example 6-1. Python XML-RPC client script (continued)

```
    rgb = (255, 255, 0)

    # use hard-coded method name
    response = conn.SetColor("rectangle", 14, rgb)
    print response

    ### 2nd call
    print "\n*** Calling Describe() ..."

    strings = (s1, s2, s3)
    numbers = (i1, f1)
    arrays = (a1, a2)
    dicts = (d1, o1)
    specials = (obj_bool, obj_dtime, obj_bin)
    groups = {
        "grp1": strings,
        "grp2": numbers,
        "grp3": arrays,
        "grp4": dicts,
        "grp5": specials
    } # alternative: submit all values in a single structure

    response = conn.Describe(strings, numbers, arrays,
                                dicts, specials)
    print response

    ### 3rd call
    # expecting a Fault response this time
    print "\n*** Calling ThisMethodDoesNotExist() ..."
    response = conn.ThisMethodDoesNotExist()
    print "NOT!"

except xmlrpclib.Fault, faultobj:
    print "Server error:", faultobj.faultCode
    print ">>> %s <<<" % faultobj.faultString

except:
    print "Client error: '%s/%s'" % (sys.exc_type, sys.exc_value)

# bye
sys.exit(0)
```

XML-RPC Servers

PythonWare XML-RPC includes the script *xmlrpcserver.py*, which implements a
simple server. In the spirit of code reuse, this script can be used as a template to
implement new XML-RPC servers. The script imports the **xmlrpclib** module,
along with the standard Python library modules **SocketServer** and
BaseHTTPServer.

Like a client, a server may need to deal with the special XML-RPC data types and, thus, with the classes `DateTime`, `Binary`, and `Boolean` defined in the `xmlrpclib` module. And like a client, a server uses the XML parser in either the `xmllib` module or the `sgmlop` module.

The script creates a `SocketServer.TCPServer` object to listen for XML-RPC method calls on a particular port. A method call is wrapped inside an HTTP POST request, so the script implements a `RequestHandler` object, derived from the class `BaseHTTPServer.BaseHTTPRequestHandler`, to process it. The `RequestHandler` object:

- Uses an XML parser to decode the incoming XML `<methodCall>` message.

- Determines the method name (a string).

- Converts each parameter from XML format to a Python data item—of a built-in Python data type or an instance of one of the above-mentioned `xmlrpclib` classes. A tuple object is created from these data items, constituting the method's argument list.

- Invokes its `call()` method, passing it the method name and the argument list.

- Packages the `call()` method's return value in an XML `<methodResponse>` message and sends it back to the client.

Setting Up an XML-RPC Server

Here's a procedure for setting up a server, by adapting the *xmlrpcserver.py* script in the PythonWare XML-RPC distribution:

1. Create a copy of the script.

2. Set a port number.

3. Recode the `call()` method to define the server's API.

4. Create functions to implement the API.

5. Run the server script.

Creating a copy of the script

Our PythonWare XML-RPC installation instructions advised you to place file *xmlrpcserver.py* in a Python development directory. Go to that directory and make a copy of the file. In the following sections, "the server script" refers to this copy—it's good practice not to modify *xmlrpcserver.py* itself.

Setting a port number

If you wish to specify a port number other than 8000, modify this line in the server script:

```
server = SocketServer.TCPServer(('', 8000), RequestHandler)
```

Don't forget to document the port number you've chosen to your potential clients.

Recoding the call() method to define the API

Each XML-RPC server implements a particular application programming interface (API). The API consists of a set of *procedures*, each of which is implemented as a Python function that accepts zero or more arguments and returns a single value to the client.

The `RequestHandler` object handles each incoming method call by invoking its `call()` method. For example, a call to method `ChangeSetting` with string parameter `priority_level` and integer parameter `5` becomes, in effect:

```
self.call("ChangeSetting", ("priority_level", 5))
```

Note that the method's parameters (in this example, two of them) are packaged into an *argument-list tuple* and are passed to the `call()` method as a single argument.

To keep things sane, it makes sense to have the `call()` method act as a dispatcher, invoking a separate *dispatch function* for each method name in the API. Thus, if your API consists of three methods—named `go`, `pause`, and `stop`—you might recode the `call()` method like this:

```
def call(self, meth_name, arg_tuple):
    ...
    if meth_name == "go":
        return do_go(arg_tuple)
    elif meth_name == "pause":
        return do_pause(arg_tuple)
    elif meth_name == "stop":
        return do_stop(arg_tuple)
```

This approach, in which you call the methods directly, can lead to a substantial "elif chain" for an API with many methods. Python's built-in `eval()` and `apply()` functions can help:

```
def call(self, meth_name, arg_tuple):
    ...
    func_obj = eval("do_" + meth_name)
    return apply(func_obj, arg_tuple)
```

This alternative approach produces much more compact code, but you pay the cost of introducing a level of indirection that can make your code more obscure.

The `elif` chain and the `apply()` approaches are not completely equivalent. If you change approaches, you must also change the way your dispatch functions process their arguments. For details, see the section "Creating dispatch functions to implement the API" later in this chapter.

With either approach, keep in mind that the return value of the `call()` method becomes the server's response to the XML-RPC method call. So, for example, it's not enough to invoke a `do_pause()` function to implement a method named "pause." You must take the return value of `do_pause()` and make it (or adapt it to be) the return value of `call()`.

As always, be sure to avoid Python keywords when selecting function names. It's fine for an XML-RPC *procedure* name to be "list" or "dict" or "range," as long as you don't define a Python function with such a name. Using `do_` or some other prefix or suffix in the function name, as illustrated previously, prevents this problem.

Creating a hierarchical API. The XML-RPC procedure-name argument passed to the `call()` method (`meth_name` in the previous examples) is just a string. You can process this string in any way you wish as you go about selecting a dispatch function. For example, suppose a "color" API consists of these methods:

```
color           # describes all the color.XXX methods
color.setRGB    # specifies a new color
color.getRGB    # reports the current color
```

To define this API, you might recode the `call()` method like this:

```
def call(self, meth_name, arg_tuple):
    # no "." in name, call "summary" function
    if string.count(meth_name, '.') == 0:
        category, func_name = meth_name, "summary"

    # one "." in name, get the two pieces
    elif string.count(meth_name, '.') == 1:
        category, func_name = string.split(meth_name, '.')

    # lookup the dispatch function and invoke it
    func_obj = double_lookup(category, func_name)
    return apply(func_obj, arg_tuple)
```

A method name that includes a dot character is split into a category and function name within that category. A method name without a dot character names the category itself (in our example, `color`), and will invoke a function that returns a summary of that category.

The hard work is in the **double_lookup()** function that:

- Looks up the category in a master dictionary, yielding a category-specific dictionary.

- Looks up the function name in the category-specific dictionary, yielding a particular dispatch function.

Python's object orientation makes the dictionary setup relatively easy. For example, the category-specific dictionary for the "color" API might look like this:

```
color_dict = {
   "summary" : do_color_summary,
   "setRGB"  : do_color_setRGB,
   "getRGB"  : do_color_getRGB
}
```

The values are function objects, not strings, so the definitions of the several **do_color_XXX** functions must precede the setting of **color_dict**.

Creating dispatch functions to implement the API

You're now faced with the task of writing the set of "dispatch functions" to implement the server's API. Let's examine the task by considering one API method named **ChangeSetting**, which accepts a string parameter and an integer parameter.

According to the scheme described previously, you'll name the dispatch function **do_ChangeSetting()**. Be careful how you code the function header:

- If your **call()** method invokes the dispatch functions directly (the elif chain approach), the header should look like this:

```
def do_ChangeSetting(arg_tuple):
    # unpack argument-list tuple
    setting_name, setting_value = arg_tuple
    ...
```

That is, the **call()** method can simply pass the argument-list tuple it has received down to the dispatch function without "unpacking" it. The dispatch function does the unpacking.

- If your **call()** method invokes the dispatch functions indirectly (the **eval()** and **apply()** approach), you can code the dispatch function to process its arguments individually:

```
def do_ChangeSetting(setting_name, setting_value):
    ...
```

Either way, make sure you define these dispatch functions at the top level of the server script. Don't make them methods of the **RequestHandler** object. This restriction follows from Python's standard local/global/built-in scoping rules for names.

In general, the function (1) processes its argument list, (2) performs some computations, and (3) returns a value. We'll discuss steps (1) and (3) only—the computing is up to you!

Processing the argument list. The RequestHandler's call() method receives the method's argument list in the form of a tuple. According to our scheme, call() passes this tuple down, unchanged, as the sole argument to the selected dispatch function.

The type of each data item in the tuple might be a Python built-in (such as string) or an xmlrpclib-defined data type (such as Boolean). Moreover, a data item can be a Python list or dictionary. It's up to you to extract each data item from the argument-list tuple and, if necessary, to extract the actual value from an xmlrpclib-defined object. Here are a couple of examples:

- Implement a ChangeSetting method that accepts two arguments, a string and an integer:

```
def do_ChangeSetting(arg_tuple):
    # assign arguments to individual variables
    which_setting, new_value = arg_tuple

    # work with the data
    print "Changing the %s setting" % which_setting
    make_the_change( ..., new_value, ... )
```

- Implement a DateStamp method that accepts a single date-time argument:

```
def do_DateStamp(arg_tuple):
    # extract ISO8601 string from first item on argument list
    dstring = arg_tuple[0].value

    # analyze the ISO8601 string
    year = int(dstring[0:4])
    month = int(dstring[4:6])
    day = int(dstring[6:8])
    ...
```

Returning a value. The value returned by the RequestHandler's call() method becomes the server's response to the XML-RPC method call. According to our scheme, call() simply passes along the value generated by a dispatch function:

```
def call(self, meth_name, arg_tuple):
    ...
    if meth_name == "DateStamp":
        return do_DateStamp(arg_tuple)
```

A dispatch function can return any individual value (a Python built-in or xmlrpclib-defined object) or an aggregate value (a list or dictionary) that incorporates individual and/or aggregate values. Consider the following examples:

- Have a `VerifyCompletion` method return a `Boolean` object to indicate a true or false answer:

```
def do_VerifyCompletion(arg_tuple):
    # process argument list; perform computations
    ...
    # return a Boolean
    if completed_flag:
        return xmlrpclib.True
    else:
        return xmlrpclib.False
```

- Have a `GetEmployeeInfo` method return a three-item list, containing a string, an integer, and a block of binary data:

```
def do_GetEmployeeInfo(arg_tuple):
    # process argument list
    ...
    # perform computations
    emp_name = string-valued computation
    emp_number = integer-valued computation
    emp_photo = load-binary-data-into-Python-string

    # return 3-item list
    return [emp_name, emp_number, xmlrpclib.Binary(emp_photo)]
```

Returning a fault value. A dispatch function can force the XML-RPC server to return a *fault* response to the client. Such a response is encoded by the server in an XML <fault> element, whose actual values are an integer (`faultCode`) and a string (`faultString`).

To force a fault response, create an instance of class `xmlrpclib.Fault`, specifying an integer and a string. Be sure to `raise` this instance; don't simply `return` it:

```
raise xmlrpclib.Fault(13, "Invalid setting")      # rightt
return xmlrpclib.Fault(13, "Invalid setting")     # wrong
```

Running the server script

Having customized the server script to define and implement a particular API, you're ready to start the server. Run the server script, for example, like this on a Unix system:

```
% python myserver.py &
```

Or like this on a Windows system:

```
C:\> start python myserver.py
```

The following lines in the server script create and activate the **TCPServer** object that listens for XML-RPC calls:

```
server = SocketServer.TCPServer(('', port), RequestHandler)
server.serve_forever()
```

It continues listening until the Python interpreter is terminated.

A Server Script

Example 6-2 shows a complete XML-RPC server script that implements a two-method API: **SetColor()** and **Describe()**. (The client script in Example 6-1 calls each of these methods.) Again, these methods don't do anything particularly interesting, but they do demonstrate basic Python XML-RPC techniques, following the process discussed in the previous section. This script is based on the *xmlrpcserver.py* script included in PythonWare XML-RPC Version 0.9.8. It is also based on code by Fredrik Lundh.

Much of the server code is dedicated to servicing HTTP requests. Two parts of this script require you to make modifications. The first is the method call, **call()**. In the archive from Secret Labs, this dispatch method is simply stubbed in and will not work without modification. The code in Example 6-2 presents a more robust dispatch method that attempts to call functions defined in the *main* package. Please note that the **call()** method is part of the **RequestHandler** class, and the functions that implement the XML-RPC API are defined in *main*. Because Python defines programming blocks with indentation, it is trivially easy to put the API implementing functions in the **RequestHandler** class accidentally.

The **do_SetColor()** and **do_Describe()** methods perform the actual work of handling client calls to the XML-RPC server. Note that most of **do_Describe()** is devoted to handling all the different kinds of arguments that can be passed to it.

The other task is to specify the TCP/IP port on which this script will listen. This is set in the call to **TCPServer()** near the end of Example 6-2.

Example 6-2. Python XML-RPC server script

```
# ora_server.py (based on xmlrpcserver.py)
#
# XML-RPC SERVER
# $Id: ch06,v 1.15 2001/06/11 16:17:01 brenda Exp aschirmer $
#
# a simple XML-RPC server for Python
#
# History:
# 1999-02-01 fl  added to xmlrpclib distribution
# 2000-10-28 jjp modified for use in O'Reilly XML-RPC book
#
```

Example 6-2. Python XML-RPC server script (continued)

```
# written by Fredrik Lundh, January 1999.
#
# Copyright (c) 1999 by Secret Labs AB.
# Copyright (c) 1999 by Fredrik Lundh.
#
# fredrik@pythonware.com
# http://www.pythonware.com
#
# --------------------------------------------------------------
# Permission to use, copy, modify, and distribute this software
# and its associated documentation for any purpose and without
# fee is hereby granted.  This software is provided as is.
# --------------------------------------------------------------

import SocketServer, BaseHTTPServer
import xmlrpclib, sys

class RequestHandler(BaseHTTPServer.BaseHTTPRequestHandler):

    def do_POST(self):
        try:
            # get arguments
            data = self.rfile.read(
              int(self.headers["content-length"])
            )
            params, method = xmlrpclib.loads(data)

            # generate response
            try:
                response = self.call(method, params)
                if type(response) != type(()):
                    response = (response,)

            except xmlrpclib.Fault, faultobj:
                # generated response was a Fault
                response = xmlrpclib.dumps(faultobj)

            except:
                # report exception back to server
                response = xmlrpclib.dumps(
                  xmlrpclib.Fault(1,
                  "%s:%s" % (sys.exc_type, sys.exc_value))
                )
            else:
                # no exception occurred:
                # send method's return value back to server
                response = xmlrpclib.dumps(
                    response,
                    methodresponse=1
                    )
```

Example 6-2. Python XML-RPC server script (continued)

```
        except:
            # internal error, report as HTTP server error
            self.send_response(500)
            self.end_headers()
        else:
            # no internal error: send back a "success" response
            self.send_response(200)
            self.send_header("Content-type", "text/xml")
            self.send_header("Content-length", str(len(response)))
            self.end_headers()
            self.wfile.write(response)

            # shut down the connection (from Skip Montanaro)
            self.wfile.flush()
            self.connection.shutdown(1)

    # def call(self, method, params):
    # override this method to implement RPC methods
    # print "CALL", method, params
    # return params

    def call(self, meth_name, arg_tuple):
        """
        XML-RPC method dispatcher
        """
        myAPI = ("SetColor",  "Describe")
        if meth_name in myAPI:
            func_obj = eval("do_" + meth_name)
            return apply(func_obj, arg_tuple)
        else:
            raise xmlrpclib.Fault(123, "Unknown method name")

##### functions that implement XML-RPC API

def do_SetColor(shape_type, shape_id, color_tuple):
    """
    implementation of "SetColor" method
    """
    message = (
      "Modifying %s number %s:\n" % (shape_type, shape_id) +
      ">> setting Red value to %d\n" % color_tuple[0] +
      ">> setting Green value to %d\n" % color_tuple[1] +
      ">> setting Blue value to %d" % color_tuple[2]
    )
    # do the work, then ...
    return message

def do_Describe(*one_or_more_args):
    """
    implementation of "Describe" method:
    describe arguments, any number of them
    """
```

Example 6-2. Python XML-RPC server script (continued)

```
from types import *

##### "Describe" internal functions
def proc_list(arg):
    """
    process a list argument (called by do_Describe)
    """
    rtn = "* Array argument:\n"
    for i in range(len(arg)):
        rtn = rtn + "    " + "%d: %s\n" % (i, arg[i])
    return rtn

def proc_dict(arg):
    """
    process a dictionary argument (called by do_Describe)
    """
    rtn = "* Dictionary argument:\n"
    for pair in arg.items():
        rtn = rtn + "    " + "%s: %s\n" % pair
    return rtn
##### end of "Describe" internal functions

# title line
console_msg = ("Called RPC method 'Describe' with %d arguments"
        % len(one_or_more_args))

# special case: empty argument list
if not one_or_more_args: return ""

# report summary of call to server console
print console_msg

# start accumulating return-value text
rtn = console_msg + ":\n\n"

# describe each parameter, distinguishing by datatype
for arg in one_or_more_args:
    if type(arg) is IntType:
        rtn = rtn + "* Integer argument: %d\n" % arg
    elif type(arg) is StringType:
        rtn = rtn + "* String argument: %s\n" % arg
    elif type(arg) is ListType:
        rtn = rtn + proc_list(arg)
    elif type(arg) is DictionaryType:
        rtn = rtn + proc_dict(arg)
    elif type(arg) is FloatType:
        rtn = rtn + "* Floating-point argument: %f\n" % arg
    elif isinstance(arg, xmlrpclib.DateTime):
        rtn = rtn + "* Date-time argument: %s\n" % arg.value
    elif isinstance(arg, xmlrpclib.Binary):
        rtn = rtn + "* Base64-text-encoded binary value\n"
    elif isinstance(arg, xmlrpclib.Boolean):
```

Example 6-2. Python XML-RPC server script (continued)

```
            if arg.value == 1:
                bool = 'True'
            else:
                bool = 'False'
            rtn = rtn + "* Boolean argument: %s\n" % bool
        else:
            rtn = rtn + "* Argument of type %s\n" % type(arg)

    # return accumulated text as value of XML-RPC call
    return rtn

if __name__ == '__main__':
    # set up and run XML-RPC server process (daemon)

    # create server
    port = 8000
    server = SocketServer.TCPServer(('', port), RequestHandler)

    # send startup message to console
    print "XML-RPC server listening on port %s ..." % port

    # start server
    server.serve_forever()
```

Integrating XML-RPC into a Web Server

The preceding section describes a standalone server—a process dedicated to handling XML-RPC method calls by listening for those calls on a dedicated TCP/IP port. One problem with this approach is that it ignores (or at least minimizes) one of XML-RPC's main design points: its use of the HTTP protocol. In many situations, the machine designated to handle XML-RPC method calls is already running a process that accepts HTTP requests—a standard web server.

One solution is to allow the web server to handle all the HTTP-level communications. A browser might retrieve a regular web page at one location on the server (for example, *http://MyStore.com/catalog/gloves.html*), while an XML-RPC client might make method calls at another location (such as *http://MyStore.com/catalogAPI*). In other words, it is quite possible to have different web-based information services running on the same server and same port.[*]

It is very easy to create CGI scripts that are Python XML-RPC listeners. If you are new to CGI programming, you may want to pick up a copy of *CGI Programming with Perl*, by Scott Guelich, Shishir Gundavaram, and Gunther Birznieks (O'Reilly,

---

[*] As we discussed in Chapter 1, there is a lot of controversy on the subject of using the same TCP/IP port to provide multiple services with different performance requirements, security requirements, etc. We'll duck those issues here and just tell you how to get the job done.

2000). Although that book focuses on Perl, it provides a great overview of how CGI works and fundamental concepts that apply to all CGI programming, regardless of language.

Example 6-3 shows a Python XML-RPC server that runs as a CGI program. Although it has many similarities to the standalone server shown in Example 6-2, much of this script deals with extracting XML-RPC requests, attempting to execute the requested procedure and then packaging up the response. The `xmlrpclib` class handles most of the protocol related tasks, but you still need to define and implement the API procedures. In Example 6-3, these API procedures, `do_SetColor()` and `do_Describe()`, are simply stubbed out.

As in the standalone script, the main program invokes `call()` to dispatch a particular function. This means you can copy the definition of `call()` from the standalone script virtually unchanged. The one difference is that in the CGI script, `call()` is an ordinary function, not a class method, so the argument list of the CGI script's `call()` method does not include an object reference.

Example 6-3. Python CGI script that implements an XML-RPC server

```
# xmlrpc_cgi.py

import xmlrpclib
import os, sys, string

#### HTTP message templates

success_msg = """
HTTP/1.1 200 OK
Content-type: text/xml
Content-length: %d

%s
"""

failure_msg = """
HTTP/1.1 500 Internal Server Error

"""

#### functions that implement XML-RPC API

def do_SetColor(shape_type, shape_id, color_tuple):
    return "hello from do_SetColor"

def do_Describe(*one_or_more_args):
    return "hello from do_Describe"

def call(meth_name, arg_tuple):
    """
    XML-RPC method dispatcher
    """
```

Example 6-3. Python CGI script that implements an XML-RPC server (continued)

```
    myAPI = ("SetColor", "Bounce", "Describe")
    if meth_name in myAPI:
        func_obj = eval("do_" + meth_name)
        return apply(func_obj, arg_tuple)
    else:
        raise xmlrpclib.Fault(123, "Unknown method name")


##### main program

if __name__ == "__main__":

    try:
        # get arguments
        data = sys.stdin.read()
        params, method = xmlrpclib.loads(data)

        # generate response
        try:
            response = call(method, params)
            if type(response) != type(()):
                response = (response,)

        except xmlrpclib.Fault, faultobj:
            # generated response was a Fault
            response = xmlrpclib.dumps(faultobj)

        except:
            # report exception back to server
            response = xmlrpclib.dumps(
              xmlrpclib.Fault(1,
               "%s:%s" % (sys.exc_type, sys.exc_value))
            )
        else:
            # no exception occurred:
            # send method's return value back to server
            response = xmlrpclib.dumps(
                response,
                methodresponse=1
                )
    except:
        # internal error, report as HTTP server error
        print failure_msg
    else:
        # no internal error: send back a "success" response
        print success_msg % (len(XML_response), XML_response)
```

Using Zope as an XML-RPC Server

Our discussion of integrating a Python-based XML-RPC service into a web server would be remiss not to mention Zope. It's a souped-up web server, designed for dynamic—including script-driven—content creation. You could call Zope a "web application server;" Zope calls itself the "Z Object Publishing Environment."

Zope is an "everything is an object" environment, whose objects know how to respond to XML-RPC method calls. (PythonWare XML-RPC is built into Zope.) Moreover, Zope recognizes Python scripts as objects, at the same architectural level as web pages.

We don't pretend that the previous paragraphs will bring you up to speed if you're unfamiliar with Zope. Nevertheless, here's a quick outline of how to port the three-method API in *ora_server.py* to Zope. We hope that, if nothing else, you'll get the idea that it's quite easy. At some location in the Zope object hierarchy, create a *folder* object named myRPC.

Within the myRPC folder, create an *external method* object named SetColor, specifying do_SetColor as the function name and myRPC_fns as the Python module. Similarly, create an external method object Describe. In Zope's *Extensions* directory (akin to a *cgi-bin* directory), create Python module file *myRPC_fns.py*. Copy the definitions of functions do_SetColor() and do_Describe() from *ora_server.py* to the new file.

You don't need to copy the call() dispatcher function or any of the HTTP or XML-RPC infrastructure code—Zope handles all this automatically. A client might invoke the Describe method like this:

```
cn = xmlrpclib.<Server("http://Zope-host/.../myRPC")
cn.Describe( arg-list )
```

7

Bridging XML-RPC and COM: XML-RPC in ASP

XML-RPC is about breaking down the barriers of language and platform. With it, you are free to use your preferred operating system with your preferred programming language to get at the computer resources you need. If you're a Unix hacker, you may be frustrated by Microsoft Windows programs that don't provide adequate support for remote usage. If you're a Windows coder, you might want a standard way to get at the resources on a Unix machine. The answer to both of these problems is XML-RPC, a protocol well-suited to creating platform-independent gateways to server resources. Designing those gateways to and from Microsoft Windows is the subject of this chapter.

This chapter demonstrates how to build XML-RPC listeners and clients using the ASP library written in VBScript. To get a flavor of the typical cross-language use of XML-RPC, Perl clients and servers are also shown briefly. If you don't understand Perl, please have a look at Chapter 4, which talks more about using Perl's `Frontier::RPC` library.

Using XML-RPC with ASP

For the impatient, Example 7-1 shows the contents of a file called *rpc_sum.asp*. It is a brief example of an ASP XML-RPC listener that merely returns the sum of the two integers passed to it.

Example 7-1. An ASP XML-RPC listener used to add two integers

```
<!--#include virtual="/jjohn/xmlrpc.asp" -->
<%
rpcserver
```

Example 7-1. An ASP XML-RPC listener used to add two integers (continued)

```
Function add_em( a, b )
  add_em = a + b
End Function
%>
```

Example 7-2 shows an ASP client, stored in the file *sum_client.asp*, that asks the listener in Example 7-1 to compute the sum of two hard-coded integers.

Example 7-2. An ASP client used to query the listener

```
<!--#include virtual="/jjohn/xmlrpc.asp"-->
<h1>Computing 3 + 5</h1>
<%
    Dim args(2), Answer
    args(0) = 3
    args(1) = 5
    Answer = XMLrpc("http://durgan.daisypark.net/jjohn/rpc_sum.asp", _
                "add_em", args)
%>
<P>The answer is <%= Answer %>
```

Figure 7-1 shows what this client page looks like when run.

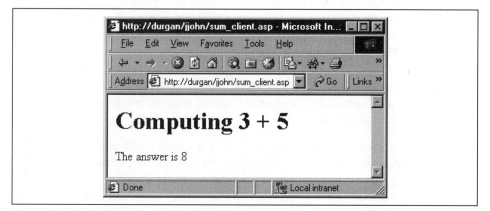

Figure 7-1. Active Server pages know math

Although just finding the sum of two numbers seems like a lot of work, this model can be used by a puny workstation to distribute larger computational tasks to a network of robust servers.

One of the most surprising aspects of producing web services in XML-RPC is the simplicity of the libraries. There aren't many devilish details to using the ASP library, but you should know some finer points before trying to build more complex XML-RPC systems.

Making Active Server Pages More Active

Creating dynamic web pages is fun. With Microsoft's Internet Information Server, the novice Windows programmer can easily create a simple HTML form and process user input with just a few Active Server Page (ASP) directives. You can do a surprising amount of work with just this simple model. Any server resource can be made available through a web page. In fact, Microsoft ships a web frontend to control IIS right now. The problem with this model is that the only resources you can twiddle from a web page have to be on the web server itself.

Now imagine if the frontend web page didn't make direct calls to the backend resource, which here is IIS, but instead made remote procedure calls. Then this frontend could talk to any number of web servers on a network. The conduit through which the frontend talks to the backend is called *middleware*. Middleware is the key to creating scalable web architectures, and XML-RPC is a simple, but powerful, middleware protocol.

From Person-to-Computer to Computer-to-Computer

To make this centralized network administration system work, we'll begin by creating an application programming interface (API) that defines the procedures that can be called, the input each procedure expects, and the output each procedure produces. An API separates how procedures are implemented from the way those procedures are called. This division of labor allows the procedure implementation to change without requiring clients who call the procedures to be rewritten. In this way, frontend code can access backend resources without any knowledge of how the backend is implemented.

In XML-RPC, the piece that implements the API is called a *listener*. The piece that makes procedure requests is called the *client*. For this fictional network administration system, all remote machines will have XML-RPC listeners waiting to service API requests. The web page that controls these remote machines makes XML-RPC client requests to the appropriate system. When you need to restart a remote server, your web page makes a request to the target remote machine to execute your command.

If an action can be performed from a web page, it can certainly be done from a standalone program, as well. Because the administration of the network is centralized, all network events (such as reboots or backups) can be scheduled from one program in one place. You will no longer have to log into ten machines to get them to reboot one hour earlier. You need to change only one script in only one place. There is no requirement in the XML-RPC specification that your manager be told of your newly found free time.

Treating ASP as a Window into Your System

To understand XML-RPC in action, let's consider a simple example. One of the earliest, and still most popular, uses for CGI is to create web User Interfaces (UI) to databases. Perhaps you have stored your small company's address book in an MS Access database. Unfortunately, when your boss is on the road, she cannot get into your network to see this Access file. She asks you to make that information accessible from a web page outside your corporate firewall. Figure 7-2 illustrates such a simple network.

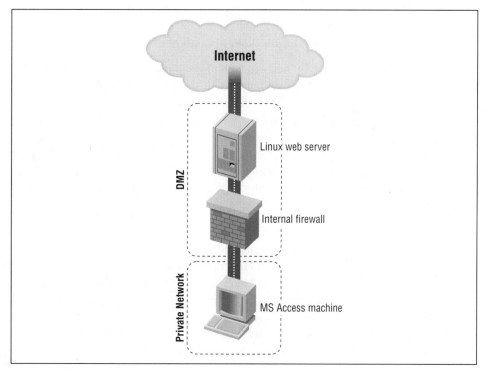

Figure 7-2. Typical small network with firewall

Unfortunately, the machine on which the address database sits is on the protected side of your firewall. Authentication and encryption issues aside, an XML-RPC bridge can help connect the external web server to the internal server holding the Access file. Although this API is put into more formal XML-RPC terms later, the following four procedures comprise the functionality needed to make this bridge work:

`dump_table()`

Returns an array of all records in your address book table

`lookup()`

Given a field and search term, returns an array of records matching the criteria `add_address()`

Adds a new record to the address book table

`remove_address()`

Given the primary key of first name and last name, removes the associated record

Just as in the centralized network administration system, the web page is going to make the API client calls. The listener will implement the API, but on which machine should it be? Clearly, the listener needs to directly manipulate the MS Access file that is on the protected side of the firewall. Because the web page your boss will use is on both a different machine and a different network from your address database, the best place for the XML-RPC listener is on the database server.

Our sample XML-RPC listener (which appears in Example 7-3, later in this chapter) uses Active Data Objects (ADO) to manipulate the address book stored in an Access file. Of course, a web page can make an ODBC connection from the web server to the MS Access database. Allowing ODBC traffic through the firewall can put your company-confidential information at risk. If one of the public machines gets hijacked, all your ODBC traffic can be watched. Worse still, if the web server with the address web page gets compromised, your firewall will not be able to detect the difference between your script's ODBC traffic and unauthorized ODBC calls made by an intruder.

XML-RPC provides some advantages in this very common situation. First, all traffic between the web server and the internal database server happens over a single TCP port, which is usually port 80. This makes configuring the firewall very simple. Second, the XML-RPC listener's API can strictly control the kind of information the web server can access. If you design your API to allow very limited actions, you will be slightly less concerned if your public web server gets compromised. Only the data that the XML-RPC listener accesses can be altered. Thus, other databases on that server are in much less danger.

Data Types and the API

APIs are unusually important in XML-RPC applications because servers and clients are often written in different programming languages hosted on different operating systems. You will find comments at the beginning of every function in the sample ASP address book listener that describe the input and output using XML-RPC data types.

The XML-RPC ASP library translates between VBScript objects and the appropriate XML. Most simple VBScript objects (such as strings, numbers, and arrays) map directly to XML-RPC tags, as illustrated in Table 7-1. XML-RPC structures are represented in VBScript as `Dictionary` objects. This will no doubt look natural to a Perl programmer but may take a C programmer a minute to get used to. They consist of a sequence of key-value pairs.

Table 7-1. VBScript objects corresponding to XML-RPC types

XML-RPC	VBScript type name
`<i4>`	`VbInteger`
`<double>`	`VbDouble`
`<dateTime.iso8601>`	`VbDate`
`<string>`	`VbString`
`<boolean>`	`VbBoolean`
`<array>`	`VbArray`
`<struct>`	`Dictionary`
`<base64>`	Any object not of type `Recordset` or `Dictionary`

A couple of notes about using data types. First, you should assume case-sensitivity whenever you make XML-RPC procedure calls or use structs. If you write the client, use the identical casing for your calls that the API has. When reading or writing structs, make sure your key names are in the same case as the API.

Another tip is to employ simple guidelines for using upper- and lowercase letters for the terms in the API. One good rule is that the names for procedures and structure fields should be in all lowercase letters, with words separated by underscores. But whatever scheme you choose, be ruthlessly consistent in your style!

It is critical to keep the XML-RPC API current with the implementation. There is no way for a client to automatically discover the API. If the client was expecting to get four arrays with four elements each, but instead got one array with four elements that were each structures of four members, there is little chance that the client program will run correctly. Even changing the capitalization of procedure names is reason enough to update the API.

XML-RPC doesn't specify how you should publish or format your API. There is nothing like a document type definition (DTD) to describe your API in XML. A simple web page often sufficesfor this. The description of the API should be implementation-language neutral. The input and output of the procedures should be specified in XML-RPC data types.

Ideally, you can keep the API documentation in the source code of the listener itself. By creating specially tagged comments, you can create a tool to extract API information and generate the API document automatically from the listener source code. Languages such as Perl and Java have facilities for doing this already (called

POD and javadoc, respectively). You could even write a Perl script to extract the comments from the ASP listener to produce the API document. Use whatever tools are appropriate in your environment.

Building an Address Book Web Service with ASP

Let's consider the problem of making an MS Access file that lies inside a protected network visible to Linux web servers that are exposed to the Internet. This problem can be solved easily with a web service using XML-RPC. Implementing the Address Book API (described in Table 7-2) with XML-RPC requires a library to handle listener-client communication. The library used here, called *xmlrpc.asp*, was written by David Carter-Tod in VBScript (available at *http://www.wc.cc.va.us/ dtod/XMLRPC*). All XML-RPC ASP pages written in VBScript use this file by using the simple server-side directive, `#include`. This IIS directive causes a file to be inserted into a web page before the ISAPI engine parses any ASP code.

All XML-RPC listeners have two important parts. The first is simply a call to the subroutine `rpcserver()`, which is defined in the XML-RPC library. This one subroutine call is responsible for extracting the client XML procedure request, translating the request into VBScript code, calling the appropriate API procedure with the given arguments, and returning the results of the procedure in XML to the client. The second part of the listener is simply the VBScript functions that implement your API. The XML-RPC library ensure that these functions get called when requested. As the creator of the listener, you never think about XML. The procedures get VBScript data as arguments and return standard VBScript data. The library handles all communication.

Although the complete code for this address book listener is only 203 lines long, it will be easier to focus on explaining one function at a time. Let's look at the API that defines remote operations allowed on the address book database, shown in Table 7-2.

Table 7-2. Address book API

Procedure	Input	Output
dump_address_book	None	An array of structs with the following members, all of which are strings: "lastname," "firstname," "phone," and "email"
lookup	Two strings: "field" and "sought"	An array of structs with the following members, all of which are strings: "lastname," "firstname," "phone," and "email"

Table 7-2. Address book API (continued)

Procedure	Input	Output
add_address	Struct with the following members, all of which are strings: "lastname," "firstname," "phone," and "email"	An i4 (1 for success, 0 for failure)
remove_address	Two strings: "firstname" and "lastname"	An i4 (1 for success, 0 for failure)

Getting the Contents of the Address Book

The natural place to begin looking at the implementation of this address book API is with the **dump_address_book()** procedure shown in Example 7-3. This procedure requires no input and doesn't change any record in the database. It also provides a look at a simple ADO SQL operation. The key to understanding how this procedure works is to look at the structure of the MS Access database.

The addresses are stored in a file called *addresses.mdb*. It has only one important table, called **directory**. This table has four fields: **firstname**, **lastname**, **phone**, and **email**. The **firstname** and **lastname** fields make up the table's primary key. If there are two "Bob Smiths" at your company, you must identify them differently (e.g., refer to one as "Robert").

Example 7-3. Implementing dump_address_book()

```
<!--#include virtual="/jjohn/xmlrpc.asp"-->

<%
  ' Globals
  Dim DB_SRC
  DB_SRC = "Driver=Microsoft Access Driver (*.mdb); DBQ=C:\addresses.mdb"
%>

<%
rpcserver

Function dump_address_book()
' Input:
'      None
' Output:
'      An array of records represented in dictionaries
'         Each dictionary will have the following fields:
'         * lastname:  (string) last name of the person
'         * firstname: (string) first name of the person
'           phone:       (string) their phone number
'           email:       (string) their email address
'         (* fields make up the primary key)

  Dim rs, query
  Set rs = Server.CreateObject("ADODB.RecordSet")
```

Example 7-3. Implementing dump_address_book( ) (continued)

```
query = "Select * from directory"

rs.Open query, DB_SRC

' our return array and index
Dim ret(10), cnt

cnt = 0
Do While Not rs.Eof
    Dim entry, i
    Set entry = Server.CreateObject("Scripting.Dictionary")

    For Each i In rs.Fields
        entry.Add i.Name, i.Value
    Next

    Set ret(cnt) = entry
    cnt = cnt + 1
    rs.MoveNext
Loop

dump_address_book = ret

End Function
```

In Example 7-3, the first line is the IIS server side include that makes the XML-RPC library available to the rest of the listener code. The small section that follows this server directive is a place to define global variables used throughout the remainder of this code. When you implement your own listener, consider declaring your global variables together in one section near the top. The next line contains a call to **rpcserver( )**, a subroutine all XML-RPC listeners need to make to handle RPC requests properly. For those who want a more complete treatment of ADO, look at Jason T. Roff's book *ADO: ActiveX Data Objects* (O'Reilly, 2001).

The procedure called **dump_address_book( )** in our API document is imple-mented in the listener code with a function called **dump_address_book( )**. In the XML-RPC library, there is a one-to-one mapping of API procedure names and ASP function names. It is often helpful to restate the API for the function in comments for future users or code maintainers. This function will merely return the entire directory table as an array of structures. To get the information out of MS Access, a new ADODB **RecordSet** object is created. The **RecordSet** method **open( )** is then passed an SQL **SELECT** query that will get every row of the directory table and the database connection string that is defined in the global variable DB_SRC. The connection string tells ADO how to communicate with the data source and indicates the ODBC driver to use and the location of the Access database file. Here's the connection string for the previous example:

```
"Driver=Microsoft Access Driver (*.mdb); DBQ=C:\addresses.mdb"
```

The API describes this procedure as returning an array of structures. In VBScript terms, this is an array of Dictionary objects. (If you are not familiar with dictionaries, they are like arrays, but indexed on strings called keys rather than linearly sequenced integers. Each key is associated with one value.) Each Dictionary holds one row of the directory table. The keys of the Dictionary are the column names of this table, and the values are the row data for those columns.

You need to know the size of VBScript arrays before using them. I define a ten-element array in this function to be returned to the calling procedure. For production code, you need to size the array to accommodate the total number of records your query returns.

To populate the return array, each row of the RecordSet object needs to be turned into a Dictionary object. You can create a locally scoped Dictionary object inside the while loop. The RecordSet method Fields returns a list of Field objects that describe the row returned from the database. There is one Field object for every column in our current row. Each Field object has a Name method that returns the column name and a Value method that returns the row data. In the inner For Each loop, the Dictionary object is populated with a new key-value pair for each column in the current row.

Once this loop has finished, the local Dictionary object has all the current row data and is ready to be appended to the return array. At the bottom of the While loop, the next row of the RecordSet is selected with the method MoveNext. If the current row is the last, MoveNext doesn't fail, but a call to the RecordSet's Eof method returns a value of false and the outer While loop ends. As with all VBScript functions, the data to be returned must be assigned to the name of the function. Recall that the XML-RPC library packs up the return value automatically and sends it back to the calling client.

Looking up Entries in the Address Book

The next procedure defined in the API is lookup(). The implementation of this function is shown in Example 7-4. lookup() is used to search for individual records by restricting the return set against one criterion. Except for this restrictive clause in the SQL statement, this procedure is identical to dump_address_book(). Although it would be possible to merge these two procedures, it is conceptually clearer to those using the API to keep these procedures separate. lookup() expects two string arguments. The first is a column name as it appears in the address database. The other is the string that is searched for in the given column. Because the SQL query uses the fuzzy match operator like, the search term may contain SQL wildcards.

Example 7-4. Implementation of lookup()

```
Function lookup( field, sought )
' Input:
'     Expects two strings:
'     field:  (string) Fieldname to search in table
'         sought: (string) Value to look for
' Output:
'         An array of records stored in dictionaries
'         that match search.
'     * lastname:  (string) last name of the person
'     * firstname: (string) first name of the person
'       phone:        (string) their phone number
'       email:        (string) their email address
'     (* fields make up the primary key)

  Dim rs, query
  Set rs = Server.CreateObject("ADODB.RecordSet")

  query = "Select * from directory where " _
      & field                        _
      & " like "
      & "'" & sought & "'"

  rs.Open query, DB_SRC

  Dim ret(10), cnt

  cnt = 0
  Do While Not rs.Eof
     Dim entry, i
     Set entry = Server.CreateObject("Scripting.Dictionary")

     For Each i In rs.Fields
         entry.Add i.Name, i.Value
     Next

     ' store this record in the return array
     Set ret(cnt) = entry
     cnt = cnt + 1
     rs.MoveNext
  Loop

  lookup = ret

End Function
```

Adding and Removing Address Book Entries

The two procedures shown so far, **dump_address_book()** and **lookup()**, are sufficient to create a read-only frontend to the address database. Casting prudence to the wind, let's see how to enable remote modifications of the address database using **add_address()** (shown in Example 7-5) and **remove_address()** (shown in Example 7-6).

To add a new address into the database using this web service, an XML-RPC client program calls the **add_address()** procedure. As seen in Example 7-5, this procedure expects to be passed a **Dictionary** object that represents the record to be inserted and returns a value of 1 for success or 0 for failure. To avoid adding a record that has the same primary key as an existing one (i.e., has the same first and last names), the table is first checked for just such a row and then the record is added. This means that **add_address()** actually makes two database calls.

Example 7-5. Implementing add_address()

```
Function add_address( entry )
' Input:
'      Expects a dictionary object with the fields:
'      * lastname:  (string) last name of the person
'      * firstname: (string) first name of the person
'        phone:        (string) their phone number
'        email:        (string) their email address
'        (* fields make up the primary key)
' Output:
'      Returns 1 for success, 0 for failure
    Dim oconn, cm1, cm2

    ' Setup a DB connection and SQL command object
    Set oconn = Server.CreateObject("ADODB.Connection")
    oconn.Open DB_SRC

    Set cm1 = Server.CreateObject("ADODB.Command")
    cm1.ActiveConnection = oconn

    Set cm2 = Server.CreateObject("ADODB.Command")
    cm2.ActiveConnection = oconn

    ' First, if a record exist with this key, abort
    Dim rs, SQLstr
    SQLstr = "select * from directory where lastname = " _
        & "? and firstname = ?"

    cm1.CommandText = SQLstr
    Set rs = cm1.Execute(, Array(entry.Item("lastname"), _
                    entry.Item("firstname")) )

    If Not rs.EOF Then
        ' Any populated record is bad, n'ok?
        If Not rs.Fields("lastname") = "" Then
            add_address = 0
            Exit Function
        End If
    End If

    ' Ok to Insert, Setup placeholders
    cm2.CommandText = "Insert into directory "            _
            & "(lastname, firstname, phone, email) " _
            & "Values (?, ?, ?, ?)"
```

Example 7-5. Implementing add_address()

```
Set rs = cm2.Execute( , Array( entry.Item("lastname"), _
                      entry.Item("firstname"),_
                      entry.Item("phone"),   _
                      entry.Item("email")    _
                    ) _
              )
  add_address = 1

End Function
```

There are many ways to use ADO to get at your data. The `RecordSet` objects (as used in Example 7-3 and Example 7-4) are well-suited for SQL `SELECT` statements because these objects provide methods for getting at the rows returned by the SQL. The alternative to using `RecordSet` objects is to use ADO `Command` objects. These objects are useful when the SQL action to be performed alters the table rather than looking up rows. ADO allows for placeholders in SQL statements. Placeholders escape SQL metacharacters found in the data to be inserted. An ADO `Command` object is needed to use placeholders.

Like the `RecordSet` object, the `Command` object needs a link to the database. The ADO `Connection` object, which uses the global variable `DB_SRC`, provides that connection. Placeholders allow SQL statements to become more generic. If in a `For Each` loop an SQL `SELECT` statement is to be executed with the value of the current list item, placeholders make the SQL much cleaner and sometimes faster. Using placeholders is simple. Everywhere in an SQL statement that data would normally be specified, a question mark is placed. When that SQL is executed, the data that replaces the question marks is passed as an array to the `Command`'s `Execute` method. The placeholders are then replaced in sequence with the list given to `Execute`. If the executed SQL statement produces rows, a `RecordSet` object is returned. Placeholders are also used in Perl's Database Interface (DBI) module in the same way and for the same reasons that ADO uses them—so it's worth the extra time to learn how to use them.

Note that if the number of placeholders doesn't match the number of arguments passed to `Execute`, you will get a runtime VBScript error. Two `Command` objects are used in `add_address()` because two very different SQL statements are needed. If a record to be inserted has the same primary key as an existing record, a runtime error occurs. To prevent this error, the database is checked with a `SELECT` statement restricted to the primary key of the record to be inserted. If no record is found, it is safe to proceed with the `INSERT` statement. Again, placeholders are used to make the code both cleaner and safer. The `Execute` method has an empty first argument. It's possible to pass in an integer variable to be populated with the number of table rows affected by the particular SQL statement.

The last procedure in the address book API is `remove_address()`, shown in Example 7-6. Not surprisingly, this is the reciprocal function of `add_address()`. The `remove_address` function expects to be passed a primary key for the directory table that consists of the first and last names of the record to be deleted. Like `add_address()`, this function uses two `Command` objects, but it first checks the database to make sure there's a record with the given primary key to delete before attempting the actual delete.

In addition to `remove_address()`, Example 7-6 also uses a nifty VBScript operator called `Array`, which produces an `Array` of its arguments on the fly. This is very useful if you need to pass a list to a method and you don't already have the data in an array.

Example 7-6. Implementing remove_address()

```
Function remove_address( firstname, lastname )
' Input:
'      Expects two strings:
'      firstname: (string) First name of the record to delete
'      lastname:  (string) last name of the record to delete
' Output:
'       Returns 1 for success, 0 for failure
  Dim oconn, cm1, cm2

  ' Setup a DB connection and SQL command object
  Set oconn = Server.CreateObject("ADODB.Connection")
  oconn.Open DB_SRC

  Set cm1 = Server.CreateObject("ADODB.Command")
  cm1.ActiveConnection = oconn

  Set cm2 = Server.CreateObject("ADODB.Command")
  cm2.ActiveConnection = oconn

  ' If a record exist with this key, abort
  Dim rs, SQLstr
  SQLstr = "select * from directory where lastname = " _
      & "? and firstname = ?"

  cm1.CommandText = SQLstr
  Set rs = cm1.Execute(, Array(lastname, firstname) )

  If Not rs.EOF Then
     ' Record must exist to delete
     If rs.Fields("lastname") = "" Then
        remove_address = 0
        Exit Function
     End If
  End If
```

Example 7-6. Implementing remove_address( ) (continued)

```
' Ok to Insert, Setup placeholders
cm2.CommandText = "Delete from directory where lastname = " _
            & "? and firstname = ?"

Set rs = cm2.Execute(, Array(lastname, firstname) )

remove_address = 1

End Function
```

What's not shown in any of these examples is how you would simply update an address. Using only these four procedures defined in the API of Table 7-2, a record is updated by deleting it with **remove_address()** and then adding with the new information using **add_address()**. For production code, you should find a more performance friendly solution, possibly by creating an **update_address()** procedure.

This section completes the discussion of the ASP address book listener. The careful reader will no doubt have noticed that the verbiage required to explain what the code does far exceeds the number of characters needed to implement the service.

Talking to MS Access from Linux

Debugging an XML-RPC listener without a client that talks to it is a little like trying to clap with one hand: it is very difficult to know when you've succeeded. Although we could have written a simple client for this listener in ASP, building a Perl client that runs from Linux provides a more dramatic example of the cross-platform aspect of web services. Example 7-7 shows the code used for this Perl test harness, a bare-bones Perl script meant to be run from the command line. With just a little digging into Perl's CGI.pm module, you could easily use the code presented in this example to create a dynamic web page. In its current form, however, the code provides a simple way to debug the ASP address book listener presented in the preceding section.

Example 7-7. Perl test script for XML-RPC listener

```
#!/usr/bin/perl --

use strict;
use Frontier::Client;
use Data::Dumper;

my $rps = Frontier::Client->new(
        url => "http://durgan.daisypark.net/jjohn/rpc_addresses.asp",
        debug => 1,
            );
```

Example 7-7. Perl test script for XML-RPC listener (continued)

```
print "\ntesting dump_address_book\n";
eval { my $hr = $rps->call(qw/dump_address_book/);
      print Dumper($hr);
    };

print "\ntesting lookup\n";
eval { my $hr = $rps->call(qw/lookup lastname %ra%/);
      print Dumper($hr);
    };

print "\ntesting add_address\n";
eval { my $hr = { lastname  => "Bush",
        firstname => "George",
        phone     => "999 666 8008",
        email     => "pres\@whitehouse.gov",
      };
      print $rps->call("add_address", $hr);
    };

print "\ntesting remove_address\n";
eval {
      print $rps->call("remove_address", "George", "Bush");
    };
```

The script in Example 7-7 begins by using Perl's XML-RPC client module and **Data::Dumper**, a library that displays the structure of arbitrarily complex variables. Then it initializes a new **Frontier::Client** object with the URL of the ASP listener. Debugging is turned on to show the XML request and response of each procedure call. Note that creating a new **Frontier::Client** object does not make any kind of network connection.

The **Frontier::Client** method **call()** is the heart of making XML-RPC calls in Perl. This method expects to be passed a list that starts with the name of the remote procedure to be called, followed by whatever parameters that remote procedure expects. Because this method decodes the XML received from the listener, each **call()** is done inside of an **eval()** to prevent an XML parsing error from halting the program.

dump_address_book() is the first API procedure tested. The Perl programmer's faithful debugging companion, **Data::Dumper**'s **Dump()** function, is used to display the arbitrarily complex data structures returned from the XML-RPC call. It is particularly useful for unrolling the array of hash references returned by **dump_address_book()**.

Next up is **lookup()**. Because this procedure is implemented on the listener side with SQL, our code can use wildcards to search for last names that contain the letter sequence "ra." Recall that **call()** expects to be passed a list of arguments.

Here, the procedure name and its arguments are wrapped in Perl's quote word `qw()` operator, which turns a space-separated string into a list. Like `dump_address_book()`, `lookup()` also returns an array of hash references.

So far, our test harness has only requested data from the listener. The real test of the system is whether we can modify the database remotely. Thus, the example features a call to `add_address()` that attempts to add the current U.S. president, George W. Bush, to the electronic rolodex. If the call succeeds, the script prints "1." Because political alliances are fleeting at best, this record is expunged in the last few lines of the program.

With the small amount of Perl code shown here, all procedures listed in the address book API can be tested. On the face of it, this code is a very serviceable debugging tool. It also shows a more subtle aspect of XML-RPC programming. Although in this case the XML-RPC listener talks to an MS Access database, the Perl code shown in Example 7-7 wouldn't change if the underlying database were switched to Oracle, MS SQL, or even to a flat text file (although the wildcard searches of `lookup()` might be harder to implement for flat text files). Because the functionality of the address book (embodied by the Perl client code) is divorced from the implementation (realized in the ASP), it becomes easier to make radical changes on either side of the API fence. If the Perl client created a web page instead of emitting plain text, programmers who specialize in HTML layout need know nothing about SQL in order to manipulate the address database. Similarly, SQL hackers don't have to know anything about HTML layout changes that need to be made to the database architecture.

An XML-RPC Client in ASP

The address book system we've been discussing involves making a Windows resource available to Linux clients. Sometimes an ASP programmer needs to access a Linux resource from an NT platform. At the risk of being repetitive, let's turn this address system inside out so the database system in which the address book information dwells is MySQL hosted on Linux, and the public web servers are NT running IIS. The API for this version of the address book web service is the same one presented in Table 7-2.

Example 7-8 presents the code for a very simple ASP interface to the address book system. For most ASP programmers, this code should look more familiar than the listener code presented in Examples 7-3 to 7-6 because it actually generates a viewable web page.

Example 7-8. An ASP XML-RPC address book client

```
<BODY BGCOLOR="#FFFFFF">
<h1>Testing the Perl Server on Marian</h1>

<!--#include virtual="/jjohn/xmlrpc.asp"-->
<%
  ' Globals
  Dim RPC_URL
  RPC_URL = "http://marian.daisypark.net/RPC2"

  ' Helper functions
Sub display_record( entry )
  Dim l
  Response.Write "<PRE>"
  For Each l in entry.Keys
   Response.Write l & ": " & entry.Item(l) & "<BR>"
  Next
  Response.Write "</PRE>"
End Sub
%>

<%
   ' We may have been asked to do something.
   Dim rc, args(2), action
   If    Not "" = Request.Form("action") Then
        action = Request.Form("action")
   Elseif Not "" = Request.QueryString("action") Then
      action = Request.QueryString("action")
   Else
      action = "no action requested"
   End If

   Select Case action

    Case "add"

       Response.Write "Attempting 'add'</BR>"
       Dim E
       Set E = Server.CreateObject("Scripting.Dictionary")

       E.Add "firstname", Request.Form("firstname")
       E.Add "lastname",  Request.Form("lastname")
       E.Add "phone",     Request.Form("phone")
       E.Add "email",     Request.Form("email")

       Call display_record( E )

       Set args(1) = E
       rc = xmlRPC(RPC_URL, "add_address", args)

       If rc = 1 Then
            Response.Write " Succeed<BR>"
       Else
```

Example 7-8. An ASP XML-RPC address book client (continued)

```
            Response.Write " Failed<BR>"
       End If

    Case "view"

       Response.Write "Attempting 'view'</BR>"
       args(1) = "lastname"
       If Not "" = Request.Form("lastname") Then
        args(2) = Request.Form("lastname")
       Else
        args(2) = Request.QueryString("lastname")
       End If

       rc = xmlRPC(RPC_URL, "lookup", args)

       Dim i
       For i=0 to UBound(rc) - 1
        Call display_record( rc(i) )
       Next

    Case "remove"

       Response.Write "Attempting 'remove'</BR>"
       args(1) = Request.QueryString("firstname")
       args(2) = Request.QueryString("lastname")
       rc = xmlRPC( RPC_URL, "remove_address", args)

       If 1 = rc Then
         Response.Write "Remove succeeded<BR>"
       Else
         Response.Write "Remove failed<BR>"
       End If

    Case "no action requested"
       ' Just fall though

    Case Else
      Response.Write "<font color=red>Don't know how to '" _
           & action & "'</font><BR>"

    End Select
%>

<P>There are this many records in the address table:
<%
   Dim null_list(0), ret2

   ret2 = xmlRPC(RPC_URL, "dump_address_book", null_list)

   Response.Write Ubound(ret2) & "<BR>"

   ' Make links to delete this records
```

Example 7-8. An ASP XML-RPC address book client (continued)

```
    Response.Write "Modify the address book?<BR><UL>"
    Dim j
    For j = 0 to Ubound(ret2) - 1
      Dim l, f
      l = ret2(j).Item("lastname")
          f = ret2(j).Item("firstname")
      Response.Write "<LI>" & f & " " & l & " " &_
                "<A HREF='http:client.asp?action=view&lastname=" & l _
            & "&firstname=" & f & "'>"                              _
              & "<small>view</small></a> | "                       _
              & "<A HREF='http:client.asp?action=remove&lastname=" _
            & l                                                     _
            & "&firstname=" & f & "'>"                             _
            & "<small>delete</small></a>"
    Next

    Response.Write "</UL>"
%>


<P>Want to add another Address?
<HR>
<P>Add a record:
<FORM method=Post Action=client.asp>
<Input Type=Hidden Name=action Value=add>
<PRE>
last name:   <input type=text name=lastname>
first name:  <input type=text name=firstname>
phone:       <input type=text name=phone>
email:       <input type=text name=email>
</PRE>
<P><INPUT TYPE=SUBMIT>
</FORM>
</HR>
</BODY>
```

Example 7-8 begins with simple HTML to set up the page. As with the ASP server, this client code must use a server-side include to draw in the XML-RPC library. A global string, RPC_URL, holds the URL path to a Perl Frontier::Daemon listener that will service this client's requests. Also, a simple debugging function called display_record prints the key-value pairs of a Dictionary object in HTML.

Because the page contains a form, what this code actually displays depends on whether the user tries to manipulate the address book. This page is both a form and a form handler. If the user updates or adds a record, the HTML parameter action is set. This page uses both GET and POST HTML methods so both ASP Request object methods Form and QueryString need to be checked for the presence of the action parameter. By default, this page displays a short listing of everyone in the address book, and paints an HTML form for adding a new record to the table, as illustrated in Figure 7-3.

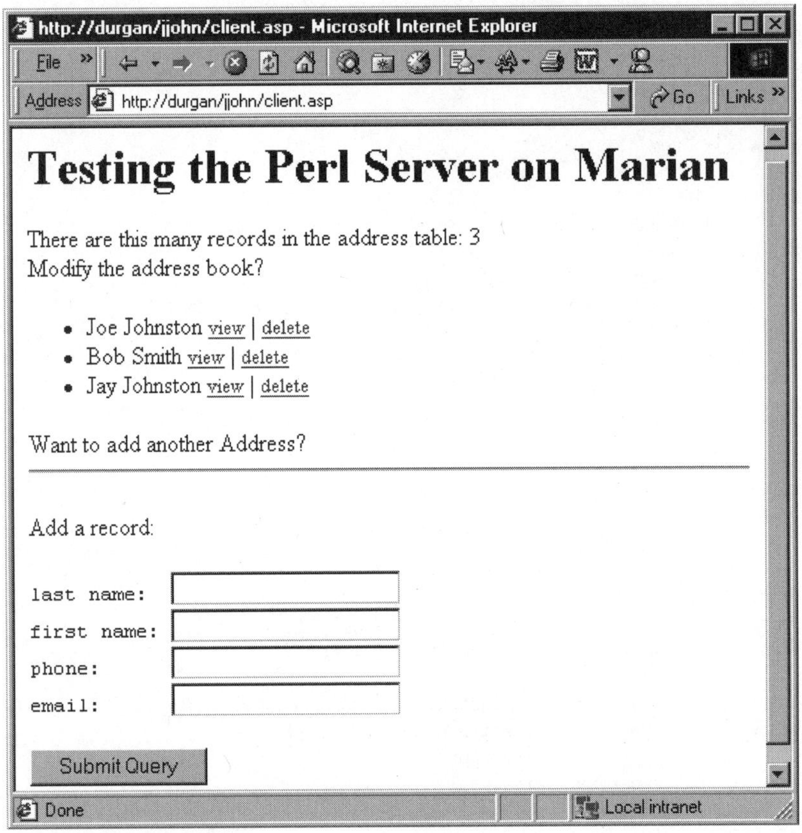

Figure 7-3. ASP address book client in action

A switch statement is used to select the appropriate action. If the variable `action` is set to `add`, the user is trying to add a record to the address book. According to the API, `add_address()` should be called with a structure containing the record to be inserted into the table. A VBScript `Dictionary` object filled with the user-supplied information is passed to this remote procedure. Performing XML-RPC client calls in ASP is only slightly more work than doing them in Perl. The XML-RPC library defines the `xmlRPC()` function, which expects three arguments: the URL to the listener, the name of the procedure to call, and an array of arguments to be passed to the remote procedure. (Note, however, that you cannot use the VBScript `Array` operator to bundle your RPC arguments in `xmlRPC()`.)

Just like its Perl counterpart, `xmlRPC()` delivers the result of the procedure call as language native data. An appropriate status message is printed based on the outcome. If the ASP page is requested to find a particular entry, a call to `lookup()` is made. The API defines this procedure's return value as an array of structures. The variant variable `rc` is assigned the result of the `xmlRPC()` call, which is an array of

`Dictionaries`. Each element of this array is then displayed with the helper subroutine `display_record()`. (Note that the `xmlRPC` call requires an array variable as the third argument. If you have a procedure with no arguments, you still need to supply a zero-length array.)

Keep in mind that regardless of whether an action was requested, the ASP page prints out a short list of all records in the database followed by links to view or delete that record. This requires an XML-RPC call to `dump_address_book()`. The resulting array of `Dictionaries` is iterated through and each record is rendered appropriately. A form through which new address records can be added appears at the bottom of the page. (No doubt the formatting of this HTML page makes graphic designers cringe, but it is functional.)

The final action is `remove`, which tries to delete the specified record. There is nothing new about the way the `remove_address()` procedure is called here. The rest of the script creates a web form in standard HTML.

This ASP page is certainly a bit larger than the Perl test harness shown in Example 7-7, but it's not particularly long or complicated. Why not use an ASP page to test an ASP listener? There are two reasons why this isn't a good strategy. First, if the ASP XML-RPC library is broken or set up incorrectly, it is difficult to figure out where the failure is occurring. Recall that in order to get this test harness to print anything, all ASP syntax must be correct, the XML-RPC library calls must also be correct, and the XML-RPC listener must be working. There are many points of failure in this path, and even a simple Perl script run from Windows would be a more reliable test of an ASP listener. The other reason not to use an ASP client for an ASP listener is that XML-RPC is most effective when used across languages. It is possible to make assumptions (that are VBScript specific in the API) that become obvious when creating a client in a different language. Don't be afraid to experiment with other languages; XML-RPC provides a good excuse to learn them.

Creating a Window to Linux

Perhaps the only thing more useless than an XML-RPC listener without a client is an XML-RPC client without a listener. Although the API is the same, some readers may be interested to see what the Perl listener for this address book system looks like. Example 7-9 contains the entire Perl listener. For a more complete discussion of the `Frontier::Daemon` class, see Chapter 4.

A few words of warning about this code: to get better debugging, every procedure defined by the API prints a message to the console describing which function was called and with what arguments. The script in Example 7-9 includes a hack of the `Frontier::Daemon` class to print out the request and redirect the resulting XML to a file in the */tmp* directory. This procedure was designed to

emulate the `Frontier::Client` debugging process. These additions to the
`Frontier::Client` class are not very portable, but they are very convenient for
debugging and demo purposes. Perhaps a future release of this Perl module will
contain a more robust debugging solution. To turn on this special debugging, the
flag `RPC_Debug` is set when the `Frontier::Daemon` object is created.

Because this chapter is about ASP and not Perl, most of the code in Example 7-9 is
presented without commentary. Readers interested in learning about details of
Perl's DBI module should pick up a copy of *Programming the Perl DBI* (O'Reilly,
2000) or consult the DBI manpage.

The first three procedures, `helloWorld`, `hash_test`, and `arg_test`, are not part
of the address book API, but do help to establish that XML-RPC communication is
happening with clients. Often, simple procedures like these help isolate client-lis-
tener connection problems quickly.

Like the MS Access database, the address information is contained in one MySQL
table called **directory** in the database **address**. Using standard DBI calls, this
table is manipulated almost identically to the way ADO handles MS Access files. In
fact, the SQL statements are exactly the same, even down to the placeholders!

Example 7-9. Perl listener script

```perl
#!/usr/bin/perl --
use strict;

use Frontier::Daemon;
use Data::Dumper;
use DBI;

sub helloWorld {
    return "Hello, $_[0]";
}

sub hash_test {
    return {
    first  => "joe",
    second => "johnston",
    };
}

sub arg_test {
    return @_;
}

sub init_db {
  # return an initialize DBI object
  return DBI->connect("dbi:mysql:addresses", "editor", "editor") ||
    die "$DBI::errstr";
}
```

Example 7-9. Perl listener script (continued)

```perl
sub dump_address_book{
  # return an array of recs
  my $dbi = init_db();

  my $sth = $dbi->prepare("Select * from directory");
  $sth->execute || return $sth->errstr;

  my @return;
  while( my $hr = $sth->fetchrow_hashref ){
    push @return, $hr;
  }

  $dbi->disconnect;
  return \@return;
}

sub lookup {
  my ($field, $sought) = @_;
  print caller, Dumper( \@_ );
  my $dbi = init_db();

  my $sth = $dbi->prepare("select * from directory where $field = ?);
  $sth->execute($sought) || return $sth->errstr;

  my @return;

  while( my $hr = $sth->fetchrow_hashref ){
    push @return, $hr;
  }
  $dbi->disconnect;

  return \@return;
}

sub add_address {
  my $entry = shift;
  print caller, Dumper( \$entry);
  my $dbi = init_db();

  my $sth = $dbi->prepare("insert into directory "        .
                  " (lastname, firstname, phone, email) ".
                  "values (?, ?, ?, ?)");

  my $rc = $sth->execute(@$entry{qw/lastname firstname phone email/});
  $dbi->disconnect;

  return (defined $rc) ? 1 : 0;
}

sub remove_address {
  my ($first, $last) = @_;
  print caller, Dumper( \$first, \$last );
```

Example 7-9. Perl listener script (continued)

```
  my $dbi = init_db();

  my $sth = $dbi->prepare("delete from directory where ".
                          "lastname = ? and firstname = ?");

  my $rc = $sth->execute( $last, $first );
  $dbi->disconnect;

  return (defined $rc) ? 1 : 0;
}

Frontier::Daemon->new( methods => {
                  helloWorld => \&helloWorld,
                  hash_test  => \&hash_test,
                  arg_test   => \&arg_test,
                  dump_address_book => \&dump_address_book,
                  lookup          => \&lookup,
                  add_address     => \&add_address,
                  remove_address  => \&remove_address,
                            },
            LocalPort => 80,
            Reuse     => 1,
            RPC_Debug => 1,
          );
```

At this point, both the client and listener side of the ASP XML-RPC library have been presented in a somewhat realistic setting. Some dirty details of XML-RPC are discussed in the next section, "Connections and Caveats," but overall, the simplicity of XML-RPC is its primary strength. There are many proprietary solutions for creating RPC calls, but none are as easy to use. Even for the incidental ASP programmer, XML-RPC should prove no harder to learn than processing CGI forms.

Connections and Caveats

Before jumping doe-eyed into a serious XML-RPC application, the following pitfalls are lurking just out of view. Some of them are more serious than others, depending on the application. Many of them can be mitigated with some additional programming effort, but all are more pleasantly discovered here by reading rather than getting blindsided by them later during development.

No Transaction Support

Although the current chapter demonstrates a database application, the careful reader will note the absence of any reference to money in the examples. XML-RPC does not guarantee the safe arrival of your data. It has no mechanisms for supporting transactions. If you need transaction support, your listener must take responsibility for it. By using a database that supports transactions like Oracle or PostgreSQL, a listener can often co-opt that functionality to prevent data corruption in the backend information store.

Furthermore, XML-RPC is stateless. If an application demands memory, use session IDs to remember program states between RPC calls. This technique will be familiar to those who have designed web shopping cart modules.

Expect Speed Hits

In the XML-RPC protocol, XML data is encoded and decoded twice by each end of the system. Although the XML messages are often quiet small, XML parsers do consume both CPU resources and memory. Plan your applications with this in mind.

Debugging is Terrible

The ASP XML-RPC library goes to great pains to shield the user from the details of the XML conversation. Unfortunately, many bugs occur because the XML is malformed, one end has gone dead, or the arguments are not in the expected format. In the current version of the ASP library, there is no "debug" switch. Some sanity checks are peppered throughout the code to make it a bit easier to find where a mistake happened, however. When in doubt, use the uncomplicated "helloWorld" procedures to see if simple XML-RPC communication is happening at all. Add code until errors occur. Repeat as necessary.

The old Unix *fortune* program, in its randomly generated wisdom, used to say: "Debugging is anticipated with distaste, performed with reluctance, and bragged about forever."

Keep the API Current

Software engineers are much disparaged for their minimalist documentation styles. If the written API for an XML-RPC application falls out of date, the application is pretty much broken to all the clients using the old API. There is little glory in fixing typos, but none in releasing an application no one can use.

Where to Find the VBScript XML-RPC Library

The ASP XML-RPC library (created by David Carter-Tod) used throughout this chapter currently can be found at:

http://www.wc.cc.va.us/dtod/XMLRPC

There is also a SourceForge project page for this library located at:

http://aspxmlrpc.sourceforge.net

Be sure to follow the installation directions. A few additional packages needed; the SourceForge site provides direct links to them.

Where to Find the COM XML-RPC Library

Steve Ivy and Joe Massey created and implemented an XML-RPC library in C++ and exposed the internals as a COM object. Once this library is installed on an NT IIS server, ASP pages will be able to access the class just like any other COM object. Unfortunately, the XML-RPC listener functionality is unstable and further work on the library seems to be halted. If this isn't a show stopper, the code can be found here:

http://redmonk.editthispage.com/xmlrpccom/

One of the most interesting aspects of XML-RPC programming is that it brings together many technologies in a terse package. A quick survey of this chapter finds topics such as ISS, ADO, COM, XML, Perl, and of course ASP, each of which commands a healthy chunk of bookstore shelving space in its own right. If Perl were the duct tape of first generation Internet programs, it is clear that web services would bind together many of the Web's next generation applications. As a wire protocol for web services, XML-RPC is an incredibly sticky, but refreshingly simple, glue.

8

XML-RPC and the Web Services Landscape

Although much of the rest of this book has explored the internals of various XML-RPC implementations and approaches, developers using XML-RPC should also look at the bigger picture. XML-RPC is one of several possible protocol choices built on XML.

The Web Services Vision

The World Wide Web is pretty well understood at this point, providing a cheap means of presenting content to human readers and allowing for a certain amount of navigation and interaction. Web infrastructures—TCP/IP, HTTP, and HTML—are widely deployed, supported, and understood. Although these infrastructures have some limitations, their widespread use has made them commodities ready for cheap reuse, and the Web Services community plans to take the model for computer-to-computer communications pioneered by XML-RPC and extend it to a wider variety of architectures and projects.

Trumpeted by conference presenters as a solution for distributing logic across networks and hyped as the foundation of new business models for application service providers, Web Services is a pretty simple set of tools at its heart. The foundations are XML and HTTP, and those two ingredients are combined for computer-to-computer communications. As the vision of Web Services has grown beyond the basic integration provided by XML-RPC, the number and kinds of specifications for Web Services have grown, as well. Specifications now include protocols used to pass object information between computers, an API that can be used to find services, and a language for describing services.

Public XML-RPC Services

XML-RPC is an integration solution used in real applications available today. Although many of the examples shown in this book are in an intranet setting, just some applications available right now that have a public XML-RPC interface are listed in the following paragraphs.

Considering that Userland was the birthplace of XML-RPC, it is no surprise to learn that Userland's content management system Manila (*http://manila.userland.com*) has a Web Services interface that allows any text editor to upload content directly into it. Those who have worked with content management systems that only use HTML's simple <TEXTAREA> tag for content composition will appreciate the significance of this Manila feature. Even a cursory read of the interface documentation (*http://www.xmlrpc.com/manilarpc*) shows that many remote procedures require a username and password argument. Public Web Services often require more attention to security than intranet applications. Because security is not a part of the XML-RPC specification, the burden of authentication and payload encryption of sensitive information will be on the web service application writer.

Web Crossing (*http://www.webcrossing.com*) is yet another content management system designed to promote threaded group discussions. It also has an XML-RPC interface that allows Web Crossing servers on different sites to exchange information and user credentials. A simple application of Web Crossing's credential passing mechanism is that a user who logs into one site may have his credentials passed on to another Web Crossing site. Thus, trust relationships can be established at the application level. Another interesting use of this interface might be a calendaring system that pushes or pulls information from other Web Crossing sites.

Content management systems aren't the only place public XML-RPC services are used. O'Reilly's Meerkat Wire Service also has a Web Service interface, which is described more fully in Chapter 5. Briefly, Meerkat collects Rich Site Summary files from many web sites and allows the user to browse that content through a consistent web interface. What's interesting about this application is that its creator, Rael Dornfest, understood that other applications might want access to Meerkat's data. Instead of making those applications go through the traditional technique of requesting Meerkat pages, parsing the HTML, and extracting the desired information, Dornfest created and documented URL line parameters that would present his application's data in a more program-friendly way. After learning about XML-RPC, Rael soon ported this functionality to this Web Service protocol. Because Meerkat's data is read-only, no authentication or security issues need special attention for this public service.

Although not exactly public, Version 2.0 of the KDE desktop environment includes support for XML-RPC scripting of KDE applications. Much like the way Microsoft exposes application functionality with COM objects, KDE's component model is called DCOP. Users can create a C++ XML-RPC server that makes DCOP calls for any XML-RPC clients. Although few desktop users want arbitrary Internet users opening up Konquor at random times on their machines, a reasonable application of this XML-RPC/DCOP bridge might be to synchronize calendars among a workgroup. Conceivably, KDE users could use the KOrganizer application to update their Web Crossing calendar. The possibilities are tantalizing.

With the emerging awareness of Web Services by software developers, the number of public XML-RPC application interfaces will only increase. Check out *XML-RPC. com*'s list (*http://www.xmlrpc.com/directory/1568/services*) of Web Service enabled applications for the latest information.

Design Considerations for Any XML-RPC Application

Although the details of using the XML-RPC implementation can differ radically from one language to another, there are some design challenges that every Web Service developer faces. Although not every application needs to address these issues, it is worth listing some of the most common XML-RPC design problems. These issues are presented in the order in which a new XML-RPC developer is likely to encounter them.

Debugging

Unlike most batch oriented or single process programs, it is impossible to test and debug an XML-RPC script without writing both a client and server. Even though you may be only interested in developing and deploying the server, you still have to get at least a primitive client working to verify the proper functioning of your server. If you don't know a scripting language yet and are serious about developing XML-RPC applications, learn one now. Perl and Python XML-RPC clients are trivial to write and debug; this convenience frees you to concentrate on getting the server to work correctly.

What is more challenging is that it is sometimes necessary to review the raw XML-RPC requests and responses to track down a "misfeature." Some languages make logging the raw XML easier than others. Some implementations, like the ASP library, don't support logging at all; the Perl library shows both sides of the XML conversation.

Network Latency

In clients, XML-RPC calls look like ordinary function or method calls. In reality, the careful reader knows that each call has to encode an RPC request in XML, send it across the network, get a response in XML, and decode it. Even on private LANs, this takes a significant amount of time. Always limit the number of XML-RPC calls that have to happen before a user receives output. Even if users can see the RX/TX lights on their workstation's NIC, rarely will they understand that to mean that their application is working correctly. Life is too short to wait for slow programs to finish.

If you control both sides of the XML-RPC application, it may be possible to combine several calls into one. It is faster to get one large XML message than several small ones. Frequently, this optimization is easy to do.

Documentation

Although documentation is the bane of most developers' lives, it is crucial to thoroughly document Web Service APIs. Although there are some efforts to automate this task, creating a detailed web page is often the best form this documentation can take.

Along with documentation is the importance of adhering to the published API of the Web Service. Although Perl can automatically promote integers to strings, other languages can't. If an API promised a string but returned an integer, some clients will break. Most XML-RPC libraries have the facility to force native language values to be encoded for transmission in a particular way. For public Web Services, be sure that your documentation and implementation agree.

Logging

Logging is important beyond the scope of debugging. After the XML-RPC application is deployed, logs are useful to application administrators for evaluating the performance of the Web Service. Application developers can gain important optimizing insights by recording each request and the time it takes to complete it. Logging is often simple to implement, so take time to do so for serious XML-RPC applications.

Authentication and Authorization

Whenever an application has to limit functionality based on who attempts to use it, one of XML-RPC's most glaring omissions manifests itself. Although authentication can be implemented by simply passing usernames and passwords along to remote procedure calls, building authorization systems from scratch can be a substantial task. If it is possible to redefine the problem so that authorization isn't necessary, the application program's life will be greatly eased.

Payloads: Big and Secret

XML-RPC works best for small and insensitive information. Can FTP be replaced by an XML-RPC service? Not really. Recall that every XML-RPC response is a complete XML document that has to be parsed before the payload can be extracted for the client. Imagine trying to send a CD-ROM image through XML-RPC. The client would need to fit that 650 MB document into memory before using it! So far, there aren't any standard ways to stream large data in XML. The application writer either has to send the data in smaller chunks or use another protocol (like raw HTTP) to transmit the requested information.

XML-RPC requests are sent in clear text across the network. If an XML-RPC message contains sensitive data, it is necessary for the XML-RPC application writer to make arrangements to ensure the privacy of that data. There are two ways to accomplish this. The first is to protect the entire XML-RPC conversation by using an SSL-enabled web server or an SSH tunnel. If SSL is used, remember that the client also has to "speak" SSL. Not all the libraries support this. The second way to protect data is to encrypt the payload with PGP or an MD5 hash. The problem with this solution is that for some platforms, getting libraries to handle these forms of encryption may be difficult. Such is the price of privacy.

Statelessness

XML-RPC comes from the procedural programming tradition. Procedures process input to produce an answer. Unfortunately, current software designers think in object-oriented terms. Objects contain data and provide methods that know what to do with them. An object can be set to different states. Although some hackery can be done to do this with procedures (using static variables or a database), most object-oriented programmers will find this unsatisfying. Still, the call and response conversation of XML-RPC is very effective for a number of real business applications.

Beyond XML-RPC

Although we think XML-RPC is a very useful set of tools (it's very difficult to write books about technologies you don't think are useful), a number of other protocols use XML to transfer information between computers, often riding the HTTP protocol, as well. Although XML-RPC seems secure in its procedure-calling niche, developers who need more capabilities than procedure calls can offer are building new proposals on similar foundations.

The use of XML for loosely coupled application integration has become a high-profile topic, crucial as it is for the future conduct of electronic business transactions. This area has seen a proliferation of activity from both consortia and individual vendors. The list below provides some of the options developers may consider as potentially competing solutions to XML-RPC, though some of these options (such as WSDL) could conceivably be used in conjunction with XML-RPC. For an up-to-date list of more protocols, described in somewhat less detail, visit the W3C's XML protocol matrix at *http://www.w3.org/2000/03/29-XML-protocol-matrix.*

SOAP: Simple Object Access Protocol

SOAP is a lightweight protocol used to exchange XML-encoded information. It has three parts: an XML-envelope used to carry the messages, rules for encoding program objects into XML, and a convention for performing Remote Procedure Calls (RPC). Whereas XML-RPC comes from a procedural tradition, SOAP is firmly rooted in the object-oriented paradigm. SOAP passes live objects, each with their own state information, across the wire. This opens up a whole new range of possible applications. Imagine a Python SOAP server that creates a customer object that can be modified by a Perl or Java client. Microsoft is so keen on SOAP that they are making sure all their future applications have SOAP interfaces. This is the keystone of their .NET initiative.

Created by Userland, IBM, DevelopMentor, Lotus, and Microsoft, SOAP has been in development for a long time. Born out of work that originally generated XML-RPC, SOAP has been through three major iterations (0.9, 1.0, and 1.1) and is now supported by IBM, Microsoft, and Sun, as well as a number of other companies.

Status
> At Version 1.1, this was submitted as input to the W3C's XML Protocol activity, software deployed; however, refer to the W3C XML Protocol *(http://www.xml. com/pub/a/2000/11/01/protocols/quickref.html#w3c)* for the latest status.

Read the specification
> W3C NOTE: SOAP 1.1 *(http://www.w3.org/TR/SOAP/).*

Read more
> Web Services and the Simple Object Access Protocol *(http://msdn.microsoft. com/xml/general/soap_webserv.asp).*

Write XML-RPC code (in various programming languages/environments)
> Perl *(http://www.geocities.com/paulclinger/soap.html)*; Java *(http://xml.apache. org/soap/)*; Windows *(http://msdn.microsoft.com/xml/general/toolkit_intro.asp)*; and Python *(http://www.pythonware.com/products/soap/).*

Community
> SOAP mailing list *(http://discuss.develop.com/soap.html).*

UDDI: Universal Description, Discovery, and Integration of Business for the Web

The UDDI group was started in July 2000 by Microsoft, IBM, and Ariba. Most other leading B2B companies have joined the effort.

UDDI provides a framework for the description and discovery of business services on the Web. It provides this framework by using distributed web-based registries of services and conventions for accessing that registry using SOAP. Think of it as an advanced search engine for web services. Every web service provider uses WSDL (see what follows) to describe their SOAP application. This is then imported into the central UDDI registry and becomes available for searches.

If this all seems a little pedantic, consider a time in the future when companies use software that is a collection of rented web services. Perhaps many vendors provide the same service. UDDI would be a marketplace for IT departments to find the components they need at the best available prices. Needless to say, this is only one possible future scenario for UDDI.

Status
  In development; initial specs are issued.

Web site
  UDDI.org (*http://www.uddi.org/*).

Read the specification
  Specifications in Word and PDF (*http://www.uddi.org/specification.html*).

Read more
  Technical White Paper (*http://www.uddi.org/pubs/Iru_UDDI_Technical_White_Paper.PDF*).

Write code
  jUDDI (*http://www.juddi.org/*), a Java-base open source implementation of a UDDI registry and client code, spearheaded by James Tauber of BowStreet (*http://www.bowstreet.com/*).

Community
  General newsgroups (*news://news.software.ibm.com/ibm.software.uddi.general*) and technical newsgroups (*news://news.software.ibm.com/ibm.software.uddi.technical*).

WSDL: Web Services Description Language

Released by Microsoft, IBM, and Ariba (the three initiators of UDDI), WSDL is an XML language used to describe network services or endpoints. WSDL 1.0 includes

bindings of service descriptions for the SOAP protocol and also for simple HTTP
GET and POST requests. WSDL supersedes IBM's NASSL and Microsoft's SCL
efforts, and it's a key part of the UDDI initiative.

Introspection is a way a web service describes its inputs, outputs, and procedure
names. Introspection is a remote procedure itself. WSDL is the SOAP way to provide this service. When a client wants to know which classes are available through a
SOAP server, it would make a request to an agreed-upon procedure name (which is
yet to be agreed on). Documenting a web service is almost as important as building
it. One noticeable gap in the XML-RPC specification is the lack of a uniform way to
publish information about a new web service. The creators of SOAP, wishing to
avoid this problem, defined WSDL to have tight integration with this web service
protocol. There is even talk of using WSDL to describe XML-RPC services!

Status
    In development.

Read the specification
    WSDL 1.0 (*http://www.w3.org/TR/wsdl*).

Write code
    The IBM Web Services toolkit (*http://www.alphaworks.ibm.com/tech/
    webservicestoolkit*).

W3C XML Protocol Activity

In response to the growing interest in the use of XML for distributed peer-level
communication, the W3C has created an XML Protocol Activity. The aim of the
activity is to develop solutions that "allow a layered architecture on top of an
extensible and simple messaging format, which provides robustness, simplicity,
reusability, and interoperability."

The first working group to be chartered within the activity is the XML Protocol
Working Group (*http://www.w3.org/2000/xp/Group/*). Broadly speaking, this WG
is chartered with producing a SOAP-like protocol for XML messaging comprising
an envelope, object serialization conventions, an HTTP transport binding, and conventions for conducting remote procedure call.

SOAP is likely to be superseded, at least in part, by the introduction of the result
of this working group, but not until the end of 2001 at the earliest.

Status
    In development.

Web site
    W3C XML Protocol Activity (*http://www.w3.org/2000/xp/*).

Read more

XML Protocol Activity Statement (*http://www.w3.org/2000/xp/Activity.html*) and XML Protocol Working Group Charter (*http://www.w3.org/2000/09/XML-Protocol-Charter*).

Community

W3C xml-dist-app mailing list (*http://lists.w3.org/Archives/Public/xml-dist-app/*).

BXXP: Blocks eXtensible eXchange Protocol

Blocks eXtensible eXchange Protocol (BXXP) offers a slightly different approach to protocols such as XML-RPC and SOAP. Instead of building on top of HTTP, BXXP is layered directly on TCP. It was designed from the start for protocols. It supports authentication, transport security, and data communication. IMXP, a protocol for instant messaging that uses BXXP, was created by BXXP's originators.

Standardization of BXXP is now pursued through the IETF (*http://www.ietf.org/html.charters/beep-charter.html*).

Status

In development. Software is deployed and RFC specifications have been issued.

Web site

See *BXXP.org*.

Read the specifications

ETF Internet Drafts and RFCs (*http://www.bxxp.org/bxxp/info/drafts.jsp*, *http://ietf.org/rfc/rfc3080.txt*, and *http://ietf.org/rfc/rfc3081.txt*).

Read more

BXXP at 30,000 feet (*http://www.bxxp.org/bxxp/info/bxxp30k.jsp*).

Write code

BXXP projects page (*http://www.bxxp.org/bxxp/projectList.jsp*).

Community

BXXP WG mailing list (*http://lists.invisible.net/pipermail/bxxpwg/*) and BXXP.org community (*http://www.bxxp.org/bxxp/community.jsp*).

Protocol Design Choices

XML-RPC's creators took one of many possible paths through the options available to designers creating XML-based protocols. In this section, we'll take a look at some of the options these protocols have available to them and why developers might need a particular approach to meet their needs. Every protocol provides its own answers to these questions, depending on what its designers had in mind, and even protocols that make similar choices on the surface have plenty of room for differences in approach and implementation that may merit further examination.

Transport is one key area where protocols diverge. XML-RPC uses HTTP to send its messages, and the specification doesn't provide for other alternatives. Other protocols have also used HTTP, though some also choose not to use HTTP or offer alternatives to HTTP. SOAP, for instance, includes a binding to HTTP, but doesn't preclude other possibilities. Blocks (BXXP) offers its own protocol built directly on TCP/IP, leaving HTTP behind. Although this situation requires the creation of more infrastructure, it also offers more efficiency, less confusion, and potentially better security and authentication.

All of these protocols use different content structures, providing different levels of flexibility. Although XML-RPC messages contain a limited set of structures identifying methods, parameters, and return values, other approaches prove more flexible. SOAP includes a foundation set of structures that can create envelopes around arbitrary XML data, rules for encoding data structures, and a set of rules for using those encodings in situations for which XML-RPC-like functionality is desired. Blocks uses XML in its transport protocol and also lets developers send arbitrary XML using that protocol. Although the XML in the underlying protocol shouldn't be tampered with, the XML in the message body can represent any needed data structure. Blocks also provides for the use of non-XML data, though its focus is clearly on XML.

Why would protocol designers choose these very different approaches? Although all these protocols can solve similar problems, they offer different combinations of flexibility, infrastructure reuse, and complexity. XML-RPC is very good at making remote procedure calls, but not capable of exchanging arbitrary XML messages. SOAP adds capabilities for encoding objects and enveloping arbitrary XML, but is a significant step up in complexity from XML-RPC. Blocks is far more flexible than either SOAP or XML-RPC, providing essential building blocks for the creation of protocols using XML, but it requires more work of developers to build simple projects. Unlike SOAP and XML-RPC, Blocks also opted to build a new transport infrastructure, making it more difficult to build Blocks applications out of commodity tools, but improving efficiency and security.

There isn't (yet) one true answer to XML protocols. Any protocol design must make compromises, and many evangelists prefer to minimize the apparent impact of these compromises during their sales pitches. Fortunately, more comparisons of XML protocols are appearing, making it easier for developers to pick the protocol that fits their needs precisely. Competition may both improve XML protocols and make clear which protocol approaches are best suited for particular niches in software development, effectively letting protocols find their homes in the computing infrastructure.

Developers who really need to get involved in the details of protocol creation have a number of options available to them. The World Wide Web Consortium (W3C) sponsors an XML Protocols Activity that conducts its activities publicly on the *xml-dist-app@w3.org* mailing list. Although SOAP will be a likely foundation for this work, the work is still in the requirements phase (as of March 2001.) The IETF is the home of work on Blocks, and information on the latest Blocks activities is available at *http://www.invisibleworlds.com*. Both activities are currently spinning off much discussion on the why and how behind these protocols—the Blocks work even has a document, "On the Design of Application Protocols," that explains the series of choices made by the Blocks designers.

XML-RPC and Web Services

It's clear that XML-RPC isn't and won't be the only protocol choice available to developers, but it seems fairly clear that XML-RPC will be around for a long time. Although it isn't the most flexible or efficient XML protocol, it has key advantages in simplicity, easy integration with existing architectures, and stability. XML-RPC is three years old and shows few signs of needing substantial change. The W3C and IETF activities creating new protocols appear to stay out of this relatively simple world, creating tools that are more useful in some situations but not necessarily competitors to XML-RPC. XML-RPC is here now, is stable, and will continue to solve its chosen set of problems for a long time.

Choosing whether or not to use XML-RPC is fairly simple because it doesn't claim to solve every problem. Generally, it's fairly easy to see which kinds of services fit well into XML-RPC and which don't. Implementing an XML-RPC solution doesn't foreclose on other possibilities, either, because the protocol is really only a thin layer supporting functionality over the network. Many projects are implementing XML-RPC for its ubiquity and ease of use, while using other protocols (SOAP, RMI, or CORBA) to meet different sets of development needs. Apart from the cost of duplicating effort (largely reduced by the packages we've explored in this book), it usually isn't very difficult to make programs speak in multiple vocabularies, using the right tool for each job.

The existence of multiple packages automatically raises questions of interoperability, especially for a specification written as informally as XML-RPC. The XML-RPC web site maintains an XML-RPC validator at *http://validator.xmlrpc.com/*, providing a foundation for testing. The XML-RPC mailing list (*http://groups.yahoo.com/group/xml-rpc*) provides a forum in which developers can discuss (and hopefully sort out) interoperability issues. In general, implementation developers have documented extra features they may have added, and have marked them as potentially incompatible with other implementations. Reading the documentation and sticking to the core set of features should keep programs using XML-RPC interoperable.

There may also be room for a standard library of XML-RPC services to appear, supplementing the basic procedure call mechanism with a means of describing which procedures are available and which parameters they take. WSDL provides a means of describing Web Services, but the specification currently focuses on SOAP, raw HTTP GET and PUT, and MIME-encoded transfers rather than XML-RPC. The PHP implementation of XML-RPC includes an introspection service (described in Chapter 5) that offers one means of performing similar services in XML-RPC, but those methods currently work only in the PHP implementation.

The XML-RPC specification's future is likely static because it addresses a relatively simple set of needs and has met those needs. Despite that stability, however, there is no shortage of new XML-RPC libraries—several of which have appeared over the course of this book's creation—and plenty of ongoing work putting XML-RPC to use in new environments. The future of applications using XML-RPC is wide open for development.

For the latest list of XML-RPC implementations, see the web site *http://www. xmlrpc.com/directory/1568/implementations.* For recent news on XML and XML-based protocols, see *http://xmlhack.com/.*

A

The XML You Need for XML-RPC

The purpose of this appendix is to introduce you to XML. Although with most XML-RPC implementations you won't ever see the XML representation of the underlying machine-to-machine communications, knowledge of what is going on underneath will help you debug and troubleshoot.

If you're already acquainted with XML, you don't need to read this appendix. If not, read on. It's obviously beyond the scope of this appendix to be a complete reference to XML, but it does present enough information to give you an understanding of how XML is used in XML-RPC.

Note that this appendix makes frequent reference to the formal XML 1.0 specification, which can be used for further investigation of topics that fall outside the scope of XML-RPC. Readers are also directed to the "Annotated XML Specification," written by Tim Bray and published online at *http://XML.com/*, which provides illuminating explanation of the XML 1.0 specification; and to "What is XML?" by Norm Walsh, also published on *XML.com*.

What is XML?

XML, the Extensible Markup Language, is an Internet-friendly format for data and documents, invented by the World Wide Web Consortium (W3C). The "Markup" denotes a way of expressing the structure of a document within the document itself. XML has its roots in a markup language called SGML (Standard Generalized Markup Language), which is used in publishing and shares this heritage with HTML. XML was created to do for machine-readable documents on the Web what HTML did for human-readable documents—that is, provide a commonly agreed-upon syntax so that processing the underlying format becomes a commodity and documents are made accessible to all users.

Unlike HTML, though, XML comes with very little predefined. HTML developers are accustomed both to the notion of using angle brackets < > for denoting elements (that is, *syntax)*, and also to the set of element names themselves (such as head, body, etc.). XML only shares the former feature (i.e., the notion of using angle brackets for denoting elements). Unlike HTML, XML has no predefined elements, but is merely a set of rules that lets you write other languages like HTML.[*] Because XML defines so little, it is easy for everyone to agree to use the XML syntax, and then to build applications on top of it. It's like agreeing to use a particular alphabet and set of punctuation symbols, but not saying which language to use. However, if you're coming to XML from an HTML background, then prepare yourself for the shock of having to choose what to call your tags!

Knowing that XML's roots lie with SGML should help you understand some of XML's features and design decisions. Note that, although SGML is essentially a document-centric technology, XML's functionality also extends to data-centric applications, including XML-RPC. Commonly, data-centric applications do not need all the flexibility and expressiveness that XML provides and limit themselves to employing only a subset of XML's functionality.

Anatomy of an XML Document

The best way to explain how an XML document is composed is to present one. The following example shows an XML document you might use to describe two authors of this book:

```
<?xml version="1.0" encoding="us-ascii"?>
<authors>
    <person id="edd">
        <name>Edd Dumbill</name>
        <nationality>British</nationality>
    </person>
    <person id="simonstl">
        <name>Simon St.Laurent</name>
        <nationality>American</nationality>
    </person>
    <person id="mysteryman"/>
</authors>
```

The first line of the document is known as the *XML declaration*. This tells a processing application which version of XML you are using—the version indicator is mandatory[†]—and which character encoding you have used for the document. In

---

[*] To clarify XML's relationship with SGML: XML is an *SGML subset.* By contrast, HTML is an *SGML application.* XML-RPC uses XML to express its operations and thus is an *XML application.*

[†] For reasons that will be clearer later, constructs such as **version** in the XML declaration are known as *pseudoattributes.*

the previous example, the document is encoded in ASCII. (The significance of character encoding is covered later in this chapter.) If the XML declaration is omitted, a processor will make certain assumptions about your document. In particular, it will expect it to be encoded in UTF-8, an encoding of the Unicode character set. However, it is best to use the XML declaration wherever possible, both to avoid confusion over the character encoding and to indicate to processors which version of XML you're using.

Elements and Attributes

The second line of the example begins an *element*, which has been named "authors." The contents of that element include everything between the right angle bracket (>) in `<authors>` and the left angle bracket (<) in `</authors>`. The actual syntactic constructs `<authors>` and `</authors>` are often referred to as the element *start tag* and *end tag*, respectively. Do not confuse tags with elements! Note that elements may include other elements, as well as text. An XML document must contain exactly one *root element*, which contains all other content within the document. The name of the root element defines the type of the XML document.

Elements that contain both text and other elements simultaneously are classified as *mixed content*. XML-RPC does not use this feature, which is more often utilized in document-centric applications. Elements in XML-RPC contain either text-only text or other elements only.

The sample "authors" document uses elements named **person** to describe the authors themselves. Each person element has an *attribute* named **id**. Unlike elements, attributes can only contain textual content. Their values must be surrounded by quotes. Either single quotes (') or double quotes (") may be used, as long as you use the same kind of closing quote as the opening one.

Within XML documents, attributes are frequently used for *metadata* (i.e., "data about data")—describing properties of the element's contents. This is the case in our example, where **id** contains a unique identifier for the person being described.

As far as XML is concerned, it does not matter in which order attributes are presented in the element start tag. For example, these two elements contain exactly the same information as far as an XML 1.0 conformant processing application is concerned:

```
<animal name="dog" legs="4"/>
<animal legs="4" name="dog"/>
```

On the other hand, the information presented to an application by an XML processor on reading the following two lines will be different for each animal element because the ordering of elements is significant:

```
<animal><name>dog</name><legs>4</legs></animal>
<animal><legs>4</legs><name>dog</name></animal>
```

XML treats a set of attributes like a bunch of stuff in a bag—there is no implicit ordering—while elements are treated like items on a list, where ordering matters.

New XML developers frequnetly ask when it is best to use attributes to represent information and when it is best to use elements. As you can see from the "authors" example, if order is important to you, then elements are a good choice. In general, there is no hard-and-fast "best practice" for choosing whether to use attributes or elements.

To keep things simple, XML-RPC uses only elements.

The final author described in our document has no information available. All we know about this person is his or her ID, **mysteryman**. The document uses the XML shortcut syntax for an empty element. The following is a reasonable alternative:

```
<person id="mysteryman"></person>
```

Name Syntax

XML 1.0 has certain rules about element and attribute names. In particular:

*   Names are case-sensitive: e.g., <person/> is not the same as <Person/>.

*   Names beginning with "xml" (in any permutation of uppercase or lowercase) are reserved for use by XML 1.0 and its companion specifications.

*   A name must start with a letter or an underscore, not a digit, and may continue with any letter, digit, underscore, or period.*

A precise description of names can be found in Section 2.3 of the XML 1.0 specification, at the URL *http://www.w3.org/TR/REC-xml#sec-common-syn*.

Well-Formed

An XML document that conforms to the rules of XML syntax is known as *well-formed*. At its most basic level, well-formedness means that elements should be properly matched, and all opened elements should be closed. A formal definition

---

* Actually, a name may also contain a colon, but the colon is used to delimit a *namespace prefix* and is not available for arbitrary use. Knowledge of namespaces is not required for understanding XML-RPC, but for more information, see Tim Bray's "XML Namespaces by Example," published at *http://www.xml. com/pub/a/1999/01/namespaces.html.*

of well-formedness can be found in Section 2.1 of the XML 1.0 specification, at the URL *http://www.w3.org/TR/REC-xml#sec-well-formed.* Table A-1 shows some XML documents that are not well-formed.

Table A-1. Examples of poorly formed XML documents

Document	Reason why it's not well-formed

`<foo>`
  `<bar>`
  `</foo>`
`</bar>`
	The elements are not properly nested because foo is closed while inside its child element bar.

`<foo>`
  `<bar>`
`</foo>`
	The bar element was not closed before its parent, foo, was closed.

`<foo baz>` `</foo>`	The baz attribute has no value. While this is permissible in HTML (e.g., `<table border>`), it is forbidden in XML.
`<foo baz=23>` `</foo>`	The baz attribute value, 23, has no surrounding quotes. Unlike HTML, all attribute values must be quoted in XML.

Comments

As in HTML, it is possible to include *comments* within XML documents. XML comments are intended to be read only by people. With HTML, developers have occasionally employed comments to add application-specific functionality—for example, the server-side include functionality of most web servers uses instructions embedded in HTML comments. XML provides other means of indicating application processing instructions,* so comments should not be used for any purpose other than those for which they were intended.

The start of a comment is indicated with `<!--`, and the end of the comment with `-->`. Any sequence of characters, aside from the string `--`, may appear within a comment.

Comments tend to be used more in XML documents intended for human consumption than those intended for machine consumption. One particularly useful aspect in the context of XML-RPC is that they may be used to carry debugging information from a server back to a client, which can then be used by people doing troubleshooting.

Entity References

Another feature of XML with which you need to be acquainted to use XML-RPC is the mechanism for *escaping* characters.

---

* A discussion of *processing instructions (PIs)* is outside the scope of this book. For more information on PIs, see Section 2.6 of the XML 1.0 specification, at the URL *http://www.w3.org/TR/REC-xml#sec-pi.*

Because some characters have special significance in XML, there needs to be a
way to represent them. For example, in some cases the < symbol might really be
intended to mean "less than" rather than to signal the start of an element name.
Clearly, just inserting the character without any escaping mechanism would result
in a poorly formed document because a processing application would assume you
were commencing another element. Another instance of this problem is that of
needing to include both double quotes and single quotes simultaneously in an
attribute's value. Here's an example that illustrates both these difficulties:

```
<badDoc>
  <para>
    I'd really like to use the < character
  </para>
  <note title="On the proper 'use' of the " character"/>
</badDoc>
```

XML avoids this problem by the use of the (fearsomely named) *predefined entity
references.* The word *entity* in the context of XML simply means a unit of content.
The term *entity reference* means just that, a symbolic way of referring to a certain
unit of content. XML predefines entities for the following symbols: left angle
bracket (<), right angle bracket (>), apostrophe ('), double quote ("), and ampersand (&).

An entity reference is introduced with an ampersand (&), which is followed by a
name (using the word "name" in its formal sense, as defined by the XML 1.0 specification), and terminated with a semicolon (;). Table A-2 shows how the five predefined entities can be used within an XML document.

Table A-2. Predefined entity references in XML 1.0

Literal character	Entity reference
<	&lt;
>	&gt;
'	&apos;
"	&quot;
&	&amp;

Here's our problematic document revised to use entity references:

```
<badDoc>
  <para>
    I'd really like to use the &lt; character
  </para>
  <note title="On the proper &apos;use&apos; of the &quot;character"/>
</badDoc>
```

Being able to use the predefined entities is all you need for XML-RPC; in general, entities are provided as a convenience for human-created XML, whereas the XML in XML-RPC is generated by a machine. XML 1.0 allows you to define your own entities and use entity references as "shortcuts" in your document, which is not permitted in XML-RPC. Section 4 of the XML 1.0 specification, available at *http://www. w3.org/TR/REC-xml#sec-physical-struct*, describes the use of entities.

Character References

You are less likely to find *character references* in the context of XML-RPC. Character references allow you to denote a character by its numeric position in Unicode character set (this position is known as its *code point*). Table A-3 contains a few examples that illustrate the syntax.

Table A-3. Example character references in UTF-8

Actual character	Character reference
1	&#48;
A	&#65;
Ñ	&#xD1;
®	&#xAE;

Note that the code point can be expressed in decimal or, with the use of x as a prefix, in hexadecimal.

Character Encodings

The subject of character encodings is frequently a mysterious one for developers. Most code tends to be written for one computing platform and, normally, to run within one organization. Although the Internet is changing things quickly, most of us have never had cause to think too deeply about internationalization.

XML, designed to be an Internet-friendly syntax for information exchange, has internationalization at its very core. One of the basic requirements for XML processors is that they support the Unicode standard character encoding. Unicode attempts to include the requirements of all the world's languages within one character set. Consequently, it is very large!

Unicode Encoding Schemes

Unicode 3.0 has more than 57,700 *code points*, each of which corresponds to a character.* If one were to express a Unicode string by using the position of each character in the character set as its encoding (in the same way as ASCII does), expressing the whole range of characters would require 4 octets† for each character. Clearly, if a document is written in 100 percent American English, it will be four times larger than required—all the characters in ASCII fitting into a 7-bit representation. This places a strain both on storage space and on memory requirements for processing applications.

Fortunately, two encoding schemes for Unicode alleviate this problem: *UTF-8* and *UTF-16*. As you might guess from their names, applications can process documents in these encodings in 8- or 16-bit segments at a time. When code points are required in a document that cannot be represented by one chunk, a bit-pattern is used that indicates that the following chunk is required to calculate the desired code point. In UTF-8 this is denoted by the most significant bit of the first octet being set to 1.

This scheme means that UTF-8 is a highly efficient encoding for representing languages using Latin alphabets, such as English. All of the ASCII character set is represented natively in UTF-8—an ASCII-only document and its equivalent in UTF-8 are byte-for-byte identical.

This knowledge will also help you debug encoding errors. One frequent error arises because of the fact that ASCII is a proper subset of UTF-8—programmers get used to this fact and produce UTF-8 documents, but use them as if they were ASCII. Things start to go awry when the XML parser processes a document containing, for example, characters from foreign languages, such as Á. Because this character cannot be represented using only one octet in UTF-8, this produces a two-octet sequence in the output document; in a non-Unicode viewer or text editor, it looks like a couple of characters of garbage.

Other Character Encodings

Unicode, in the context of computing history, is a relatively new invention. Native operating system support for Unicode is by no means widespread. For instance, although Windows NT offers Unicode support, Windows 95 and 98 do not have it.

XML 1.0 allows a document to be encoded in any character set registered with the Internet Assigned Numbers Authority (IANA). European documents are commonly

---

* You can obtain charts of all these characters online by visiting *http://www.unicode.org/charts/*.

† An *octet* is a string of 8 binary digits, or bits. A *byte* is commonly, but not always, considered the same thing as an octet.

encoded in one of the *ISO Latin* character sets, such as ISO-8859-1. Japanese documents commonly use *Shift-JIS*, and Chinese documents use *GB2312* and *Big 5*.

A full list of registered character sets may be found on the Web at *http://www.isi. edu/in-notes/iana/assignments/character-sets*.

XML processors are not required by the XML 1.0 specification to support any more than UTF-8 and UTF-16, but most commonly support other encodings, such as US-ASCII and ISO-8859-1. Although most XML-RPC transactions are currently conducted in ASCII (or the ASCII subset of UTF-8), there is nothing to stop XML-RPC clients and servers talking to one another in, say, Japanese. You will, however, probably have to dig into the encoding support of your computing platform and XML-RPC libraries to find out if it is possible for you to use alternate encodings.

Validity

In addition to well-formedness, XML 1.0 offers another level of verification, called *validity*. To explain why validity is important, let's take a simple example. Imagine you invented a simple XML format for your friends' telephone numbers:

```
<phonebook>
  <person>
    <name>Albert Smith</name>
    <number>123-456-7890</number>
  </person>
  <person>
    <name>Bertrand Jones</name>
    <number>456-123-9876</number>
  </person>
</phonebook>
```

Based on your format, you also construct a program to display and search your phone numbers. This program turns out to be so useful, you share it with your friends. However, your friends aren't so hot on detail as you are, and try to feed your program this phone book file:

```
<phonebook>
  <person>
    <name>Melanie Green</name>
    <phone>123-456-7893</phone>
  </person>
</phonebook>
```

Note that, although this file is perfectly well-formed, it doesn't fit the format you prescribed for the phone book, and you find you need to change your program to cope with this situation. If your friends had used **number** as you did to denote the phone number, and not **phone**, there wouldn't have been a problem. However, as it is, this second file is not a *valid* phonebook document.

For validity to be a useful general concept, we need a machine-readable way of saying what a valid document is; that is, which elements and attributes must be present and in what order. XML 1.0 achieves this by introducing *document type definitions* (DTDs). For the purposes of XML-RPC, you don't need to know much about DTDs, but it is useful to be able to read a basic DTD.

Document Type Definitions (DTDs)

The purpose of a DTD is to express the allowed elements and attributes in a certain document type and to constrain the order in which they must appear within that document type. A DTD is generally composed of one file, which contains declarations defining the *element types* and *attribute lists*. (In theory, a DTD may span more than one file; however, the mechanism for including one file inside another—*parameter entities*—is outside the scope of this book.) It is common to mistakenly conflate *element* and *element types*. The distinction is that an element is the actual instance of the structure as found in an XML document, whereas the element type is the *kind of element* that the instance is.

Element type declarations

The form of an element type declaration is:

```
<!ELEMENT element-name contentspec>
```

The allowable content defined by **contentspec** is defined in terms of a simple grammar, which allows the expression of sequence, alternatives, and iteration within elements. For a formal definition of the element type declaration, see Section 3.2 of the XML 1.0 specification, at *http://w3.org/TR/REC-xml#NT-elementdecl*. Table A-4 introduces the most common constructs.

Table A-4. Element type content specifications

Content specification	Meaning
`<!ELEMENT e (#PCDATA)>`	The element may contain character data—that is, text.
`<!ELEMENT e EMPTY>`	The element has no content—that is, it can only appear as `<e/>`.
`<!ELEMENT e ANY>`	The element may contain character data or any other element defined in the DTD.
`<!ELEMENT e (a,b*,c)>`	The element must contain the following sequence: one *a* element, followed by zero or more *b* elements, followed by one *c* element. The asterisk means "zero or more."
`<!ELEMENT e (b|#PCDATA)>`	The element may contain either a *b* element or character data.
`<!ELEMENT e (a|b|c)*>`	The element may contain zero or more *a*, *b*, or *c* elements, in any order.

Attribute list declarations

Inside a DTD, permissible attributes are specified on a per-element basis. An attribute list declaration takes this form:

```
<!ATTLIST element-name attribute-definitions>
```

The attribute definitions themselves take the form of the attribute's name and type whether the attribute is optional or required, and, if necessary, the attribute's default value. Unlike elements, you can specify defaults for attributes, which are inserted by an application when it parses the XML document, even if they're not explicitly written in the document.

Table A-5 shows some common attribute definitions.

Table A-5. Attribute definitions

Attribute definition	Meaning
`attrname CDATA #REQUIRED`	This attribute must always be present and it should contain only character data. It has no default value.
`attrname CDATA #IMPLIED`	This character data attribute is permissible, but not compulsory. It has no default value.
`attrname (scissors|paper|stone) "stone"`	This attribute may take only the values "scissors," "paper," or "stone." If it is not specified, it is assumed to take the default value "stone."
`attrname CDATA #FIXED "purple"`	This attribute must take the value "purple." If it is not specified on the element, the processing application provides "purple" as a default value.

Here's a complete declaration for a fictitious "animal" element, which must have a name, either two or four legs, and, optionally, a note field:

```
<!ATTLIST animal name CDATA #REQUIRED legs (two|four) "four"
          notes CDATA #IMPLIED>
```

As we have noted, XML-RPC itself does not use attributes in its message format, so coverage of attributes has been kept necessarily brief. As ever, formal definitions can be found in the W3C XML 1.0 specification.

Putting It Together

To demonstrate a complete DTD, here's the DTD for the XML document we used at the beginning of the chapter to list the authors of this book:

```
<!ELEMENT name (#PCDATA)>
<!ELEMENT nationality (#PCDATA)>
```

```
<!ELEMENT person (name,nationality)*>
<!ATTLIST person id CDATA #REQUIRED>
<!ELEMENT authors (person)*>
```

The final step is to link the document to its defining DTD. This is done with a document type declaration `<!DOCTYPE ...>`, inserted at the beginning of the XML document, after the XML declaration:

```
<?xml version="1.0" encoding="us-ascii"?>
<!DOCTYPE authors SYSTEM "http://example.com/authors.dtd">
<authors>
    <person id="edd">
        <name>Edd Dumbill</name>
        <nationality>British</nationality>
    </person>
    <person id="simonstl">
        <name>Simon St.Laurent</name>
        <nationality>American</nationality>
    </person>
    <person id="mysteryman"/>
</authors>
```

This example assumes the DTD file has been placed on a web server at *example. com*. Note that the document type declaration specifies the root element of the document, not the DTD itself. You could use the same DTD to define "person," "name," or "nationality" as the root element of a valid document. Certain DTDs, such as the DocBook DTD for technical documentation,[*] use this feature to good effect, allowing you to provide the same DTD for multiple document types.

A *validating XML processor* is obliged to check the input document against its DTD. If it does not validate, the document is rejected. To return to the phone book example, if your application validated its input files against a phone book DTD, you would have been spared the problems of debugging your program and correcting your friend's XML, because your application would have rejected the document as being invalid.

Chapter 2 explains how the structure of legal XML-RPC messages can be described by a DTD. Not all XML-RPC tools actually validate against a DTD; instead they have custom programming to perform the checking. You can see from the phone book example that in circumstances when you have a simple document type, unlikely to change over time, hard-coding validation might be preferable to using a DTD—to achieve a smaller code footprint.

For your own applications, to have to write a DTD parser and an XML parser yourself simply to use XML is a large overhead. Instead, you can choose to build your application on top of existing XML processors. The next section gives a brief

---

[*] See *http://www.docbook.org/*.

overview of these tools. In general, you won't need them to use XML-RPC because many XML-RPC processing libraries are already written, but if you decide to implement your own XML-RPC code or experiment further with XML, you may find them a good starting point.

Tools for Processing XML

Unless you work in a very specialized environment, there can be few reasons for writing all your code to handle XML from scratch. Many parsers exist for using XML with many different programming languages. Most of these tools are freely available, the majority being Open Source.

Selecting a Parser

An XML parser typically takes the form of a library of code that you interface with your own program. You hand the XML over to the parser, and it hands you back information about the contents of the XML document. Typically, parsers do this either via *events* or via a *document object model*.

With event-based parsing, the parser calls a function in your program whenever a parse event is encountered. Parse events include things like finding the start of an element, the end of an element, or a comment. Most Java event-based parsers follow a standard API called SAX, which is also implemented for other languages such as Python and Perl. You can find more about SAX at *http://www.megginson.com/SAX/*.

Document object model (DOM) based parsers work in a markedly different way. They consume the entire XML input document and hand your program back a tree-like data structure that you can interrogate and alter. The DOM is a W3C standard; documentation is available at *http://www.w3.org/DOM/*.

Choosing whether to use an event- or DOM-based model depends on your application. If you have a large or unpredictable document size, it is better to use event-based parsing for reasons of speed and memory consumption (DOM trees can get very large). If you have small, simple XML documents, using the DOM leaves you less programming work to do. Many programming languages have both event-based and DOM support.

As XML matures, hybrid techniques that give the best of both worlds are emerging. The best way to find out what's available and what's new for your favorite programming language is to keep an eye on the following online sources:

XML.com Resource Guide: *http://xml.com/pub/resourceguide/*
XMLhack XML Developer News: *http://xmlhack.com/*
Free XML Tools Guide: *http://www.garshol.priv.no/download/xmltools/*

XSLT Processors

Many XML applications involve transforming one XML document into another or into HTML. The W3C has defined a special language called XSLT for doing transformations. XSLT processors are becoming available for all major programming platforms.

XSLT works by using a *stylesheet*, which contains templates that describe how to transform elements from an XML document. These templates typically specify what XML to output in response to a particular element or attribute. Using a W3C technology called XPath gives you the flexibility not just to say "do this for every 'person' element," but to give instructions as complex as "do this for the third 'person' element whose 'name' attribute is 'Fred'".

Because of this flexibility, some applications have sprung up for XSLT that aren't really transformation applications at all, but take advantage of the ability to trigger actions on certain element patterns and sequencers. Combined with XSLT's ability to execute custom code via extension functions, the XPath language has enabled applications such as document indexing to be driven by an XSLT processor. It would be possible to write a specialized XML-RPC server with XSLT, but it probably isn't the most convenient way of implementing one!

The W3C specifications for XSLT and XPath can be found at *http://w3.org/TR/xslt* and *http://w3.org/xpath*, respectively.

Is That All There Is?

The general overview of XML given in this appendix should be sufficient to enable you to work with XML-RPC in most situations. In fact, if you only use XML-RPC in one programming language and only within your own networks, you will have very few XML-specific issues to deal with. However, when your programs start communicating with XML-RPC servers on different machines, using different programming languages, and probably in different countries, a little XML knowledge will serve you well.

Most of this book deals with implementing clients and servers with XML-RPC libraries already in existence. If, however, you need to work in an environment for which no such support exists, then this appendix and Appendix B will provide you with the knowledge you need to create your own XML-RPC client and server code. For further information about XML, the O'Reilly books *Learning XML* (2001) and *XML in a Nutshell* (2001) are invaluable guides, as is the weekly online magazine *XML.com*.

B

The HTTP You Need for XML-RPC

Instead of creating an entirely new transport protocol, XML-RPC avoids rein-venting the wheel by reusing a commonly available wheel: HyperText Transfer Protocol (HTTP). HTTP is better known as the transport protocol for the World Wide Web (WWW), and HTTP tools are available for nearly every network-aware programming language and operating system. XML-RPC uses only a subset of HTTP's features, but even the use of that subset has proven controversial in some quarters. We'll explore how HTTP works in general, and then focus on the details you need to create, read, and analyze HTTP transactions.

By using HTTP for its transport mechanism, XML-RPC takes advantage of nearly a decade of protocol development and implementation. HTTP is widely deployed, relatively well understood, and supported by infrastructures from clients to servers to firewalls to cache engines, though some of that support isn't necessary for XML-RPC. XML-RPC arrived after HTTP 1.1 had stabilized, letting it take advantage of some critical features for two-way communications that hadn't existed in earlier versions. We'll take a brief look at HTTP in its normal web environment before exploring ways to reuse that infrastructure in an XML-RPC context.

A Bit About TCP/IP

HTTP is built on a foundation of the Transmission Control Protocol and Internet Protocol (TCP/IP). Although it is the protocol suite on which the Internet and many smaller networks are built, TCP/IP often seems mysterious, especially when you get into the details of where and how your information gets to you, but fortu-nately HTTP takes care of all those details for you. If you know all about TCP/IP already, you may be able to apply some of that knowledge in your XML-RPC endeavors; if you don't know much about TCP/IP, the amount you need to learn is fairly small.

TCP/IP lets programs send information between computers, which are typically identified by four-byte identifiers, called IP addresses. IP addresses are commonly written with dots between each byte value, such as 10.251.27.4, 127.0.0.1, or 192. 168.142.100. Although this notation is a little strange, it's much easier than reading the large numbers that four bytes (32 bits) can represent. For normal human consumption, we tend to hide these numbers behind human-readable names, such as *example.com, a.jaundiceeye.com, xmlhack.com,* or *www.simonstl.com.* A vast distributed infrastructure, the Domain Name Service (DNS), provides the necessary translations between names and addresses and back again.

There are a few addresses you might want to know about for testing purposes and to follow the examples in this book. 127.0.0.1, or *localhost*, is a stand-in number that always represents the local system. If I ping 127.0.0.1, I'm pinging the computer on which I'm typing right now. If I telnet into another computer and ping 127. 0.0.1, I'm pinging the computer where my telnet session is taking place. The other range you'll see here occasionally is 192.168.*x.x.* The addresses beginning with 192. 168 are *private* addresses, useful for working on networks behind firewalls.

IP addresses typically identify a single computer, but there are cases when a single computer may host many IP addresses, or when companies share a small set of IP addresses among a larger group of computers, not all of which are connected at any given time. Network Address Translation (NAT), a technique often used by firewalls for hiding entire networks behind a single IP address, can also add to the chaos. Fortunately, most of these complex cases are easy to deal with. You can treat a computer with many different IP addresses much the same as many computers and not worry about its multiple identities. Shared IP addresses are usually dealt with by the software that implements them, and you may not be able to tell the difference between these kinds of IP addresses in your XML-RPC transactions. The only case you really need to watch out for is a computer you need to communicate with that changes its address among different transactions—a rare case, and one that usually requires a network administrator to assign a fixed address.

TCP/IP provides a framework that allows a single IP address to support multiple services and different kinds of communications. Transmissions are not directed at an IP address generically—instead, they are directed at a combination of an address and a port. Although the IP portion of TCP/IP makes certain that packets can move from computer to computer, the TCP part understands ports. Every IP address has 65,535 port numbers available for TCP-based protocols. TCP isn't your only option for sending information over IP, but it's the protocol HTTP uses.

There are numerous standard "well-known" port numbers, 80 for HTTP, 23 for Telnet, and 25 for SMTP, along with others, like the 8080 often used for experimental HTTP servers. In an example later in the chapter, we'll use 1234. By providing port numbers, TCP/IP helps establish communication not just between machines, but between particular services on those computers.

For the "well-known" protocols, port numbers don't need to be specified. The URL *http://www.simonstl.com* connects to port 80 on the system identified by the name *www.simonstl.com*. In other cases, port numbers can be specified explicitly. HTTP services don't have to run on port 80 just because the protocol is well known. If I wanted to connect to a web server running on port 8080 of *www.simonstl.com*, the URL would read *http://www.simonstl.com:8080*. (And yes, *http://www.simonstl.com:80* produces the same results as *http://www.simonstl.com.*)

In XML-RPC, you use HTTP for all of this. The network information you'll need to know is limited to the names or IP addresses of the systems you'll connect and which port number you use *if* you're using something other than the default port 80. If the network pathway between the two systems includes firewalls or other barricades, you may need to talk with your network administrators for more detail, but fortunately managing HTTP transactions with proxies, firewalls, and address translation is pretty well understood, if a bit arcane at times. Basically, you need to have URLs for every machine you want to contact—not that different a situation from the level of network management knowledge needed to make web browsers behave. For more details on TCP/IP, see Craig Hunt's *TCP/IP Network Administration, 2nd Edition* (O'Reilly, 1998).

HTTP at the Start of the Web

When HTTP first appeared, it was an astoundingly simple. Clients could make requests to a server on port 80, sending a single request terminated by a carriage return and a line feed:

```
GET /docs/mydoc.html
```

The server would respond by sending an HTML file as ASCII text and close the TCP/IP connection, ending the session. Error messages were just reported as human-readable text returned to the client.*

Although this simple functionality was undoubtedly limited, lacking even the basic two-way functionality used by XML-RPC, it was enough to get the Web off the ground.

---

* To see how simple a retrieval process this was, visit *http://www.w3.org/Protocols/HTTP/AsImplemented. html*, or even the slightly more complex formal specification at *http://www.w3.org/Protocols/HTTP/HTTP2. html*.

Adding Two-Way Communications

The next major revision of HTTP, 1.0, brought much more sophisticated communications to the Web. Although HTTP 1.0 added support for documents of various MIME types (not just HTML files), perhaps the most important change was support for sending information from users' browsers back to the server in ways that allowed more sophistication than a basic query string. HTTP 1.0 provided support for much more complex and much larger information-collection schemes using HTML forms.

HTTP 1.0 went through a much more intensive design process at the Internet Engineering Task Force (IETF) and concluded with the publication of Informational RFC 1945 (available at *http://www.ietf.org/rfc/rfc1945.txt*). It reflects a few years of development beyond the pioneering work of HTTP 0.9 and uses some approaches, notably text-based headers, taken from previous IETF work, such as the Simple Mail Transfer Protocol (SMTP). Just like SMTP, HTTP headers are not case-sensitive, nor does order (except the top line) matter.

A Richer Set of Headers

HTTP 1.0 transactions include more than the simple GET method, though most HTTP 1.0 processors accept the simple syntax used by HTTP 0.9. HTTP 1.0 supports GET, for simple retrieval and the use of query strings for form-based information; POST, for more sophisticated sending of information from client to server; and HEAD, which allows clients to collect information about what they'll get from the server without having to retrieve the entire document. (PUT, DELETE, LINK, and UNLINK are defined in an appendix, as well.) HTTP 1.0 also introduced a much more complete set of status error messages (including the famous 404 Not Found) to replace the human-readable messages used by HTTP 0.9.

Even a simple HTTP 1.0 GET request has many more parts than its HTTP 0.9 counterpart. HTTP 1.0 adds information about the protocol in use, the kind of software making and handling the request, acceptable MIME content types for transfer, and other kinds of information about the transaction. A simple HTTP request is shown below:

```
GET docs/mydoc.html HTTP/1.0
User-Agent: Mozilla/4.7 [en] (WinNT; I)
Host: www.simonstl.com
Accept: */*
```

The Host header isn't actually part of HTTP 1.0, but HTTP 1.0 made it relatively easy to add headers. Using Host makes it possible for servers that support multiple domains to sort out requests without needing an IP address for every domain.

If your XML-RPC servers use the same IP address to host multiple domains, you need to use the Host header.

The server response is also fairly simple, though it contains identifying information that didn't exist in HTTP 0.9, stored in headers that look like the request headers:

```
HTTP/1.0 200 OK
Date: Sun, 29-Apr-01 12:27:43 GMT
MIME-version: 1.0
Content-type: text/html

<html>
<head><title>My Document</title></head>
<body><h1>My Document</h1></body>
</html>
```

HTTP 1.0 was a simple request-response protocol. When the server finished sending the document, it closed the connection. It could also indicate the number of bytes that were in that content with a Content-Length header, though this is not required. If a page required multiple resources from the same server, the client would open multiple connections as necessary.

POST: the Key to XML-RPC

HTTP 1.0 uses a similar set of headers to handle transactions based on forms. Forms that use query strings and the GET method generate conversations that look very much like the previous one, but forms that use the POST method send different kinds of information. Simple forms send information that looks just like a query string, except that it's stored at a different location in the transaction.

To demonstrate the different ways that clients can send information to the server, we'll explore a few basic forms and send some simple information. One minor hassle in doing so is that seeing the information in its raw state requires either a network packet sniffing tool or a custom server. Writing custom servers is a nuisance, but because we're only exploring what the client is sending, the server can be *very* simple. The following bit of Java code listens to port 1234, reports what it receives, and shuts down when the client hits the stop button. It's not an HTTP server *per se*, but it lets us see what we need:

```
import java.net.*;
import java.io.*;

public class test
  {
  public static void main(String[] asArgs)
    {
    try
```

```
        {
        ServerSocket ss=new ServerSocket(1234);
        Socket s=ss.accept();
        InputStream is=s.getInputStream();

        while(true)
          {
          int i=is.read();
          if(i==-1) break;
          System.out.write(i);
          }

        System.out.println("\n\nConnection closed");
        }
    catch(IOException ioe)
        {
        System.err.println("Exception:");
        ioe.printStackTrace();
        }
      }
   }
```

(Thanks to Sam Marshall (*S.Marshall@open.ac.uk*) for this handy public-domain viewer.)

Once you start this listener from the command line, you can send it HTTP requests and view them in the terminal window. We'll send it requests from three HTML forms to see how clients can send information to servers using the POST method. The first form includes three fields—two single-line text input areas and a multi-line text area—and doesn't specify any special encoding for sending the information:

```
<html>
<head><title>Testing POST - form information</title></head>
<body>
<form method="POST" action="http://192.168.124.14:1234">
<p>Given name:<input name="given" type="text" maxlength="20"></p>
<p>Family name:<input name="last" type="text" maxlength="30"></p>
<p>Other information:</p>
<textarea name="other" cols="20" rows="5" ></textarea>
<input name="Post it" type="submit">
</form>
</body></html>
```

The form, shown in a browser in Figure B-1, is very simple.

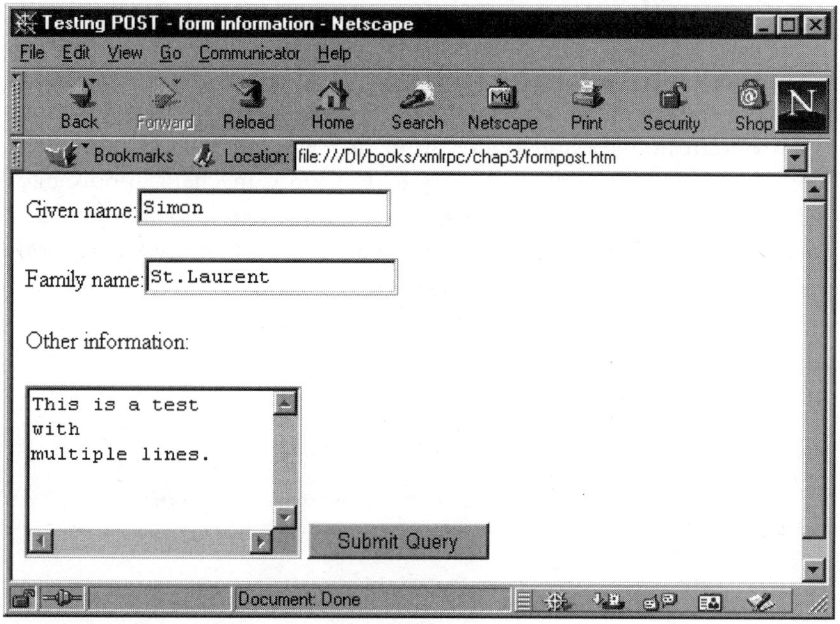

Figure B-1. A simple form for testing the POST method

When we fill out the form as shown in Figure B-2 and send it to our bit of reporting Java code, we get the following:

```
POST / HTTP/1.0
Connection: Keep-Alive
User-Agent: Mozilla/4.7 [en] (Win95; I)
Host: 192.168.124.14:1234
Accept: image/gif, image/x-xbitmap, image/jpeg, image/pjpeg, image/png, */*
Accept-Encoding: gzip
Accept-Language: en
Accept-Charset: iso-8859-1,*,utf-8
Content-type: application/x-www-form-urlencoded
Content-length: 100

given=Simon&last=St.Laurent&other=This+is+a+test%0D%0Awith%0D%0Amultiple+lines.
&Post+it=Submit+Query


Connection closed
```

The most important pieces here are the **Content-Type** and **Content-Length** headers, followed by the form contents. The **Content-Type** header tells the HTTP server that it will get form information in URL encoded form—effectively, exactly what would have been appended to the URL as a query string if the form had specified the **GET** method rather than the **POST** method. The **Content-Length** header tells it how many bytes to expect in the rest of the message, so the server has an idea when the transmission from the client will be complete. After all the headers and a blank line, the content of the form is presented, followed by a few blank lines.

Although that approach is useful for many cases (especially when forms contain too much information for the query string to be used reliably), sending XML through URL encoding is inefficient, at best. The forms mechanism built into most browsers offers another mechanism, used to support users who are uploading files to servers through the browser. By specifying an encoding of "multipart/form-data" in the form element's **enctype** attribute, we can tell the browser to send the information in a different format:

```
<html>
<head><title>Testing POST - form information</title></head>
<body>
<form method="POST" action="http://192.168.124.14:1234"
      enctype="multipart/form-data">
<p>Given name:<input name="given" type="text" maxlength="20"></p>
<p>Family name:<input name="last" type="text" maxlength="30"></p>
<p>Other information:</p>
<textarea name="other" cols="20" rows="5" ></textarea>
<input name="Post it" type="submit">
</form>
</body></html>
```

When loaded, this form looks exactly like the form shown in Figure B-1. When we fill it with the same data and send it to our test reporter, however, we get a very different representation of the same information:

```
POST / HTTP/1.0
Connection: Keep-Alive
User-Agent: Mozilla/4.7 [en] (Win95; I)
Host: 192.168.124.14:1234
Accept: image/gif, image/x-xbitmap, image/jpeg, image/pjpeg, image/png, */*
Accept-Encoding: gzip
Accept-Language: en
Accept-Charset: iso-8859-1,*,utf-8
Content-type: multipart/form-data; boundary=------------------------365478912630
Content-Length: 482

--------------------------365478912630
Content-Disposition: form-data; name="given"

Simon
--------------------------365478912630
Content-Disposition: form-data; name="last"

St.Laurent
--------------------------365478912630
Content-Disposition: form-data; name="other"
```

```
This is a test
with
multiple lines.
--------------------------365478912630
Content-Disposition: form-data; name="Post it"

Submit Query
--------------------------365478912630--
```

The top few headers are identical, but the last two change significantly. Instead of a `Content-Type` of "application/x-www-form-urlencoded," we now have a `Content-Type` of "multipart/form-data," whose parts are specified to have the boundary:

```
--------------------------365478912630
```

The `Content-Length` has expanded significantly, to 482 bytes. The content itself is no longer URL encoded; instead, each part appears as plain text with a `Content-Disposition` header identifying it as `form-data` and providing the name of each piece. (It even provides information about the Submit Query button!)

Why would we want to nearly quintuple the number of bytes used to send a simple (even stupid) form transaction? Although it may be less efficient, this approach allows you to send different kinds of information, notably files that users will upload. For our next example, we'll look at uploading information using this approach, bringing us a significant step closer to the kinds of XML transfers we need for XML-RPC.

The next form, rather than collecting name information, collects files. Users can send any file they like to the server, which will then do something (undefined, for now) with it. Like the previous form, the form element specifies an enctype of `multipart/form-data`. Unlike the previous form, this form contains an input of type `file`, which (with a little help from the browser) can be used to select a file and send it to the server when the Submit Query button is pushed:

```html
<html>
<head><title>Testing POST - files</title></head>
<body>
<form method="POST" action="http://192.168.124.14:1234"
      enctype="multipart/form-data">
<input name="the file" type="file"><br>
<input name="post it" type="submit">
</form>
</body></html>
```

This simple HTML form is shown in Figure B-2.

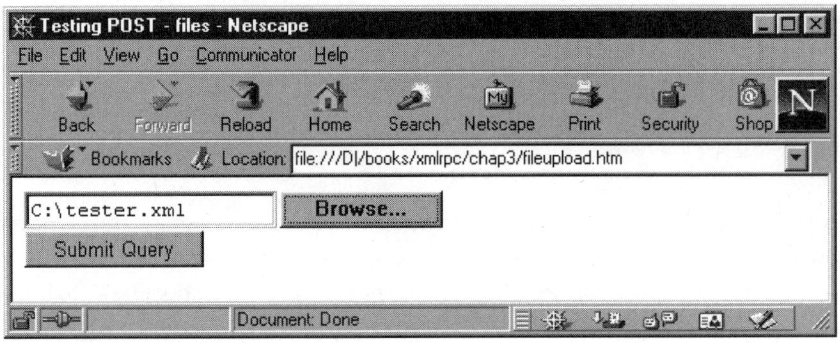

Figure B-2. A simple form for uploading files using POST

To test it out, we'll send the very simple XML file shown here as our test file:

```
<test>This is a test, only a test.</test>
```

The results are somewhat like those for the name form, but with a significant difference. We now have an XML document sent to the server, identified as `text/xml`!

```
POST / HTTP/1.0
Connection: Keep-Alive
User-Agent: Mozilla/4.7 [en] (Win95; I)
Host: 192.168.124.14:1234
Accept: image/gif, image/x-xbitmap, image/jpeg, image/pjpeg, image/png, */*
Accept-Encoding: gzip
Accept-Language: en
Accept-Charset: iso-8859-1,*,utf-8
Content-type: multipart/form-data; boundary=----------------------224083090527703
Content-Length: 350

------------------------224083090527703
Content-Disposition: form-data; name="the file"; filename="C:\tester.xml"
Content-Type: text/xml

<test>This is a test, only a test.</test>

------------------------224083090527703
Content-Disposition: form-data; name="post it"

Submit Query
------------------------224083090527703--
```

This isn't a very efficient approach because we're using, excepting headers, 350 bytes to transmit a payload (the XML file) of 41 bytes, though the filename might be of some use as well. Despite those inefficiencies, which grow less significant as files grow longer, HTTP 1.0 has taken some significant steps toward allowing clients to send XML files to servers. Because servers can send back anything they like as body content, that end of the equation will be much easier to address. XML-RPC will build on this basic infrastructure and streamline it significantly.

Strictly speaking, HTTP 1.0 is all you need to make XML-RPC work. Because much of the world has moved on to HTTP 1.1, however, you'll most likely implement your work using tools that are built for HTTP 1.1.

Making Two-Way Communications Efficient

Although HTTP 1.0 really built the Web as we know it today, it had some significant efficiency problems. Loading a page that included multiple graphic images, even if they were all in the same directory on the same server, meant opening a new HTTP connection for each file. The overhead of establishing, breaking, and maintaining TCP/IP connections became significant on larger servers. HTTP 1.0 also provided only limited support for redundancy-reducing projects, such as caching information locally.

HTTP 1.1 added an enormous amount to HTTP 1.0. RFC 1945, which defines HTTP 1.0, is 59 pages long; RFC 2616, which defines HTTP 1.1, is 176 pages long. (RFC 2617, which adds authentication to HTTP 1.1, is another 33 pages long.) The most significant improvements, from the perspective of typical web users, are sustained connections (ending the need to close and reopen connections on every file) and much better support for caching.

XML-RPC doesn't require HTTP 1.1, nor are the improvements in HTTP 1.1 particularly appropriate to XML-RPC transaction. Caching procedure call results makes far less sense than caching relatively stable documents, and XML-RPC doesn't take advantage of HTTP 1.1's "keep-alive" feature to retrieve multiple documents in the same transaction. For the kinds of simple transactions XML-RPC is designed to process, all of these possibilities are overkill.

Some of the possibilities opened up by HTTP 1.1 can be useful for some cases in which RPC is used. XML-RPC's larger sibling, SOAP 1.1 (*http://www.w3.org/TR/SOAP/*), uses HTTP 1.1 and provides for the use of HTTP Extension Frameworks, which are defined in RFC 2774.

Making the Infrastructure Do Something Different

Although XML-RPC uses the infrastructures shown earlier, it both subsets that infrastructure and changes the way it is used. XML-RPC creates a request-response relationship in which no human reader may be present.

A typical XML-RPC request uses some of the headers shown previously in the
HTTP 1.0 section, but changes the nature of the information sent through the
POST method to create a more efficient transmission. The following code represents one possible request, sent in a way that is somewhat similar to the HTTP 1.0
file upload, but involves many fewer bytes:

```
POST /RPC HTTP/1.0
User-Agent: MyCustomXMLRPCtool
Host: www.example.com
Content-type: text/xml
Content-length: 111

<?xml version="1.0" encoding="UTF-8"?>
<methodCall>
   <methodName>example.getServerName</methodName>
</methodCall>
```

Because the request identifies the `Content-Type` as `text/xml` rather than
`multipart/form-data`, we avoid separators, repetitive description, and other
overhead. The `Content-Length` header still indicates the number of bytes, but
there are far fewer. The `Accept-` headers are unnecessary in this context because
the understanding that this is an XML-RPC call should limit responses to XML-RPC
responses.

An XML-RPC server should respond with something that looks like:

```
HTTP/1.0 200 OK
Server: MyCustomXMLRPCserver
Date: Fri, 27 Apr 2001 04:23:01 GMT
Content-Type: text/xml
Content-Length: 177

<?xml version="1.0" encoding="UTF-8"?>
<methodResponse>
   <params>
     <param>
       <value><string>My Custom XML-RPC Server</string></value>
     </param>
   </params>
</methodResponse>
```

The response is more conventional than the request because specifying various
content-types and returning different kinds of content, XML included, is perfectly
consistent with typical web server behavior. Using XML content from the request
to determine the content of the response is a bit different, but that's what makes
XML-RPC work.

Infrastructure Details

Basic HTTP requests and responses aren't especially complex, even with the many options available for headers and the various versions of HTTP. A number of pieces of HTTP might be attractive for particular applications (perhaps better termed mutations) of XML-RPC. Some of these pieces are used in part by XML-RPC; others are never mentioned by the XML-RPC specification, but wouldn't be difficult to use in conjunction with XML-RPC.

MIME Types

As we saw earlier, both the request and response portions of HTTP 1.0 and HTTP 1.1 transactions use content-type identifiers to alert applications to the kind of information that follows the headers. These identifiers come from Multipurpose Internet Mail Extensions (MIME), showing HTTP's heritage from mail transport once again. MIME defines identifiers that can be used to describe packages within messages, allowing mail, HTTP, and other protocols to carry traffic that uses multiple formats. MIME content-type identifiers have two levels, the first of which provides a general category (text, image, application, multipart, etc.), and the second of which provides a more detailed description of the type within that category.

(MIME is defined by the Internet Engineering Task Force in RFCs 2045 through 2048. Current rules for XML MIME types are described by RFC 3023, and updates may appear at *http://www.imc.org/ietf-xml-mime/.*)

XML-RPC's most distinctive use of MIME types is its use of `text/xml` within the request. Although most web browser-server interactions limit themselves to `application/x-www-form-urlencoded` and `multipart/form-data`, those limitations aren't built into the HTTP 1.0 specification itself. In general, all you need to know about MIME types for XML-RPC is that both the request and the response are identified as `text/xml`.

HTTPS, VPNs, and Other Security Measures

Developers who want to build secure web connections don't typically switch over completely to entirely new protocols. Instead, they use one of a number of techniques for encrypting traffic that avoids disrupting HTTP itself, with a security layer underneath HTTP or wrapped around it. These approaches typically allow web developers to design interactive content without having to learn entirely new vocabularies for secure transactions.

Different kinds of security measures may require different approaches to XML-RPC. If you build your content in an environment (like Java Server Pages or Active Server Pages) that can handle the extra work involved in maintaining a secure connection over HTTPS, you may not have any additional issues to consider—apart from using *https://* instead of *http://* and remembering that you've moved to port 443. On the other hand, if you work in an environment where you're responsible for managing the entire transactions, exchanging and checking certificates and dealing with encryption may be more than you want to handle.

Many approaches to establishing secure point-to-point communications don't require any work of the web server or client, either by relying on lower transport layers to handle security (like IPsec) or by wrapping all transmissions into secure packages that can then be sent across open networks, such as many Virtual Private Networks. (It might also be possible to increase XML-RPC's security by encrypting the content sent within its payloads, but this would be up to individual methods and is not part of the XML-RPC specification.)

The XML-RPC specification doesn't directly provide for any security. If you want to send XML-RPC messages securely, you need to find an appropriate tool for your particular network architecture and security needs.

Things XML-RPC Leaves Out

XML-RPC uses only a small subset of the features provided by HTTP 1.0 and an even smaller subset of the features provided by HTTP 1.1. XML-RPC ignores all efficiency-enhancing features provided by HTTP 1.1, including connections that remain open, on-the-fly content compression using *gzip*, and support for caching. Even within HTTP 1.0, XML-RPC uses only a few key headers, the POST method, and the overall protocol framework.

XML-RPC can operate inside a full-fledged web server or as a much smaller component custom-built to support only the basic needs of these simple transactions. Although developers might be able to devise ways to take advantage of more HTTP features in an RPC context, XML-RPC's subset is a very well-understood and highly interoperable set of tools. By sticking to the basics, XML-RPC reduces the implementation cost substantially while making it easier for those implementations to be interoperable.

Index

Symbols

; colon, 21
. dot, 21
/ slash, 21
_ underscore, 21

A

acceptClient( ), 44
Access, 146
  talking to from Linux, 154–156
Active Data Objects (ADO), 144
add_address( ), 147, 150–152
addHandler( ), 48
addParam( ), 97
address book
  client for in ASP, 156–161
  creating as web service, 146–154
  entries
    adding to/removing from, 150–154
    looking up in, 146, 149
    updating, 154
  getting contents of, 147–149
  listener for in Perl, 161–164
Address Book API, 146
addresses.mdb file, 147
ADO (Active Data Objects), 144
anyArea handler, 39
Apache::XMLRPC, 65

APIs (application programming interfaces), 142, 144

APIs (application programming
    interfaces), 142, 144
  Address Book, 146
  keeping current, 165
  providing documentation for, 170
AreaHandler class, 52, 54
array data, preparing, 70
Array operator, 153
arraymem( ), 94
arrays, 17, 93
arraysize( ), 94
ASP scripting environment, 140–166
  creating XML-RPC listeners in, 140–146
  data types, 144–146
  library for, 165
associative arrays, 18
asynchronous system, 12
AuthenticatedXmlRpcHandler interface, 50
authentication, 25, 170
  XML-RPC handler with support for, 50
authorization, 170
Authorization header, 25
automatic registration, creating handlers
    using, 48

B

base64( ), 69
bignums, 13

We'd like to hear your suggestions for improving our indexes. Send email to *index@oreilly.com.*

About the Author

Simon St.Laurent is a web developer, network administrator, computer book author, and XML troublemaker living in Ithaca, NY. His books include *XML: A Primer*; *XML Elements of Style*; *Building XML Applications*; *Cookies*; and *Sharing Bandwidth*. Simon is a contributing editor to *XMLhack.com* and an occasional contributor to *XML.com*.

Joe Johnston is a software engineer at O'Reilly & Associates. A graduate of the University of Massachusetts in Boston with a B.A. in computer science, he is a teacher, web designer, and author of articles for *The Perl Journal, Perl.com,* and IBM's *DeveloperWorks*. Joe helps maintain the ASP XML-RPC library and wrote the Perl module, Frontier::Responder.pm.

Edd Dumbill is managing editor of *XML.com*, part of the O'Reilly Network, and founding editor of *XMLhack.com*, a daily news site for XML developers. He maintains the XML-RPC support classes for the PHP scripting language. Edd lives in York, England.

Colophon

Our look is the result of reader comments, our own experimentation, and feedback from distribution channels. Distinctive covers complement our distinctive approach to technical topics, breathing personality and life into potentially dry subjects.

The animal on the cover of *Programming Web Services with XML-RPC* is a jellyfish. A member of the phylum *Cnidaria*, jellyfish are found in all oceans and many freshwater lakes and rivers. The name "jellyfish" refers to the animal's adult stage of development, when it acquires a bell- or umbrella-shaped body and long tentacles. The animal's body (including tentacles) is about 95 percent water and ranges in size from less than an inch to over 100 feet. Jellyfish feed by paralyzing their victims with nematocysts—stinging, harpoon-like cells located in their tentacles. The sting, though lethal to its prey, protects the jellyfish; its body is so fragile that it cannot endure a struggle and must render its prey motionless before feeding. This sting has given the jellyfish a bad reputation among swimmers, some of whom are seriously injured by brushing against the animal's tentacles. Most jellyfish are harmless to humans, though, and are noted more for their fragile beauty than for their sting.

Ann Schirmer was the production editor and proofreader for *Programming Web Services with XML-RPC*. Paulette Miley was the copyeditor. Claire Cloutier, Sarah Jane Shangraw, and Jeffrey Holcomb provided quality control. Brenda Miller wrote the index.

Ellie Volckhausen designed the cover of this book, based on a series design by Edie Freedman. The cover image is a 19th-century engraving from the Dover Pictorial Archive. Emma Colby produced the cover layout with QuarkXPress 4.1 using Adobe's ITC Garamond font.

David Futato designed the interior layout based on a series design by Nancy Priest. Anne-Marie Vaduva converted the files from Microsoft Word to FrameMaker 5.5.6 using tools created by Mike Sierra. The text and heading fonts are ITC Garamond Light and Garamond Book; the code font is Constant Willison. The illustrations that appear in the book were produced by Robert Romano and Jessamyn Read using Macromedia FreeHand 9 and Adobe Photoshop 6. This colophon was written by Ann Schirmer.

Whenever possible, our books use a durable and flexible lay-flat binding. If the page count exceeds this binding's limit, perfect binding is used.

XML

HTML & XHTML: The Definitive Guide, 4th Edition

By Chuck Musciano & Bill Kennedy
4th Edition August 2000
677 pages, ISBN 0-596-00026-X

This complete guide is full of examples, sample code, and practical hands-on advice for creating truly effective web pages and mastering advanced features. Web authors learn how to insert images, create useful links and searchable documents, use Netscape extensions, design great forms, and much more. The fourth edition covers XHTML 1.0, HTML 4.01, Netscape 6.0, and Internet Explorer 5.0, plus all the common extensions.

Learning WML & WMLScript

By Martin Frost
1st Edition October 2000
208 pages, ISBN 1-56592-947-0

The next generation of mobile communicators is here, and delivering content will mean programming in WML and WMLScript. *Learning WML & WMLScript* gets developers up to speed quickly on these technologies, mapping out in detail the Wireless Application Environment (WAE), and its two major components: Wireless Markup Language (WML), and WMLScript. With these two technologies, developers can format information in almost all applications for display by mobile devices.

Web Programming

PHP Pocket Reference

By Rasmus Lerdorf
1st Edition January 2000
120 pages, ISBN 1-56592-769-9

The *PHP Pocket Reference* is a handy quick reference for PHP, an open-source, HTML-embedded scripting language that can be used to develop web applications. This small book acts both as a perfect tutorial for learning the basics of PHP syntax and as a reference to the vast array of functions provided by PHP.

Web Programming

Designing Active Server Pages

By Scott Mitchell
1st Edition September 2000
360 pages, ISBN 0-596-00044-8

Designing Active Server Pages is written for developers who have already mastered the basics of ASP application development and are ready to take the next logical step. It is sure to become an indispensable part of every web developer's library.

ASP in a Nutshell, 2nd Edition

By A. Keyton Weissinger
2nd Edition July 2000
492 pages, ISBN 1-56592-843-1

ASP in a Nutshell, 2nd Edition, provides the high-quality reference documentation that web application developers really need to create effective Active Server Pages. It focuses on how features are used in a real application and highlights little-known or undocumented features.

JavaServer Pages

By Hans Bergsten
1st Edition December 2000
572 pages, ISBN 1-56592-746-X

JavaServer Pages shows how to develop Java-based web applications without having to be a hardcore programmer. The author provides an overview of JSP concepts and illuminates how JSP fits into the larger picture of web applications. There are chapters for web authors on generating dynamic content, handling session information, and accessing databases, as well as material for Java programmers on creating Java components and custom JSP tags for web authors to use in JSP pages.

Web Programming

CGI Programming with Perl, 2nd Edition

By Shishir Gundavaram
2nd Edition July 2000
470 pages, ISBN 1-56592-419-3

The Common Gateway Interface (CGI) is one of the most powerful methods of providing dynamic content on the Web. CGI is a generic interface for calling external programs to crunch numbers, query databases, generate customized graphics, or perform any other server-side task. Based on the best-selling *CGI Programming on the World Wide Web*, this edition has been completely rewritten to demonstrate current techniques available with the CGI.pm module and the latest versions of Perl.

Dynamic HTML: The Definitive Reference

By Danny Goodman
1st Edition July 1998
1088 pages, ISBN 1-56592-494-0

Dynamic HTML: The Definitive Reference is an indispensable compendium for Web content developers. It contains complete reference material for all of the HTML tags, CSS style attributes, browser document objects, and JavaScript objects supported by the various standards and the latest versions of Netscape Navigator and Microsoft Internet Explorer.

Writing Apache Modules with Perl and C

By Lincoln Stein & Doug MacEachern
1st Edition March 1999
746 pages, ISBN 1-56592-567-X

This guide to web programming shows how to extend the capabilities of the Apache web server. It explains the design of Apache, mod_perl, and the Apache API, then demonstrates how to use them to rewrite CGI scripts, filter HTML documents on the server-side, enhance server log functionality, convert file formats on the fly, and more.

JavaScript: The Definitive Guide, 3rd Edition

By David Flanagan
3rd Edition June 1998
800 pages, ISBN 1-56592-392-8

This third edition of the definitive reference to JavaScript covers the latest version of the language, JavaScript 1.2, as supported by Netscape Navigator 4 and Internet Explorer 4. JavaScript, which is being standardized under the name ECMAScript, is a scripting language that can be embedded directly in HTML to give Web pages programming-language capabilities.

Programming ColdFusion

By Rob Brooks-Bilson
1st Edition August 2001 (est.)
900 pages (est.), ISBN 1-56592-698-6

Programming ColdFusion covers everything you need to know to create effective web applications with ColdFusion, a powerful tool for rapid web site development. The book starts with the basics and quickly moves to more advanced topics, providing numerous examples of common web application tasks, so you can learn by example.

JavaScript Application Cookbook

By Jerry Bradenbaugh
1st Edition September 1999
476 pages, ISBN 1-56592-577-7

JavaScript Application Cookbook literally hands the Webmaster a set of ready-to-go, client-side JavaScript applications with thorough documentation to help them understand and extend the applications. By providing such a set of applications, *JavaScript Application Cookbook* allows Webmasters to immediately add extra functionality to their Web sites.

Web Programming

Webmaster in a Nutshell, 2nd Edition

By Stephen Spainhour & Robert Eckstein
2nd Edition June 1999
540 pages, ISBN 1-56592-325-1

This indispensable book takes all the essential reference information for the Web and pulls it together into one volume. It covers HTML 4.0, CSS, XML, CGI, SSI, JavaScript 1.2, PHP, HTTP 1.1, and administration for the Apache server.

Java Servlet Programming, 2nd Edition

By Jason Hunter with William Crawford
2nd Edition April 2001
780 pages, ISBN 0-596-00040-5

The second edition of this popular book has been completely updated to add the new features of the Java Servlet API Version 2.2, and new chapters on servlet security and advanced communication. In addition to complete coverage of the 2.2 specification, we have included bonus material on the new 2.3 version of the specification.

How to stay in touch with O'Reilly

1. Visit Our Award-Winning Web Site

http://www.oreilly.com/

★ "Top 100 Sites on the Web" —*PC Magazine*
★ "Top 5% Web sites" —*Point Communications*
★ "3-Star site" —*The McKinley Group*

Our web site contains a library of comprehensive product information (including book excerpts and tables of contents), downloadable software, background articles, interviews with technology leaders, links to relevant sites, book cover art, and more. File us in your Bookmarks or Hotlist!

2. Join Our Email Mailing Lists

New Product Releases

To receive automatic email with brief descriptions of all new O'Reilly products as they are released, send email to:
ora-news-subscribe@lists.oreilly.com
Put the following information in the first line of your message (*not* in the Subject field):
subscribe ora-news

O'Reilly Events

If you'd also like us to send information about trade show events, special promotions, and other O'Reilly events, send email to:
ora-news-subscribe@lists.oreilly.com
Put the following information in the first line of your message (*not* in the Subject field):
subscribe ora-events

3. Get Examples from Our Books via FTP

There are two ways to access an archive of example files from our books:

Regular FTP
- ftp to:
  ftp.oreilly.com
  (login: anonymous
  password: your email address)
- Point your web browser to:
  ftp://ftp.oreilly.com/

FTPMAIL
- Send an email message to:
  ftpmail@online.oreilly.com
  (Write "help" in the message body)

4. Contact Us via Email

order@oreilly.com
To place a book or software order online. Good for North American and international customers.

subscriptions@oreilly.com
To place an order for any of our newsletters or periodicals.

books@oreilly.com
General questions about any of our books.

software@oreilly.com
For general questions and product information about our software. Check out O'Reilly Software Online at **http://software.oreilly.com/** for software and technical support information. Registered O'Reilly software users send your questions to: **website-support@oreilly.com**

cs@oreilly.com
For answers to problems regarding your order or our products.

booktech@oreilly.com
For book content technical questions or corrections.

proposals@oreilly.com
To submit new book or software proposals to our editors and product managers.

international@oreilly.com
For information about our international distributors or translation queries. For a list of our distributors outside of North America check out:
http://www.oreilly.com/distributors.html

5. Work with Us

Check out our website for current employment opportunites:
http://jobs.oreilly.com/

O'Reilly & Associates, Inc.
101 Morris Street, Sebastopol, CA 95472 USA
TEL   707-829-0515 or 800-998-9938
          (6am to 5pm PST)
FAX   707-829-0104

International Distributors

http://international.oreilly.com/distributors.html

UK, EUROPE, MIDDLE EAST AND AFRICA (EXCEPT FRANCE, GERMANY, AUSTRIA, SWITZERLAND, LUXEMBOURG, AND LIECHTENSTEIN)

INQUIRIES

O'Reilly UK Limited
4 Castle Street
Farnham
Surrey, GU9 7HS
United Kingdom
Telephone: 44-1252-711776
Fax: 44-1252-734211
Email: information@oreilly.co.uk

ORDERS

Wiley Distribution Services Ltd.
1 Oldlands Way
Bognor Regis
West Sussex PO22 9SA
United Kingdom
Telephone: 44-1243-843294
UK Freephone: 0800-243207
Fax: 44-1243-843302 (Europe/EU orders)
or 44-1243-843274 (Middle East/Africa)
Email: cs-books@wiley.co.uk

FRANCE

INQUIRIES & ORDERS

Éditions O'Reilly
18 rue Séguier
75006 Paris, France
Tel: 1-40-51-71-89
Fax: 1-40-51-72-26
Email: france@oreilly.fr

GERMANY, SWITZERLAND, AUSTRIA, LUXEMBOURG, AND LIECHTENSTEIN

INQUIRIES & ORDERS

O'Reilly Verlag
Balthasarstr. 81
D-50670 Köln, Germany
Telephone: 49-221-973160-91
Fax: 49-221-973160-8
Email: anfragen@oreilly.de (inquiries)
Email: order@oreilly.de (orders)

CANADA (FRENCH LANGUAGE BOOKS)

Les Éditions Flammarion ltée
375, Avenue Laurier Ouest
Montréal (Québec) H2V 2K3
Tel: 00-1-514-277-8807
Fax: 00-1-514-278-2085
Email: info@flammarion.qc.ca

HONG KONG

City Discount Subscription Service, Ltd.
Unit A, 6th Floor, Yan's Tower
27 Wong Chuk Hang Road
Aberdeen, Hong Kong
Tel: 852-2580-3539
Fax: 852-2580-6463
Email: citydis@ppn.com.hk

KOREA

Hanbit Media, Inc.
Chungmu Bldg. 210
Yonnam-dong 568-33
Mapo-gu
Seoul, Korea
Tel: 822-325-0397
Fax: 822-325-9697
Email: hant93@chollian.dacom.co.kr

PHILIPPINES

Global Publishing
G/F Benavides Garden
1186 Benavides Street
Manila, Philippines
Tel: 632-254-8949/632-252-2582
Fax: 632-734-5060/632-252-2733
Email: globalp@pacific.net.ph

TAIWAN

O'Reilly Taiwan
1st Floor, No. 21, Lane 295
Section 1, Fu-Shing South Road
Taipei, 106 Taiwan
Tel: 886-2-27099669
Fax: 886-2-27038802
Email: mori@oreilly.com

INDIA

Shroff Publishers & Distributors Pvt. Ltd.
12, "Roseland", 2nd Floor
180, Waterfield Road, Bandra (West)
Mumbai 400 050
Tel: 91-22-641-1800/643-9910
Fax: 91-22-643-2422
Email: spd@vsnl.com

CHINA

O'Reilly Beijing
SIGMA Building, Suite B809
No. 49 Zhichun Road
Haidian District
Beijing, China PR 100080
Tel: 86-10-8809-7475
Fax: 86-10-8809-7463
Email: beijing@oreilly.com

JAPAN

O'Reilly Japan, Inc.
Yotsuya Y's Building
7 Banch 6, Honshio-cho
Shinjuku-ku
Tokyo 160-0003 Japan
Tel: 81-3-3356-5227
Fax: 81-3-3356-5261
Email: japan@oreilly.com

SINGAPORE, INDONESIA, MALAYSIA AND THAILAND

TransQuest Publishers Pte Ltd
30 Old Toh Tuck Road #05-02
Sembawang Kimtrans Logistics Centre
Singapore 597654
Tel: 65-4623112
Fax: 65-4625761
Email: wendiw@transquest.com.sg

ALL OTHER ASIAN COUNTRIES

O'Reilly & Associates, Inc.
101 Morris Street
Sebastopol, CA 95472 USA
Tel: 707-829-0515
Fax: 707-829-0104
Email: order@oreilly.com

AUSTRALIA

Woodslane Pty., Ltd.
7/5 Vuko Place
Warriewood NSW 2102
Australia
Tel: 61-2-9970-5111
Fax: 61-2-9970-5002
Email: info@woodslane.com.au

NEW ZEALAND

Woodslane New Zealand, Ltd.
21 Cooks Street (P.O. Box 575)
Waganui, New Zealand
Tel: 64-6-347-6543
Fax: 64-6-345-4840
Email: info@woodslane.com.au

ARGENTINA

Distribuidora Cuspide
Suipacha 764
1008 Buenos Aires
Argentina
Phone: 5411-4322-8868
Fax: 5411-4322-3456
Email: libros@cuspide.com